Contents

Acknowledgments

This book would never have been completed without the support and advice of a number of very busy people. First and foremost, I should like to thank Professor Ken Robinson and Professor Fred Inglis, who gave of their time, were generous in their encouragement and honest in their criticism, throughout the project's duration. I wish, too, to acknowledge the influence on my work and on my thinking of Dr Jonothan Neelands, Dr Michael Golby and Professor Jack Zipes. I am grateful to Professor Cecily O'Neill and Dr Michael Fleming for their critical scrutiny of the text and their testing questioning of it; to Dr Eleanor Nesbitt and Dr Victor Quinn for sharing with me the knowledge of their particular specialist fields; to Barbara Juster Esbensen for her kind responses to my inquiries and to my wife, Gill, and my children, Matthew and Sally-Anne, for their patience and tolerance over the many long months, when the book all too often loomed as large in their lives as it did in mine.

The following articles, published in academic journals, have arisen from earlier versions of chapters in this book.

CHAPTER 4 has appeared in an earlier version as: Recasting the Phaedra Syndrome: Myth and Morality in Timberlake Wertenbaker's 'The Love of, the Nightingale' in *Modern Drama, vol. XXXVIII, no. 4*, Winter 1995.

CHAPTER 5 has appeared in an earlier version as: Emotion, Reason and Moral Engagement in Drama in *Research in Drama Education, vol. 1, no. 2*, August, 1996.

CHAPTER 10 Part 1 has appeared in an earlier version as Whose Story? Whose Culture? Moral and Cultural Values in Barbara Juster Esbensen's 'The Star Maiden' in *Children's Literature in Education, vol. 27, no. 2*, June 1996.

Drama, Narrative and Moral Education:
Exploring Traditional Tales in the Primary Years

Joe Winston

RoutledgeFalmer
Taylor & Francis Group

LONDON AND NEW YORK

First published in 1998
By RoutledgeFalmer,
2 Park Square, Milton Park, Abingdon, Oxon, OX14 4RN

Transferred to Digital Printing 2005

A catalogue record for this book is available from the British Library

ISBN 0 7507 0793 3 cased
ISBN 0 7507 0794 1 paper

Library of Congress Cataloging-in-Publication Data are available on request

Jacket design by Caroline Archer

Typeset in 10/12pt Garamond
Graphicraft Typesetters Ltd., Hong Kong.

Introduction

Early in 1992, I was asked to do some drama work with a class of 8–9-year-old children in a primary school local to the university where I work. The teacher wanted the drama to be centred around *The Pied Piper* and to stretch over four one-hour sessions. Looking again at Browning's (1993) version of the traditional tale, I was amused by the witty and ironic moralizing at the end of the poem but was also impressed by the ambivalent moral tensions created by the story. It managed to strike chords within me which could both celebrate the Piper's vengeance and yet feel sympathy for those who suffer such dire punishment, appealing at once to my rational sense of justice and my natural human sympathies.

I wondered if our drama might explore these conflicting moral tensions and, after some deliberation, decided to start the drama where the story ends, in the country to where the children are led beyond the mountain. Using freeze-frame,[1] the children created images of a paradise in which they had everything they could possibly want, and chose to depict a land of ice-cream trees, computer games, funfairs and seemingly infinite leisure facilities. I decided to work against these images which represented happiness in purely materialistic terms. Casting myself in role as a small boy, I created my own image of an unhappy child, gazing broodingly into the distance and clutching a small, sponge ball in my hand. When asked to speculate, the children quickly agreed that this had been a gift from my parents, that I was home-sick and, after some questioning of the boy, they decided that they, too, would like to return home and see their families again. But how could they do this? In the ensuing drama, the children 'borrowed' the Piper's flute as he lay asleep, only to discover that its magic would not work for them. When confronted by myself in role as the angry and indignant Piper, they listened to his complaints against their parents and, in particular, the Mayor and agreed that the people of Hamelin had been wrong to break their promise but insisted that it was equally wrong for him to make them, the children, suffer for it. If they would agree to bring the Mayor back to face justice, would the Piper be prepared to let them go? The Piper was unsure as to whether he could trust them to return; and they were unsure whether he would release them if they did. Eventually both parties agreed to trust one another — but back in Hamelin the children found the Mayor to be a broken man, worn out and sick with worry and guilt over the catastrophe he had caused. Furthermore, he no longer had any money to pay

1

the Piper as it had all been spent on searching for the children. Up to this point, I had been in role as the Piper but now two children, a boy and a girl, took on this role collectively as I continued to play the Mayor.[2] They listened with great seriousness to the story and then forgave the Mayor on the understanding that he must never break a promise again; and, to help ensure that he wouldn't, the boy-Piper announced that he intended to settle down at last and live in Hamelin, which would enable him to keep an eye on the Mayor. As Mayor, I accepted these conditions and the drama ended with a celebratory dance, as the jubilant children were piped back to their homes in Hamelin.

This turned out to be one of those dramas which leave the teacher with a warm glow and the gut-feeling that something significant has been created and shared between teacher and children. The children had worked with enthusiasm and their reactions and responses both inside the drama and after the lessons showed that they had enjoyed and appreciated the whole experience; but I was most pleased by the way they had apparently engaged with the moral content of the drama, exploring as it did issues of justice and vengeance, trust and forgiveness, and the nature of happiness. At the time, I was particularly struck by the children's improvisation at the end of the drama. In portraying the Mayor as weak, ill and repentant, instead of as the selfish tyrant the children had expected, I was deliberately trying to make the moral choices difficult for them. In the event, the compassion and sensitivity articulated by the two 8-year-olds was both surprising and moving to me, as teacher. They wanted justice but not revenge and, on hearing how poor and miserable Hamelin had become, the girl in role as the Piper replied: 'That will all stop when the children return. Just as my pipe could away happiness, it can pipe away sadness, too'. Here, it seemed to me, was an impressive celebration of fairness, forgiveness and social harmony.

On evaluating these sessions, it occurred to me how many of my more successful dramas with young children took traditional stories — usually fairy stories such as *Rumplestiltskin* and *Jack and the Beanstalk* — as their source material and had at their heart the exploration of moral issues. It was evident from the literature of drama in education that this was an experience common to other primary school drama practitioners.[3] However, it was equally evident that little had been written to explore the two questions which interested me most. First of all, why should traditional stories lend themselves so readily to moral exploration through drama? My experience as a teacher and as a head in primary and middle schools was that stories were, indeed, associated with moral education but usually in assemblies, where tales from such volumes as Bailey (1981) carried a straightforward didactic message designed to illustrate that, for example, lying could be dangerous, that humility was a virtue and that flatterers should not be trusted. The traditional tales that could be found in such volumes tended to be from religious sources, such as the *Bible* or the *Qu'oran*, or from books of fables, such as those written by Aesop.

What had been of interest in the story of *The Pied Piper*, however, was the moral ambivalence of the piper and it was this ambivalence, I was sure, that had made the drama possible. But the nature of this ambivalence was surely different from that found in the fairy tales I had worked with, where there were moral ambiguities implicit to the narrative often far richer than the moral lessons that the stories were apparently supposed to illustrate. This provoked a number of associated questions. How common was this ambivalence in literary versions of traditional tales? Where did it come from? When these tales had been written, had their purpose been moral instruction or fantasy entertainment? Were stories a good way to teach children to be moral and, if so, in what sense? As drama seemed to work so effectively with traditional tales, what theoretical grounds were there for seeing a special relationship between them?

The second area which interested me, and about which I could find very little theoretical analysis, was how drama and dramatic processes contribute toward moral learning. This was perhaps the more surprising as it is a common assumption in schools and among drama teachers that drama has a place in the personal, social and moral education of children. There were a number of published examples of lessons in which teachers illustrated how they had used drama for moral purposes but they were usually written in the spirit of advocacy rather than of critical analysis and their intentions were often as didactic as those of the school assembly (Hall, 1988). Some of their claims struck me as dubious and their interpretations open to challenge and I wondered if the same criticisms could be levelled at my own reading of *The Pied Piper* drama.

With a more sceptical frame of mind, I speculated as to whether the drama had reduced the rich, moral ambivalence of Browning's poem to humourless political correctness and I considered afresh the final activity that had so impressed me at the time. I had tried, indeed, to render both the Mayor and the Piper as morally ambiguous, wanting the children to explore a moral situation which was not as straightforward as it first appeared. On reflection, however, a decision which ought to have been very difficult for the Piper had not proven at all difficult for the children in role. After all, the Mayor had appeared as everything a child at school is taught to feel sorry for; old, infirm, pitiable, sad. It would have been heartless indeed for these well-adjusted 8-year-olds to do anything other than forgive him and, whatever else it might have achieved, the drama did not seem to have deepened their understanding of the Piper's feelings of injustice. Unintentionally, I had created a dilemma which was not much of a dilemma at all. As a celebration, the end of the drama might well have been successful; as a challenging, moral thought process, perhaps somewhat less so. Here was a rich area for research into theory and practice but one where there were dangers of making educational claims which might be difficult to defend. And at the heart of it all were values — cultural, moral, professional and personal.

I have begun with this short summary not only because this particular drama contributed to the genesis of the book which follows, but because it also signals some of the more problematic elements within its scope. Its specific focus is the relationship between drama and traditional stories and their potential contribution, when used together, to the moral education of young children.

By traditional stories, I mean those literary versions of tales which originated from oral sources. As I will show, this study has necessitated an inquiry into aspects of narrative theory; cultural, literary and theatre history; moral theory; moral developmental theory; the practice and theory of drama in education; and issues relating to reflective practitioner research. The outcome will, I hope, be of interest not only to practitioners and academics who specialize in educational drama but also more broadly to all those who have a professional interest in how stories, drama and the arts in general can contribute to the moral development of young children.

Moral education has become a contentious and problematic area in contemporary British society, characterized as it is by increasingly secular attitudes and cultural pluralism.[4] Within this climate, many teachers have become uncomfortable with a traditional perspective which associates moral learning closely with conventional Christianity. Influential academics have identified these uncertainties and conflictual perspectives as characteristic of the postmodern condition. Their argument is that, traditionally, belief in religion or philosophies such as liberal humanism have provided western society with a form of coherent agreement upon the values which should inform the moral guidance of its members. Such an agreed values system is defined by Lyotard as a *metanarrative*, 'the principal way a culture or a collectivity legitimates itself' (Connor, 1989, p. 32). According to Lyotard, postmodern society has witnessed the weakening of the metanarratives which define and attempt to uphold their dominant cultural values at the centre of contemporary society. In contrast, marginal cultures have proliferated and strengthened and we have consequently seen 'a shift from the muffled majesty of grand narratives to the splintering autonomy of micronarratives' (Connor, 1989, p. 32). This state of affairs, characterized by moral relativism and uncertainty, is one which many teachers will recognize and the tensions this creates can only be exacerbated when political pressure is brought to bear in an attempt to reassert dominant cultural and moral values.

Indeed, at the time of writing, the question of the role of schools in the promotion of moral values has resurfaced at the forefront of political and media attention in the wake of a debate in the House of Lords on July 5th, 1996, led by Dr George Carey, the Archbishop of Canterbury. A brief look at the tone of the debate and at its presentation in the press does, I believe, present us with a snapshot of the complex tensions that underlie the area of moral education in contemporary Britain and the resultant confusion over what form it should take.

Dr Carey's main concern was the climate of moral relativism which pervades much of public and private life in what he described as 'a world in which there are no rights and wrongs except what we individuals deem to be true for ourselves' (*The Times*, 6 July 1996, p. 9). He affirmed his belief that most people wanted a fightback against moral relativism and that, for this to happen, children needed to be taught rules and a moral code, and he held up the Ten Commandments as the best model we have of such a code. He also emphasized the need for a shared, moral discourse to permit people to talk publicly about religion and morality. In acknowledging the importance of schools in the teaching of moral matters, he welcomed the consultation initiative on moral values recently undertaken by the Schools Curriculum and Assessment Authority (SCAA) and argued that an initiative was needed in training teachers to bring out 'the moral and spiritual aspects of many different subjects'.

Carey's speech was heralded on the front page of *The Daily Telegraph* under the headline 'Carey crusade to teach children right from wrong' (*The Daily Telegraph*, 5 July 1996, p. 1), and the following day the 'Morality Debate' was given a two page spread in *The Times*. Here a similar headline: 'Man who wants schools to focus on right and wrong' (*The Times*, 6 July 1996, p. 9), profiled Nicholas Tate, Chief Executive of SCAA. These headlines signal a revealing, politically motivated simplification of the agenda. By emphasizing right and wrong, the implication is that there exist straightforward absolutes which schools are failing to teach or pay sufficient attention to. The emotive use of the word *crusade* and the presentation of Tate as a lone man taking on these faceless and failing institutions was intended to cast in a heroic light those who would apparently support such an absolutist agenda. The concept of right and wrong is integral to a code of rules and those parts of Carey's speech which emphasize rules were given prominence in the press. For example, the *Telegraph* explained:

> Dr Carey will attack the modern assumption that, while trivial occupations like football need rules, life does not. The young need to be taught these rules so that they can handle moral dilemmas that will confront them through their lives. (*The Daily Telegraph*, op. cit.)

The strong implication here is that moral dilemmas result from a lack of knowledge of moral rules and that the moral life would be relatively straightforward if we had internalized them. The intellectual weakness of such an argument is immediately apparent. In the first place, knowing a rule will not automatically ensure that I keep it, even if I believe that it is morally right to do so; in the second place, a moral dilemma involves making a choice when it is difficult to know exactly what *is* right. In such circumstances, a knowledge of moral rules might be justifiably seen as making the choices more, not less, difficult for the individual involved. Carey's speech in the Lords did, in fact, make this very point. 'We all know that the toughest moral decisions are not always between right and wrong but between two rights which pull in different directions' (*The Times*, op. cit., p. 9). Rules, states Carey, are not in themselves enough; children must learn 'the *judgment* to confront the constant dilemmas of life' (op. cit., my emphasis). Which amounts to a firm acknowledgment that moral education is more problematic than the learning of rules and codes.

This small example is indicative of an overall tension between a political desire to order the process of moral education along absolutist and straightforward principles in the face of a reality which refuses to be anything other than complex and problematic. So, as part of this urge for absolutism and simplicity, the purpose of SCAA's investigation into moral values is reported as 'the production of a public statement of moral rules' (*The Times*, op. cit., p. 8), and the place of moral learning within the curriculum is seen as situated firmly within the dominant traditions of RE (Religious Education) and the school assembly. This latter point was made evident by Gillian Shepherd, the Secretary of State for Education and Employment, who contributed to the debate by suggesting that, if the daily act of collective worship enshrined in the 1988 Education Act were to be properly enforced, then moral standards in schools would improve ('Today' BBC, 6 July 1996).

This desire for simplicity is detectable within Carey's own words but so, too, is a recognition that morality persists in remaining an area of complexity which continues to generate profound disagreement. When, for example, he addresses directly the issue of moral values rather than moral rules, he is compelled to ask the questions: 'Do we know what our shared values are? Do we have any? If we do, do we have a vocabulary that people are comfortable in using in order to describe them?' (*The Daily Telegraph*, 5 July 1996, p. 29). Shared values, of course, are fundamental to any agreed rule system but they will be difficult to codify, let alone teach, if it is open to debate as to whether there exists even a language to describe them in contemporary society.

A close look at the substance of Carey's argument, therefore, reveals that, despite his Christian stance, three tenets emerge: that the teaching of rules by themselves is insufficient for a proper moral education; that we have a need to develop a language by which we can explore what our shared moral values might be; and that moral education has a place 'in many different subjects', not simply RE. Each of these tenets is of central concern to this book, which aims to explore why and how stories which are secular in their nature and originate from different cultural sources may be used to help children articulate moral values and explore moral problems through the art form of extemporary drama. A premise to this study is that values are inescapable and pervasive: as Connor expresses it: 'We are claimed always and everywhere by the necessity of value in an active and transactional sense' (1992, p. 8).

Values are present within the stories, within the children as members of family, school and peer group communities and within myself as teacher, researcher and writer. To talk of values is to talk the language of feeling as well as reason, of commitment and conviction as well as duty and obligation. It is in the area of values where the various interests which inform the debate on moral education meet: the political, the professional, the academic, the personal, the cultural, creating the network of tensions and contradictions within which teachers find themselves needing to operate and being called increasingly to account. The writing of this book and the research which has informed it have been undertaken in a spirit of recognition and acceptance of this complexity but also in the belief that, as political interest in moral education becomes more intense, contributions from professionals based upon research and reflective practice become more urgent. Sound professional knowledge is needed to inform a contentious and emotive area and it is my hope that this study will contribute to such knowledge.

The interdisciplinary nature of my inquiry has meant that it has been selective rather than comprehensive in the broad and distinctive areas of moral education and drama education, looking for areas of overlap rather than attempting an exhaustive coverage. Nor do I attempt to prove that participation in drama practices will make children more moral in their behaviour. Experience has led me to believe that, because of the very nature of drama, children who participate in dramatic activities can learn to cooperate, gain a social identity, learn responsibility to others, understand the need for rules and self-discipline and grow in self esteem. All of these are important aspects of moral growth which lie outside the specific interests of this book. The focus here is on a particular form of literary narrative and its potential for moral learning; on those moral theories which best inform us how the moral life is expressed in this literary form; how it relates to the art form of drama; and how, within a dialogical relationship between drama and traditional stories, children can interpret, negotiate and articulate moral meanings.

The research proceeded along two connected fronts, theoretical inquiry and practical fieldwork, the one influencing and informing the other. It was a major aim of mine to sustain a dialogical relationship between theory and practice throughout the process and, in particular, to avoid approaching the fieldwork as a test of a pre-ordained, theoretical agenda. To paraphrase Lorraine Code (1991), my fear was that such an approach might close off more possibilities for discernment and action than it might create.[5] However, for the purposes of logical argument, the finished text is presented in two halves. Part 1 consists of a broadly theoretical argument for using drama and traditional stories for the moral education of primary-aged children. The fieldwork and related analyses are presented in Part 2, which consists of a rationale for the pedagogy of process drama and a series of three detailed case studies undertaken during 1993 and 1994.

Chapter 1 offers a brief examination and critique of cognitive developmental theories of moral education, in particular those expounded by Lawrence Kohlberg. I suggest that, when analysed from the critical perspectives of postmodern consciousness, the rational moral principles it proposes as universal truths are open to question as are the rigid developmental categories it advocates. I propose that, in the work of Carol Gilligan and, in particular, Alasdair MacIntyre, we are presented with alternative models of the moral life which are more inclusive of emotion, context and particularity and within which we can find the discourse necessary to develop moral understanding. This discourse emphasizes the role of narrative understanding and the language of the virtues.

Chapter 2 examines how literary narratives can educate for moral understanding, drawing upon theories offered by Bruner, Goldberg and in particular Bakhtin, with subjunctivity and dialogism emerging as key relevant concepts. It is evident, however, that traditional tales are resistant to these concepts and that debate over their moral significance is characterized by profound disagreements over their didactic purposes. I analyse these disagreements and propose that the narrative form is inappropriate to moral teaching of a straightforward, didactic nature.

In Chapter 3, I pursue an argument which offers a perspective informed by the mythic and oral origins of the tales as best disposed to help our understanding of how they can be harnessed for the purposes of moral learning. I explore historical and cultural reasons for understanding the fairy tale as myth and the relationship between myth, dramatic performance and moral values at the origins of western theatre practices and within the performative nature of the oral tradition. This analysis emphasizes the need to regard mythical tales as historical and cultural constructs open to change rather than as carriers of universal truths. I conclude that, for historical and artistic reasons, drama can be seen to be part of a process of moral learning which takes the form of a dialogical engagement with the values of traditional tales. By way of a case study to illustrate how myth is still being reinterpreted and renewed for moral purposes in contemporary British theatre, in Chapter 4 I analyse Timberlake Wertenbaker's *The Love of A Nightingale* as a feminist re-evaluation of the Phaedra myth. I propose that it demonstrates how theatre can be used either to educate and empower or to miseducate and oppress; and how a reassessment of our shared mythology, as enshrined in canonical texts, is a social and a moral necessity and one of the potent functions of the communal art form of drama.

Neo-Aristotelian ideas have influenced the moral and methodological theories underpinning this study yet, in the field of drama in education, Aristotle continues to exert very little influence. Chapter 5 attempts a reassessment of this situation and begins with a critique of the objections to Aristotelian theatre raised by Brecht and Boal, two of the theorists who most influence educational drama. It proceeds to focus upon the cognitive nature of emotion and, in particular, upon how this relationship can inform our understanding of *catharsis*. Drawing upon the work of Martha Nussbaum, I argue that catharsis is more accurately viewed as a process of cognitive illumination through the emotions rather than as one of purgation or political repression. Reflecting upon the significance of this for drama teachers, I propose that Beckerman's theory of iconic and dialectic action presents us with a perspective of moral engagement in drama which permits teachers to be informed by Brecht, Boal *and* Aristotle.

Part 2 begins with Chapter 6, in which I argue for the moral exploration of fairy tales through participatory forms of educational drama. I find it necessary to address the arguments of those critics who have questioned the value agendas and universalist preoccupations of its more famous practitioners, notably Dorothy Heathcote and Gavin Bolton. I reject the accusations that universalism is inherent to the form but acknowledge that there is a danger in drama teachers unwittingly imposing their own value agendas and hence making questionable assumptions about their teaching.

In the light of the problems analysed in the previous chapter, I present in Chapter 7 a rationale for my fieldwork, rejecting positivist research paradigms and arguing for an ethnographic approach through case study. This, I propose, is a method of inquiry which makes possible the interpretation and analysis of value-oriented actions in value-laden contexts. I detail the methodological practices used to gather data, listing and explaining those specific to each case study.

Chapters 8, 9 and 10 provide accounts of three case studies. Each is centred around a drama using as pre-text different literary versions of traditional tales taken from Indian, British and Native American sources. The mix of cultural origin was intended as a deliberate and positive response to the contemporary challenges of pluralism and cultural diversity and the stories were chosen for the dramas they suggested as well as the problems posed by their moral values. Each case study consists of an analysis of the problematic value agenda of each tale; an account of the drama lessons and the context within which each took place; and a reflective analysis of the lessons, focusing on issues and themes emerging out of the recorded data rather than from a predetermined, theory-driven agenda. The main thrust of the first case study is how two classes of 8 and 9-year-old children were able to read the hidden values of a literary version of an Indian fable and how the process of drama enabled them to articulate new moral meanings from it. The second case study looks at the tension between carnival folk humour and didactic authorial intentions in versions of *Jack and the Beanstalk* and how a drama with some 6-year-old children used carnivalesque humour to energize an exploration of these moral tensions. The final case study explores issues associated with the translation of moral and cultural values from one tradition into another in narrative and representational forms.

Finally, the conclusion attempts to draw together the implications of the book's overall thesis and, in recognizing what it has left unexplored, I make suggestions as to what further research might usefully build upon its findings and as to how schools might benefit from its arguments.

Notes

1 Freeze frame is a commonly used convention in classroom drama, also known as tableau or still image. See Neelands (1992) p. 57 for a brief description.
2 Another common drama strategy, where more than one person plays one character simultaneously. See Neelands, op. cit., p. 60.
3 The literature of primary school drama would appear to testify to the popularity of *The Pied Piper* as a drama topic, particularly centred around moral issues of one sort or another. See Fleming (1994) chapter 1, pp. 28–30, Davies (1983) and Tarlington and Verriour (1991).
4 In an opinion poll conducted by Gallup and published in the *Daily Telegraph* on July 5th, 1996, less than 10 per cent of those questioned answered that the church had had any influence on their moral thinking and 49 per cent felt that the church's moral guidance was inadequate.
5 Code, L. (1991). This paraphrase is taken from her comments on feminist moral critiques on moral theories. See p. 107.

Part 1

Theoretical Considerations

Chapter 1

Narrative and the Moral Life

Problematizing Moral Cognitive Developmental Theory

In the winter of 1987 educationalists around the world were shocked to learn that Lawrence Kohlberg, the most influential researcher into moral education of his generation, had committed suicide. This act was a poignant and ambiguous footnote to the life of an academic who had striven to establish the universal principles of moral development. In his later years, the epistemological vision which had underpinned his research had come under increasingly vocal criticism. His was a modernist project, founded upon a faith in grand theory and a belief in the existence of rational, universal laws to explain human development and human behaviour. In retrospect it is tempting to see his suicide as tragically symbolic, to view it if not as an admission of failure, then at least as a testimony to doubts in what he had achieved.

Lawrence Kohlberg was foremost of a number of theorists and researchers who attempted to apply cognitive developmental theories of learning to moral growth.[1] Rejecting both the teaching of moral habits, which he dismissed as the 'bag of virtues' approach to moral education, and also the relativistic-emotional approach, where children's moral health is believed to develop natur-ally from the fulfilment of their emotions and needs, Kohlberg began his theory from a different philosophical premise. His claim was that, at heart, morality represents a set of rational principles of judgment and decisions *valid for every culture*, the principles of welfare and justice. In addition, he claimed that his research showed how individuals acquire and refine their sense of justice by passing through a sequence of six invariant developmental stages. These were divided into three levels which he named the *Pre-conventional*, the *Conventional* and the *Post-conventional*. Each stage, Kohlberg argued, is characterized by a particular structure of thinking and he proposed that moral development should be understood as linear progression, capable of arrestation at any level. What characterizes this progression, according to Kohlberg, is an individual's increasing ability to reflect autonomously and selflessly upon the moral prin-ciples which need to be applied to specific moral dilemmas or problems.[2] The highest stage of moral development is reached when a person appreciates and is able to apply what he labelled as *universal ethical principles*, those prin-ciples which he argued any human being would agree to if able to view a situation quite impartially; in the words of the philosopher John Rawls (1977), 'from behind a veil of ignorance'.

Kant had first proposed with his *categorical imperative* a universal principle of moral law based upon justice and reason; and that: 'moral imperatives exercise absolute or universal and not merely particular or contingent authority' (Carr, 1991, p. 81). Kohlberg's understanding of morality was Kantian in its form but the source of his cognitive developmental approach to the acquisition of moral knowledge was the work of Jean Piaget. It was Piaget himself, in fact, who had first undertaken the task of structuring a theory to explain the universal principles of children's moral growth (Piaget, 1932). Piaget saw rules as the basis of all moral action and suggested that his research showed a growth in attitude to rules and rule-keeping from *heteronomy*, where rules are given by external authority, to *autonomy*, where they are mutually agreed, accepted and internalized. Kohlberg openly acknowledged his indebtedness to Piaget and saw his own research as a continuation of the work he had begun. But he was not the only cognitive developmental theorist to gain credence during the 1950s, 1960s and 1970s; Selman (1976) and Loevinger (1976) both proposed stage theories to explain personal and moral growth but one of the earliest to do so was Erikson, who in 1950 proposed eight levels of development which he termed the *Eight Ages of Man* (Erikson, 1977, pp. 222–43). There is rather more Freud than Piaget in Erikson's theory, but, like Kohlberg, his developmental stages are heirarchical, sequential and culminate in a universal model of fully developed, moral humanity; in Erikson's case, this highest stage of moral being is characterized by *Ego Integrity*, where, coupled with what he calls the virtue of wisdom: 'The style of integrity developed by his culture or civilization thus becomes the "patrimony of the soul", the seal of his moral paternity of himself' (1977, p. 242).

Aware as we now are of feminist theory, we may well wince at the pre-eminence of male, patriarchal references in such a description of the moral universe. Of course, Erikson was writing before contemporary sensibilities had been subjected to a feminist critique of language usage; but it is this very need to judge it within the context of its time which undermines the universalist claims it makes.

Cognitive, moral developmental theories sought to establish objective, universal laws to account for the moral growth of the personality; however, it is far from proven that the structural categories their creators proposed were the fundamental laws they claimed them to be. The research of Margaret Donaldson, for example, has revealed a deep flaw in the overarching structure of Piagetian developmental stage theory which premised both his and Kohlberg's moral projects. Donaldson showed that the rigid hierarchy of cognitive progression which Piaget claimed to have proven did not hold. For example, Piaget had observed an inability in children under the age of 6 to decentre, but Donaldson could describe tests which showed that, given situations which were contextualized in such a way as to make human sense, children much younger than 6 and 7 could, indeed, see things from another's perspective (Donaldson, 1978, pp. 19–24). Her stress on the inadequacy of the research tasks set by Piaget, and his lack of recognition of the importance of contextual details in children's thinking, were to have an important echo later, in criticisms of Kohlberg's research methodology, as we shall see.

There is, of course, much that is empirically logical in many of the observations made by developmental theorists. So Kohlberg's vision of the moral progression of the child which sees a movement from reliance on authority toward a position where one can oneself assume those responsibilities which pertain to the exercise of authority makes eminent and recognizable sense in our own, democratic, western society. However, this does not mean that such a progression is structurally implicit to moral growth for it assumes the human universality of the moral principles it promotes. Both Erikson and Kohlberg use a discourse which is notably modernist; rationalist, searching to provide an all-embracing grand narrative to explain moral action, irrespective of such important constituents of the human moral identity as culture and gender, and prescribing universal moral precepts which are tacitly but notably congruent with the values of western liberalism. Thus the perfect human being according to Kohlberg's and Erikson's moral categories would be an impartial, unprejudiced, calm, considerate philosopher, self-sufficient, autonomous and socially well-integrated, a perfect citizen in a twentieth century western democracy but somewhat out of place in Homeric Greece or, indeed, in a modern day, fundamentalist, Islamic community. Their theories are susceptible to a poststructuralist critique and to the criticisms, summarized by Benhabib, which characterize postmodern thought:

> If there is one position which unites postmodernists from Foucault to Derrida to Lyotard it is the critique of western rationality as seen from the perspective of the margins, from the standpoint of what and who it excludes, suppresses, delegitimates, renders mad, imbecilic or childish. (cited in Nicholson, 1993, p. 19)

This does not disprove *per se* either Kohlberg's or Erikson's views of what constitutes the moral human being but it shows that the foundations of their theories are far from the value-free, objective perspectives they claimed them to be. In the postmodern world, grand theories are under siege from feminists, cultural minorities and the many voices on the periphery. The whole concept of morality argued by both theorists can be disputed from the perspective of any of these voices.[3] It is unsurprising, therefore, that the most coherent critique of Kohlberg's system has come from one of these voices, that of his one-time collaborator, the feminist moral researcher, Carol Gilligan.

Gilligan's Ethic of Care and Narrative Moral Theory

In her book *In a Different Voice*, published in 1982, Gilligan claimed that, when developing his theories, Kohlberg's research was gender-biased; she argued that both Piaget's research into games and rules and her own subsequent interviews with female respondents revealed that a developmental theory which concentrated on the principle of impartial Justice was discriminatory toward the way women approached moral dilemmas. Her overall thesis, developed in subsequent research and publications, has been summarized by Flanagan and Jackson thus[4]:

> Gilligan describes a moral universe in which men, more often than women, conceive of morality as substantively constituted by obligations and rights and as procedurally constituted by the demands of fairness and impartiality, while women, more often than men, see moral requirements as emerging from the particular needs of others in the context of particular relationships. (1993, p. 70)

This view of morality she defines as '*an ethic of care*' and although her research saw it as expressed mainly by women, her intention was not to place men and women within different moral universes but to challenge Kohlberg's Kantian view of the nature and origin of moral action.

> For Gilligan each person is embedded in a web of ongoing relationships, and morality, importantly if not exclusively, consists in attention to, understanding of, and emotional responsiveness toward the individuals with whom one stands in these relationships. (Blum, 1993, p. 50)

Not surprisingly, Gilligan's work has found favour with postmodernists and feminists, who see in it a powerful assault on the Enlightenment project. She has had a profound impact on the perspectives of feminist researchers into moral education (Noddings, 1984; Noddings and Witherell, 1991) and on others who have sought to view moral growth as other than linear in nature and hierarchical in structure. Instead, Gilligan and her followers have sought to place *narrative* at the centre of the moral life. A look at what Blum sees as the major differences between her own theories and those of Kohlberg is a useful prelude to understanding why this should be.

According to Blum (1993, pp. 50–3), there are seven such differences and I paraphrase them below:

1 For Gilligan, the moral self is *thick* rather than *thin*, defined by historical connections and relationships. Whereas Kohlberg defines the moral point of view as totally impersonal and objective, for her it is anchored in particularity.

2 For Gilligan this radical particularization of the self extends to the other, whose moral significance cannot be reduced, as Kohlberg would have it, to general categories such as 'friend' and 'person in need'. Moral action, therefore, is irreducibly particular.

3 Gilligan sees the understanding of the other as a far more difficult and complex moral task than does Kohlberg and one that necessitates a stance informed by care, empathy, compassion and emotional sensitivity.

4 Whereas Kohlberg proposes a rational, autonomous self subject to the laws of abstract principle, Gilligan sees the self as 'approaching the world of action bound by ties and relationships (friend, colleague, parent, child) which confront her as, at least to some extent, givens'. (ibid., p. 52)

5 For Kohlberg, formal rationality generates moral action, whereas Gilligan sees it as necessarily involving an inseparable intertwining of emotion, cognition and action.

6 Gilligan rejects Kohlberg's universalistic principles of right action in favour of a notion of 'appropriate response', appraisable by non-subjective standards of care and responsibility.

7 For Gilligan, morality is founded in the caring connections between persons, whereas Kohlberg sees right principle as the initial touchstone from which moral action needs to be judged.

Gilligan, then, defines morality in terms of relatedness rather than autonomy and embraces particularity, complexity, and emotional attachment as opposed to Kohlberg's insistence on universality and rationality. In her vision, justice *and* care co-inhabit morality and we need to listen to and explore a multiplicity of moral voices if we are to understand its nature and its processes in different socio-cultural contexts. Viewed in this light, moral knowledge is not apprehended and understood through the exercise of reason alone; it is too disparate and complex a form of knowledge to fit Kohlberg's developmental paradigm. She and her followers argue that narrative story-telling is the form best suited to hold and convey such knowledge. To understand why, we need to appreciate something of the cognitive nature of narrative and its pervasiveness in our lives.

> Narrative, is present in every age, in every place, in every society . . . narrative is international, transhistorical, transcultural; it is simply there, like life itself.
> (Roland Barthes, 1977, p. 79)

In the words of Barbara Hardy (1977), narrative is a 'primary act of mind', which implies that it is one of the key ways by which we attempt to organize and make sense of our experience. Jerome Bruner (1986) has argued that there are, in fact, two modes of thought or ways of knowing, the one *paradigmatic*, the other *narrative*, each of which provides a distinctive way of ordering experience and of constructing reality. Bruner proposes that the concerns and parameters of the two modes of thought are very different. We judge a story using criteria distinct from those we use to judge a scientific hypothesis. Whereas the latter strives for well-formed, logical argument, for universal truth conditions, the former aims for verisimilitude. Inquiring more specifically into the narrative mode of thought, he suggests that 'Narrative deals with the vicissitudes of human intention' (ibid., p. 16) and that the narrative imagination leads to: 'good stories, gripping drama, believable (though not necessarily "true") historical accounts' (ibid., p. 13). Arguing that we should regard the self as deeply cultural in its nature, he draws the following conclusion:

> Insofar as we account for our actions and the human events that occur around us principally in terms of narrative, story, drama, it is conceivable that our sensitivity to narrative provides the major link between our own sense of self and our sense of others in the social world around us. (ibid., p. 69)

Given Gilligan's emphasis upon the socio-cultural embeddedness of moral knowledge, her belief that it is founded and constructed within particular relationships of care and connection, then narrative discourse as defined by Bruner becomes the natural form through which we make moral sense of our lives. Like Gilligan, Bruner sees such knowledge as simultaneously rational *and* affective, enabling us to 'perceive, feel and think at once' (1986, p. 69). Narrative, therefore, can convey the messiness of reality and the moral life and also something of its thickness and complexity.

Theorists and researchers who have been influenced by Gilligan have concluded that it is through the *narrative* mode of thought that the moral life can be broached, understood and explained; and that it is through stories that our ethical propensities develop (Day, 1991a, 1991b; Freeman, 1991, 1993; Tappan, 1991a, 1991b; Noddings and Witherell, 1991; Witherell and Pope-Edwards, 1991). The focus of their attention tends toward people's storying of their own moral experience, not their understanding of it through works of narrative fiction. They concentrate upon narrative as a way of thinking, not upon works of literature; upon the content of personal narratives as the way to find and define an individual moral voice. This approach, mistrusting any ideological imposition of moral values, seeing values as shifting and unstable, respecting difference and choice, resonates strongly with the sentiments of postmodernism and a climate of moral relativism.

Alasdair MacIntyre and the Aristotelian Tradition

If Gilligan's theories emanate from her critique on Kohlberg, those of Alasdair MacIntyre arise from a more direct attack on Kohlberg's philosophical antecedent, Immanuel Kant, and upon the Enlightenment Project which he instigated in an attempt to establish a basis for morality founded upon reason alone. MacIntyre's aim is to refute the moral relativism and emotivist thinking which permeates contemporary thinking and, from his historical and philosophical investigations into the failure of the Enlightenment Project, he proposes an alternative moral tradition as the best example we possess of a coherent moral epistemology. In doing so, he places narrative at the heart of his concept of the unity of the moral life and at how morality is learned.

Like a number of other recent ethical theorists (for example Nussbaum, 1986; Taylor, 1989), MacIntyre sees the Aristotelian tradition as providing us with the best guide to the moral life. He argues that contemporary western society suffers from a lack of any coherent agreement around which moral debate can take place and he explains this by pointing to how Emotivism, a philosophy which recognizes no objective or impersonal moral standards, has become embedded in our culture. According to emotivist thinking, if I say *Arson is wrong*, I am uniting a factual statement (that arson destroys property) with a moral judgment that such destruction is wrong. Only the factual statement can be seen as true or false, the moral judgment being no more than an expression of attitude or feeling (MacIntyre, 1981, p. 12). What characterizes contemporary moral debate is its tendency to argue from rival premises so that it ceases to be argument and descends into assertion and counter-assertion; premises that invoke justice and equality, for example, are often at odds with those which evoke success and liberty but we have no way of agreeing on what the correct initial premise should be. This lack of coherence he traces back to the breakdown of the Aristotelian tradition and the subsequent and inevitable failure of the Enlightenment Project to replace it with a new tradition based upon reason. The book consists of a detailed re-examination and a re-affirmation of this tradition, which lasted from early Classical Greece until the late Middle Ages.

Kant took as the prime, moral question 'What rules ought we to follow?' whereas Aristotle took it to be 'What sort of person am I to become?' (ibid., p. 118). This shift in emphasis moves us away from universal maxims toward central human purposes and a concept of man as a functional being.

> According to that tradition to be a man is to fill a set of roles each of which has its own point and purpose: member of family, citizen, philosopher, servant of God. It is only when man is thought of as an individual prior to and apart from all roles that 'man' ceases to be a functional concept. (ibid., p. 59)

In this way, moral qualities can be seen to have factual value, inasmuch as we can define the qualities of a good member of a family in much the same way as we can define the qualities of a good watch. However, such an understanding disappears when the notion of central human purposes is removed from concepts of morality; for MacIntyre, this was one of the key errors of Kantian philosophy. Moral truth, therefore, is not definable as an abstract, universal principle but is best understood as locatable within the social roles that individuals inherit and create for themselves, within their own particular *telos* which they either succeed or fail in fulfilling. And in his explanation of how an individual life can come to be seen as morally coherent, he argues that such coherence is captured in the form of a narrative.

MacIntyre contends that the Aristotelian meaning of virtue is only intelligible as a characteristic of the unitary life and that this unitary self is only comprehensible through narrative, a narrative which is unavoidably historical and social in its nature.

> We are never more (and sometimes less) than the co-authors of our own narratives.... In life ... we are always under certain constraints. We enter upon a stage which we did not design and we find ourselves part of an action that was not of our making. (ibid., p. 213)

(The fact that he is drawn toward using specifically dramatic imagery while expressing this point is something I shall return to in a later chapter). The unity of such a life is the unity of a narrative quest which seeks answers to the two related questions, 'What is good for me?' and 'What is good for man?' and what is good for me has to include what is good for someone who inhabits the social roles I am a part of. This narrative view of the self, therefore, brings together the historical and social identities of the individual and emphasizes community rather than autonomy. Individuals can move forward from their moral particularities in search of the universal but cannot obliterate them and escape into a realm of entirely universal maxims, as Kant suggested they could. When they try, they usually behave worse than they otherwise would; (whether this maxim be *Socialism in One Nation* or the *Irresistibility of Market Forces*, recent western experience would appear strongly to support this view).

MacIntyre's thesis gives central importance not only to the theory of narrative as a moral life lived but to the importance of a canon of stories to shape and inform the moral direction of this life. The reason lies in his concept of tradition and the relationship between individuals and their social roles. As his argument here deals with themes central to this particular book, I quote it at some length.

> Man is in his actions and practice, as well as in his fiction, essentially a story-telling animal. He is not essentially, but becomes through history, a teller of stories that aspire to truth. But the key question for men is not about their own authorship; I can only answer the question 'What am I to do?' if I can answer the prior question 'Of what story or stories do I find myself a part?' We enter human society, that is, with one or more imputed characters — roles into which we have been drafted — and we have to learn what they are in order to be able to understand how others respond to us and how our responses to them are apt to be construed. It is through hearing stories about wicked stepmothers, lost children, good but misguided kings, wolves that suckle twin boys, youngest sons who receive no inheritance but must make their own way in the world and eldest sons who waste their inheritance on riotous living and go into exile to live with the swine, that children learn or mislearn both what a child and what a parent is, what the cast of characters may be in the drama into which they have been born and what the ways of the world are. Deprive children of stories and you leave them anxious stutterers in their actions and in their words. Hence there is no way to give us an understanding of any society, including our own, except through the stock of stories which constitute its initial dramatic resources. (ibid., p. 216)

Our ability to author the moral self is therefore dependent upon our understanding of the virtues embedded in the social roles we are born into and these are learned in part from the stories which are part of our heritage. Like Oakeshott (1962), MacIntyre understands a tradition as a living argument, not as a set of precepts to enforce conformity. Stories, therefore, inform our choices in life, they do not dictate them. It is perfectly consistent with his book that the examples he lists come from legends, parables and fairy tales, from those stories generally grouped under the portmanteau term 'traditional' and it is upon such genres of tales that I now wish to concentrate. Before proceeding, however, I shall attempt to summarize and extend the implications of what has been argued so far and make some tentative proposals of my own.

Moral cognitive developmental theory, with its stress upon the autonomous, rational subject operating within a framework of universal values, has been seriously challenged in the postmodern era by moral theories which place a particular stress upon narrative ways of knowing. From this perspective, the moral self is seen as intricately woven into social and historical networks of relationships (Gilligan) and roles (MacIntyre). Gilligan and her followers see the areas of affect — care, compassion, emotional sensitivity — as inextricably bound to the rational intellect within the domain of moral experience and they view such experience as unavoidably particular and resistant to generalization according to abstract moral principles. They see the moral domain as multi-faceted; have a shared interest in the narratives of lived moral experiences; see language and culture as the fundamental constituents and mediators of moral meaning; and see the problem of interpretation of moral meaning as a deep problem in post-structuralist and postmodernist terms. They argue for a greater use of personal narratives in education and educational research to enable students and researchers to understand better how the moral life finds expression. MacIntyre has a similar view on the socio-historical particularity of the moral life and rejects the Kantian quest for universal maxims. Whereas those moral theorists influenced by Gilligan present their voices as adjuncts to or critiques of Kohlberg's paradigmatic theory, MacIntyre locates his theories of narrative as part of an alternative, Aristotelian tradition which, he argues, presents a coherent philosophy for living the moral life according to virtues, not maxims, which are only expressible from within social roles. These virtues, — courage, honesty, integrity, loyalty, practical wisdom and kindness, to name some of the more obvious — conform largely to what Bernard Williams (1985) describes as *thick* concepts, specific ethical notions which constitute a *system of ethics* as opposed to *a morality system*. This is an important distinction and one which, at this point, needs to be pursued.

Williams describes morality as a peculiarly modern version of ethical thought.[5] The thicker, ethical concepts are, he argues, vague by their very nature. This is not a weakness, for:

> although evaluative and action-guiding, (they) are also 'world-guided' in the sense that their proper application 'is determined by what the world is like.' (Scheffler, 1996, p. 13)

In contrast, the morality system which pervades modern thought demands a sharp boundary for itself and is dominated by restrictively abstract and 'thin' concepts which seek to represent all ethical conclusions as statements of obligation. Williams argues that, unlike judgments within the morality system, those which use thick concepts amount to a body of knowledge as they embrace both fact and value and are based upon notions of the world as it actually is. He, too, is drawn to narrative, to Homer, Sophocles and Thucydides, as they represent:

> human beings as dealing sensibly, foolishly, sometimes catastrophically, some-
> times nobly, with a world that is only partially intelligible to human agency
> and in itself is not necessarily well adjusted to ethical aspirations. (cited in
> Scheffler, op. cit., p. 13)

To advocate the centrality of narrative in the moral education of young school-children is, therefore, to propose that we concentrate on the broader, 'thicker' field of ethics rather than the narrower, 'thinner' field of the morality system.

Such advocacy does not imply an abandonment of institutional rules and practices intended to develop a sense of community, responsibility and auto-nomy. What I am proposing is that such practices are compatible with a view of moral education akin to a system of ethics, as advocated by Williams, MacIntyre and Gilligan; and that stories have a particularly important role in enabling children to explore the nature of the ethical life as it is experienced. One of the major problems with the morality system at the centre of the Kohlberg/Kantian approach, seeking as it does to bind together duty, practical necessity and logical consistency, is that it presents morality as though it were a rational puzzle, a series of dilemmas we preside over as impartial judges. It therefore fails to capture the *feel* of the moral impulse, with its attendant urgency and commitment but also the confusion and messiness of it all. The Aristotelian view, summarized here by Nussbaum, is sensitive to this:

> what we find in practice is not a sharp contrast between absolute claims and
> claims that can be avoided with ease but a messier continuum of claims
> judged to have various degrees of force and inevitability. (1986, p. 30)

Kohlberg, although accepting the sharp reality of moral dilemmas, neverthe-less proposes that this continuum of claims can be rationally resolved into a hierarchy. By contrast, the ethical system, I would suggest, presents a model which will make sense to both teachers and children, recognizing as it does the existence of conflicting moral feelings without suggesting that this conflict is solely due to our own poor reasoning powers. Nor does it propose that all claims are relative and therefore beyond judgment and evaluation.

Intrinsic to the argument of MacIntyre and to feminist moral theorists such as Gilligan and Noddings is the location of morality within the social world; the fact that the social world will provide different roles and relationships for each of us to fulfil; and that these roles and relationships will bring different moral pressures to bear on us, none of which may be any the less binding than another. Hence ethical judgment is particular, problematic and dependent upon context; for many of Gilligan's followers, irremediably so. Aristotle, however, insists that generalizations are possible, but that they must be informed by observations and experiences of the particular. A medical analogy may be helpful. Each case of cancer a doctor may need to treat is specific, different but is of necessity informed by other similar cases. The understanding the doctor gains from them is dependent upon an appreciation of both difference and similarity. But what is important is that the *particular* is not synonomous with the *unique*. Thus stories — or, in a medical context, case studies — inform the doctor how to act. And so, too, with the moral life. It may be difficult to argue for universal laws as Kohlberg understood them, but that does not imply that we must avoid making moral generalizations. Stories inform our capacity to make such generalizations.

Aristotle's concept of the virtues presents us with a moral vocabulary which is at once precise and problematic, open to development and to debate. For example, we may all agree that *courage* is a virtue; but what characterizes it and how it will be expressed in different circumstances and contexts will vary according to individual perceptions shaped by personal, cultural and historical experience. Hence its *thickness* as a concept, its ability to embrace fact *and* value, and the role of stories in helping us to explore the depth and complexity of this thickness. Whether we describe our present-day, British society as post-structuralist, postmodern or just contemporary, there is little doubt that the dominant ideas of the old grand narratives — religious, political, ideological — are under question as we witness an increasingly pluralistic proliferation of culture and belief. As Fred Inglis argues:

> The individualizing of values which is the inevitable product of a global cul-
> ture made up of dozens of maps of local knowledge means that none of the
> old structures of morality and the education they fathered can hold.... In
> these circumstances, a moral education composed of relatively secure precepts
> and maxims will not serve. Each individual must act morally but without maxims.
> (1993, p. 212)

In such a world, he sees stories as the only resource we have left to provide us with moral guidance.

> The guide (the) individual needs is the canon of the world's stories. The route
> from impersonal morality to personal life is marked by the narrative.... The
> stories we tell ourselves about ourselves are not just a help to moral education;
> they comprise the only education which can gain purchase on the modern
> world. (ibid., pp. 213–214)

Inglis' assertion moves us into the specific areas of biography and literature and thus raises further questions as to what kind of moral learning *literature* offers us and whether this applies to the canon of the world's fairy stories; for, notwithstanding the endorsement of MacIntyre, to argue the specific case for using fairy stories in the moral education of young children must take into account their nature as fictional narratives and whether this is compatible with the moral potential of narrative as defined within the human sciences.

Notes

1 For a full and readable account of the philosophical and educational principles underpinning Kohlberg's ideas, with selective details from his research findings, see Kohlberg, L. (1971).

2 In the appendices to the above article, Kohlberg provides definitions of the moral stages with examples of the type of reasoning which illustrates their attainment, together with a list of what he defines as the universal aspects of morality. See op. cit., pp. 86–92.

3 As an illuminating example, I quote from Erikson, (1977, p. 239), where he describes how, in Stage 6, the healthy individual achieves the stage of *Intimacy*. One of the goals of this stage is the *Utopia of genitality*. This, Erikson explains, should include:
   1. mutuality of orgasm
   2. with a loved partner
   3. of the other sex
   4. with whom one is able and willing to share a mutual trust
   5. and with whom one is able and willing to regulate the cycles of
      a. work
      b. procreation
      c. recreation
   6. so as to secure the offspring, too, all the stages of a satisfactory development.
   Homosexuals may well have criticized such a perspective when Erikson wrote *Childhood and Society*, but their criticisms would be seen as far more mainstream than marginal today.

4 There has been a great deal written about Gilligan's theories in recent years and Gilligan herself has revised and developed them. See Hekman, S. (1995) for a comprehensive overview of this development.

5 See Williams (1985) pp. 6–7 for his discussion of the difference between an ethical system and a morality system. See also Scheffler (1996) for an excellent summary of this and of Williams' ideas on the nature of 'thick' concepts.

Chapter 2

Moral Meanings in Literary Narratives and in Myths and Fairy Tales

The recent depth of interest in narrative shown by the human sciences sees in it a natural form for the human mind to apprehend reality as lived experience, regarding it, as we have seen, as 'a primary act of mind'. Paul Ricoeur has shown us how the principal property of a narrative is its sequentiality, its meaning being constructed from the overall configuration of a sequence of events, whether these events be real or imaginary (Bruner, 1990, pp. 43–44). Moreover, White has argued (1981) that to create a narrative is inherently to make a plea for moral legitimacy. As Bruner puts it: 'To tell a story is inescapably to take a moral stance, even if it is a moral stance against moral stances' (1990, p. 51).

Both real and imaginary narratives share these qualities and, according to Bruner, good stories, whether real or imaginary, share additional intrinsic qualities; they subjunctivize experience, inviting the reader to reconstruct what might have happened, opening up rather than closing down possibilities:

> To make a story *good*, it would seem, you must make it somewhat uncertain, somehow open to variant readings, rather subject to the vagaries of intentional states, undetermined. (ibid., p. 54)

This subjunctivity constitutes what the Russian formalists called 'literariness', the literariness of printed stories, far more 'artfully' shaped than the recounted experiences or oral anecdotes which are equally narrative in their form. If all stories must hold a moral stance, then in a *good*, or effective, literary narrative, it must be in such a way so as not to reduce the story's subjunctivity.

Sam Goldberg has explored the type of moral understanding to be gained from literature and his argument is compatible with Bruner's emphasis on subjunctivity. 'Literature', he writes, 'does its moral thinking in the particulars it imagines; and it has to' (1993, p. xv). This is because, whereas philosophy and psychology concentrate on *conduct-morality*, viewing people as moral agents and focusing on their voluntary, intentional actions, narrative literature fuses this vision with a more elusive *life-centred* view of morality. Conduct morality, he argues, deals with issues of *how* to live, while life morality is concerned with how to *live*. If the former centres around matters of right and wrong in human actions, of how the virtues and vices constitute moral character, then the latter characterizes and evaluates modes of living. It deals with:

> the value of manifold capacities, potentialities, wants and needs of human beings; about what is 'truly' human, or what the 'perfection' or 'well-being' of a life consists in, or what are the finest and fullest modes of human vitality. (ibid., p. 36)

What he means by this is best illustrated by his assessment of Jane Austen's achievement in *Mansfield Park*:

> Matters of sensibility, feeling, attraction, grace and ease, hoping and fearing, and desiring, even some sense of fatedness, become inter-twined in each character with matters of judgment, choice, principle and deliberate intentional action; and responsibility is found (by those capable of caring about it and finding it) to apply to the whole of what one is, to how and what one sees things to be, to the life in one as one lives it out. (ibid., p. 285)

Goldberg's emphasis on narrative as 'irreducibly particular and individual' (ibid., p. 282) is conterminous with his view of the moral life as it is actually lived. It is also very much in the same mode of thinking as Gilligan and MacIntyre, stressing the need to understand the moral life in the particular historical, social and cultural conditions which render its actions unitary rather than merely sequential:

> it is such and such a life lived within these and those particular social institutions, practices, beliefs and attitudes, for example, and within these or those personal, sexual and familial relationships. (ibid., p. 43)

He argues that to approach a literary narrative as something embodying preconceived ideas, thought out in the abstract and then illustrated within a text, is erroneous because of: 'the inability of that kind of thinking by itself to make moral sense of people' (ibid., p. xvii). In other words, as this is not how people think and act morally, it is not how stories should be morally constructed or interpreted.

A theory which does much to explain the novel's potential for moral subjunctivity was developed by Mikhail Bakhtin in his reassessment of the work of Dostoevsky (see Kelly, 1992). Bakhtin argued that the early nineteenth century novel was *monological* in its structure, with the omniscient author regulating the interpretation of characters on behalf of the reader. Dostoevsky's novels, on the other hand, are characterized by *polyphony*, where no single voice within a narrative is the bearer of a definitive truth. The perspective of the omniscient author is muddied, the central characters are given a special kind of autonomy through what he described as a *dialogic penetration* of their personalities. Bakhtin's concept of dialogism, as Aileen Kelly explains, amounts to a reinterpretation of the nature of the self:

> He held selfhood to be intrinsically 'dialogical': the self cannot be understood or expressed except in relation to an audience whose real or imagined

responses continually shape the way in which we define ourselves. (Kelly, 1992, p. 44)

The dialogical nature of the self contextualizes it in specific social and historical circumstances and any attempt to monologize it, through such authoritarian discourses as we find in religious, political or moral dogma, are ultimately false attempts to *finalize* it, to resolve its struggle between competing values. Hence Bakhtin's belief that it is through becoming increasingly responsive to the particularities of individual cases that we become more moral, not through our adoption of a set of pre-ordained moral maxims; and hence the real potential of the novel as a source of moral education. What he termed the 'prosaic wisdom' of the novel was:

> its ability to convey the fundamental 'messiness' of the world, the flux of events that cannot be reduced to any set of explanatory principles. (Kelly, op. cit., p. 46)

In such a novel, no view is incontestable and, as in the real world, people's moral stature is expressed through their ability to respond meaningfully to the ambivalence of ordinary existence.

Not surprisingly, Bakhtin's ideas have gained in influence with the advance of postmodernist discourse and they re-emphasize the cultural and historical specificity which other narrative theories of moral understanding hold as a central tenet. The novel convinces by problematizing morality, by countering any attempt to render it straightforward and facile. The theory of dialogism fits well with Iris Murdoch's perspective on the moral function of literature, which she sees as providing 'a renewed sense of the difficulty and complexity of the moral life and the opacity of persons' (1970, p. 49).

The potential for moral learning inherent to literary narratives can be understood, therefore, to rest in their ambiguity and indeterminacy on the one hand and in their contextual particularity on the other. However, such a view presents us with a problem when we turn to traditional tales for it is immediately evident that they by-pass both subjunctivity and historical specificity. They are populated by a range of instantly identifiable, stock characters, such as wolves and witches, princesses and kings, heroes and fools, and are noticeably devoid of the dialogical open-endedness characteristic of the great literary novels, as a delightful short story from Saki (1986) will remind us.

In *The Story Teller*, a beleaguered aunt on a train journey attempts to quieten her unruly charges by telling them a story in which a virtuous girl is saved from an enraged bull by neighbours, who run to her aid because they admire her goodness so much. The tale is not a success; the children listen to it reluctantly and criticize it unsparingly when the aunt has finished. A man sharing the compartment then relates the tale of a girl called Bertha who was 'horribly good', so good that she was awarded medals for her goodness and invited to walk in the king's garden as a special reward. While there, however, she encountered a vicious wolf. Running to the safety of some nearby bushes she hid and almost escaped; but her trembling caused her medals to clink one against the other, betraying her presence to the wolf who promptly ate her. The aunt is outraged, condemning the story as 'improper'; the children, on the other hand, love it. 'That is the most beautiful story I have ever heard!' proclaims the eldest daughter, wistfully. The tale is witty, cynical and very entertaining, debunking as it does the tendency in some Victorian fairy tales for facile moralizing, a pious representation of conventional virtues and a sentimental view of childhood. The children's preference for an improper story is presented as a liberating tonic to the oppressive and tedious didacticism of the aunt's tale and helps explain the popularity of Roald Dahl's stories among children today. Saki's point is that stories do not educate when they are used as vehicles for preaching conventional morality; instead, they bore their listeners and fail to convince.

Saki's parody, then, would appear to contest the enthusiastic endorsement of MacIntyre for traditional tales, underlining instead their shortcomings as sources of moral learning. However, if we are to appreciate more fully the moral discourse of the fairy tale, we must first locate it not as a poor cousin of the literary novel but as a distinct genre in a tradition that includes mythic and folk tales. Unlike the novel, which is a product of educated, literate, western society and can be analysed as such, the literary fairy tale has roots which lie in oral, pre-literate cultures and its cultural, historical and political links with myth and folk tale are complex and disputed, mirroring contradictory claims for the ethical potential of the tales in both historical and contemporary contexts. Significantly, these claims fall into two camps and reflect the universality/particularity dichotomy which characterizes the contemporary debate in moral educational theory. For there are those who see the tales as bearers of spiritual wisdom and universal, eternal truths, embodied within their archetypes and symbolisms; and those who examine their historical and cultural roots, seeing their moral meanings as transient, political and open to change. Although the emphasis in this study is on fairy tales, it is necessary to locate them within this tradition by first looking at their more ancient relatives, myths and folk-tales.

Folk Tales and Myth

There is no agreement among scholars on how to differentiate the genre of myth from that of folk tale, and the term myth, in particular, has connotations so broad, depending upon the context of its use, that a whole thesis could concentrate on these connotations alone. For the purposes of this brief résumé, I propose a bald definition of myth as a fantastic, highly symbolic story, an intricate part of a culture's belief system, expounding values significant to that culture, with central characters who are heroic or God-like. Like myths, folk-tales are ancient and contain similar patterns of fantasy, symbol and magic, forming part of an oral, folk tradition but with central protagonists who originate from humble backgrounds. Thompson (1977) argues that there is some validity for seeing a distinction between the two genres in the case of the Greek and Hindu tales but none whatsover with regard to the tales of the North American Indians. Propp (1984, p. ixx) saw the folk-tale as a 'desacralized myth'; and Benjamin (1992) saw them as an oppressive, socializing agency in primitive societies, performing the same political function as religion in contemporary society. Kirk (1970, pp. 36–41), like Benjamin, attempts to differentiate myth and folk-tale largely in terms of content and both detect a distinctly lighter tone in the folk-tale. Myths, Kirk argues, have serious underlying purposes, whereas folk-tales, although they might reflect upon recurrent social dilemmas, such as how to circumvent a malicious stepmother or a jealous sibling, are never pro-found in their intentions. He perceives the persistence of magic in such tales as 'just a special type of ingenuity' (p. 38) whose purpose is primarily a func-tional one, to provide 'a feeling of satisfaction at the neatness and finality with which an awkward situation is resolved or an enemy confounded' (p. 38). He acknowledges, however, how both magic and trickery serve to exemplify another major feature of European folk-tales, that of wish-fulfilment fantasy, where great material rewards are gained by small but often highly moral actions. 'Morality is one quality left open to the under-privileged' (p. 39) he quips. The fact that rewards for moral actions centre on wealth and riches is, he argues, due to the material poverty of the tellers and listeners in the folk tradition; as the aristocratic myths reflect a society and an audience with no lack of wealth, wish-fulfilment does not take on such a materialistic form in many such tales.

There is some agreement, therefore, that Eurasian folk-tales are optimistic in their content and point to the possibility of material happiness achieved through a mixture of good fortune and moral merit. Whether such rewards, or the nature of the morality they portray, can be judged as moral by conven-tional contemporary standards is, of course, another matter. Tales of the Native North American are different and, as Thompson points out, their mythical and folk traditions merge into each other. As their cultures embody such an attach-ment to and appreciation of the Earth, its beauty and resources, their stories express these values and have attracted the attention of educators in recent years, particularly those concerned with environmental issues in the USA. Musser and Freeman (1989) see the stories of the Plains Indians in precisely these terms and Caduto and Bruchac (1988) have developed an environmental teaching programme centred around a collection of these stories. Referring to Gilligan's ethic of care, they see the tales as material for teaching: 'a sense of being a part of the lives of other people and the Earth, and of wholism and interdependence' (1988b, p. 7).

One of the great scholars of religion and myth was Mircea Eliade (1963). He believed that myths related a sacred history set in primordial time, narrating the deeds of supernatural beings in ways which set examples for humans to codify and order their lives. Myths, he argues, provide religious experiences by being enacted and hence incorporated into the present, which enactment enables humans to be transported into sacred time. Campbell (1949) embraces all the mythologies of the world in a grand, universal theory and sees no real distinction between the function of mythology or folk-tale and, like Eliade, he sees this function as a deeply spiritual one. Drawing freely on the theories of Freud and Jung, he proposes an interpretation of mythical stories as spiritually therapeutic and health-giving. The human subconscious he defines as 'the basic, magic ring of myth' (p. 3) and the function of mythical symbolism is 'to carry the human spirit forward' (p. 11). The central, universal symbol of myth is the figure of the hero and Campbell proposes a typology for the pattern of his heroic quest which is also universal in its application. Every culture in every age needs its own heroes but the universal nature of their individual quests has been captured symbolically in myth, each of which is a 'local carrier of universal themes' (p. 231).

> In myth, the problems and solutions shown are valid for all mankind. (p. 19)
> The heroes of all time have gone before us; the labyrinth is thoroughly known; we have only to follow the thread of the hero-path. (p. 25)

The hero's journey is a model for us all to follow, if we have the courage to undertake it. Its reward is a gift of enlightenment, to be shared with a society, an 'ego-shattering, life-redeeming elixir' (p. 216) but one which will often meet with the harsh rejection by good people at a loss to comprehend its significance. Campbell's perspective is openly religious and his emphasis on symbol is equalled by his emphasis on mystery, revelation and salvation.

Campbell, like Levi-Strauss, attempts a universal theory of myth but Kirk strongly contests such theories, believing that; 'myths differ enormously in their morphology and social function' (1970, p. 7). He examines in detail not only theories of mythological function and meaning — including the ideas of Levi-Strauss, Jung and Freud — but he also draws evidence for his conclusions from a systematic study of mythologies from a diversity of cultural sources. Some myths, he suggests, originated from ritual and ceremonial use, others confirmed the memory of and provided authority for tribal customs; still others had a speculative or explanatory purpose, offering symbolic solutions to problems or asserting visions of a Truth through evocative imagery (pp. 252–259). He offers a very different form of typology from Campbell and one which holds out no privileged position for myth as a bearer of psychological or universal truth, moral or otherwise. Instead, through analysis and example, he proposes that any moral values propounded in myths were local in perspective and form. So, for example, the pervasive presence of the Gods in Greek mythology: 'provided a continuing commentary on human aspirations and limitations and the absurd conflicts between them' (p. 193). Hindu myth, on the other hand, tends to teach explicit lessons from its own belief system:

that worldly affairs are unimportant in relation to the whole of time, that men will be reborn, that reality is equivocal, that the gods are superior, that sex and fertility are good, but that destruction is also necessary. (p. 213)

Unlike Campbell (and Freud and Jung), who see the complex, dream-like symbolism of myth as central to its significance, Kirk sees its narrative story-telling as the primary point of focus. He holds an evolutionary view of myth which lays stress on:

the gradual development of narrative structures, of stories, with complex symbolic implications coming in almost incidentally. (p. 280)

Whereas Campbell sees mythology primarily in symbolic and psychological terms, Kirk scrutinizes it from a perspective which concentrates on cultural and historical meaning, a contrast in approach and emphasis mirrored by different theorists in the field of the fairy story.

Fairy Stories

The term *fairy tale* is nebulous and often used to embrace myth and folk tale: and, whereas MacIntyre equates all traditional tales as important to a child's moral education, Benjamin would apparently dispute such an assertion, evoking the fairy tale and its special kind of 'liberating magic' as the direct opponent of the oppressive teachings of myth (1992, p. 101). Moreover, the contextual referencing of Benjamin, in fact, shows that he clearly had in mind folk tales as well as fairy tales and the differences between the two genres are significant.

Jack Zipes, among others, has documented how the fairy tale is, in fact, a literary phenomenon, emerging in the seventeenth century, when writers began to use oral folk tales as source material for stories, transforming their meanings and their functions in the process of writing them down. Further-more, neither the original western fairy stories, nor the folk tales from which they were derived, were intended exclusively for an audience of children. When writers such as Charles Perrault and the Brothers Grimm began to collect oral folk tales and publish them in collections, it became evident that a new reading public, that of literate children and their parents, enjoyed such tales and thus began a debate which has continued to this day on their moral suitability. Alison Lurie has commented on how this concern has continued to be the prerogative of 'highminded, progressive people' for over two hundred years. She points to how in the eighteenth century, for example, a tale such as *Cinderella* was condemned for painting 'some of the worst passions that can enter a human breast . . . such as envy, jealousy . . . vanity, a love of dress etc.' (1990, p. 17). A more recent attack on the tale finds different values to criticize:

> Why is the stepmother shown to be wicked and not the father? Why is
> Cinderella essentially passive? . . . Why do girls have to quarrel over a man? . . .
> Are all men handsome? Is marriage the end goal of life? Is it important to
> marry rich men? (Zipes, 1979, p. 173)

However, as much as the fairy tale has had its detractors on moral grounds,
it has had its moral apologists. G.K. Chesterton saw them as 'spiritual explorations' (cited in Bettelheim, 1976, p. 24) and Eliade as expressions of psycho-
dramas 'that answer a deep need in the human being' (ibid., p. 35). There are,
in fact, two camps which I shall term the *revisionists* and the *traditionalists*. By
exploring their theories and by looking at how they have influenced writers
and educators, we can begin to map out the moral maze which the field of the
fairy tale has become.

The Revisionist Case

By revisionists, I refer to those writers and critics who are suspicious of the
moral values within the narrative of fairy tales and therefore propose that the
stories need to be revised, or sanitized for an audience of children. Such views
are particularly prevalent today and, as Lurie indicates, their moral objections
may have changed their nature over the years but they form part of a long
tradition; paradoxically, perhaps, it is the work of earlier revisionists that today's revisionists often object to.

Jack Zipes is one of the major contemporary theorists who openly advocates the need to revise fairy tales. In a number of books, he traces their roots
back to the peasant oral folk tradition, where their role, he suggests, was a
subversive one. As part of the peasants' communal property, they embodied
the people's needs and wishes, bridging a gap in their understanding of social
problems, projecting a possible fulfilment of utopian longings within the fantastic imagery of a familiar narrative mode. However, when the tales began to
be written down, their previous malleability became fixed. Whereas they had
formerly been adapted by tellers to the needs and desires of specific communities, writers of the tales, in obliterating the original folk perspective, endowed
the contents of the tales with a new ideology. To illustrate what he means
by this, it is worth referring to his comments on the history of the Red Riding
Hood story. This was first turned into a literary tale by Perrault, who endowed
it with 'an earnest moral purpose' (1993, p. 27). Such a moral purpose needs
to be viewed not only in terms of Perrault's own personal preferences but as
shaped by French social history and the aristocratic taste of the time. Stringent
codes of class and behaviour were being developed into which children needed
to fit. Consequently, the forthright, brave and shrewd heroine of the original
folk narrative was changed into a pretty, passive, innocently gullible little girl.
Perrault's tale became a warning to all little girls to beware of strangers, to
obey their parents and, within its imagery, it suggests that if they were ever

seduced and raped, it would be through their own negligence and compliance. Having created such a powerfully symbolic tale, the numerous versions which succeeded it throughout the nineteenth century built upon its potential to socialize little girls in a particular direction. This potential is succinctly summarized by Tatar:

> Foucault has taught us the extent to which socialization produces 'docile bodies' that subject themselves to self-discipline and productive labors (sic). By internalizing a disciplinary regime in each subject, socialization staves off the need for coercive action or repressive measures. (1992, p. 235)

What Zipes objects to is precisely the tale's ability to introject a moral code so successfully; for this moral code he sees as ideologically oppressive. He draws on the writings of numerous feminists, who have a particular interest in the fairy tale due to the type of female images it tends to perpetuate and summarizes their objections thus:

> Not only are the tales considered to be too sexist, racist and authoritarian, but the general contents are said to reflect the concerns of semi-feudal, patriarchal societies. (1983, p. 170)

Zipes points with approval to the work of recent writers who deliberately set out to challenge and reverse some of the expectations in the genre, thus restoring to it its 'emancipatory' and 'liberating' potential (1983, p. 191). In the tale *Prince Amilec*, for example (Zipes, 1986), the archetypal male figures of the king and the prince are portrayed as unintelligent and incompetent, the beautiful princess as bad-tempered and ultimately undesirable and the witch as pro-active, generous and sexually attractive enough to win the prince's hand.

In her analysis of the historical evolution of fairy tales, Maria Tatar points to negative female role models and to a proliferation of images of cruelty and violence, particularly toward women, typifying an outmoded pedagogy of fear. The violent images fairy tales use were taken from a folk-tale tradition where they were an instrument for anarchic humour, before later writers attempted to pervert them into the service of behavioural socialization. In the spirit of Foucault, she makes the point that:

> the entire project of childrearing, including the telling of tales, is invested in a micro-physics of power and is therefore never really in the best interest of the child. Any attempt to pass on stories becomes a disciplinary tactic aimed at the child. (1992, p. 236)

Such a blanket statement would appear to leave no-one, not even the most radical revisionist, with any room for manoeuvre except, perhaps, to shut up and leave the child be. However, she declares herself in favour of: 'breaking the magic spell that traditional tales weave around their listeners' (ibid., p. 237).

> Despite the stabilizing power of print, fairy tales can still be told and retold
> so that they challenge and resist, rather than simply reproduce, the constructs
> of a culture. Through playful disruptions, it is possible to begin transforming
> canonical texts into tales that empower and entertain children at the same
> time that they interrogate and take the measure of their own participation in
> a project to socialize the child. (ibid., p. 236)

The tale of Prince Amilec would evidently fall into this category, as would
publications by Sciezska and Johnson (1991) who, in *The Frog Prince (continued)*, for example, uses parody, ironic humour and shock to subvert the
traditional tale.

Tatar's historical analysis is thorough and she quotes instances of nineteenth century writers, revisionists themselves, such as George Cruikshank,
who had felt compelled to rewrite *Puss-in-Boots* for, as it stood, the tale was
a clever lesson in lying! What she does not note, however, is that the result of
such a layering of moral discourse is bound to be unsatisfactory: deceit and
trickery have to remain intrinsic to the tale because of their strong and persistent
narrative function, a point recognized by both Kirk (1970, p. 38) and Bruner
(1986, p. 20). Consequently, and paradoxically, such tampering often succeeds
in enhancing the ambivalent morality of the tale rather than diminishing it.

Both Tatar and Zipes, therefore, are distinctly post-structuralist in their
perspectives. They attack the oppressive moralizing of the literary fairy tale
and the outmoded values they embody, advocating new, more radical tales to
restore the original role of the folk tale, one whose moral force lies in its drive
toward social and cultural liberation.

The Traditionalist Case

The traditionalist case argues that the canon of the great fairy tales has a
central place in the social and moral education of children and its most influential exponent of recent times has been Bruno Bettelheim whose book, *The
Uses of Enchantment*, has been described as 'profound and illuminating' by
Mary Warnock, well-known for her active interest in moral education.

Bettelheim argues that the importance of these tales goes deeper than
issues of role models and moral didacticism.

> The paramount importance of fairy tales for the growing individual, resides in
> something other than teachings about correct ways of behaving in the world
> ... The fairy tale's concern is not useful information about the external world,
> but the inner processes taking place in the individual. (1976, p. 25)

These inner processes are the workings of the preconscious and subconscious, as propounded by Freud. The most popular fairy tales are 'purveyors
of deep insights that have sustained mankind through the long vicissitudes of

its existence' (ibid., p. 26). They have come to address, in symbolic form, what he calls 'the eternal questions':

> What is the world really like? How am I to live my life in it? How can I truly be myself? (ibid., p. 45)

For this reason, they should not be revised or tampered with. Furthermore, within the parameters of these bigger questions, the symbolic portrayal of good and evil has a fundamental place.

> Contrary to what takes place in many modern children's stories, in fairy tales evil is as omnipresent as virtue. In practically every fairy tale good and evil are given body in the form of some figures and their actions, as good and evil are omnipresent in life and the propensities for both are present in every man. It is this duality which poses the moral problem, and requires the struggle to solve it. (ibid., p. 9)

There is no ambivalence in the classic fairy tales favoured by Bettelheim; the good win, the bad lose. The use of unambiguous characters and the lack of psychology are important features of this process. As the good figure is straightforwardly and obviously the hero or heroine, the child will identify with it.

> The question for the child is not 'Do I want to be good?' but 'Who do I want to be like?' The child decides on the basis of projecting himself wholeheartedly into one character. If this fairy-tale figure is a very good person, then the child decides that he wants to be good, too. (ibid., p. 10)

Much of the power within fairy tales, he argues, resides in the way they enable a child to work through anti-social urges in symbolic form. He gives the example of a young boy who enjoyed the exploits of Jack the Giant Killer because his subconscious saw the Giants as symbolically representative of grown-ups (ibid., p. 27). Rather than this leading to a desire to commit violence, it purged him of any frustrations and rages that adults, in their role as agents of social control, might have provoked within him. The story showed him that one day he, too, would be like the giant and acquire the same powers. We should not, therefore, worry about the violence in the tales; its purpose is intended and responded to as symbolic rather than literal. What matters is that the figure who represents the force of good is eventually triumphant.

Bettelheim's case for the traditional fairy tale is based upon an orthodox Freudian perspective and his view of the moral development of children is very different from Kohlberg's but similar in its tacit acceptance of social hegemony and the dominant moral discourse. Behind the quasi-mystical regard he holds for fairy tales, his moral perspective is conventional in its intended outcomes, namely the socialization of the child into the necessary givens of dominant, western culture. As such, there is an assumption in his work that the social and moral values within the tales are favourable. Such an outlook, on the surface at least, would appear to be closer to MacIntyre than to Benjamin.

For MacIntyre, what matters are the symbolic roles represented in the tales which present children with the kind of moral choices and decisions which they can expect to face as they grow. Benjamin, too, stresses the types found in fairy tales but for very different reasons; each reveals symbolically how man can escape from the oppressive force of myth; the fool shows how we can act dumb towards it, the wiseacre how the questions myth poses are simple-minded, and so on. By analogy, he implies that a myth is any regulatory socio-religious system of thought used to order the individual against his best interests. In this he shows himself to have more in common with Zipes and Tatar, seeing the moral force of the fairy tale in essentially political terms.

Conclusion

In the field of the human sciences, then, narrative is seen as the form best suited to capture the contextual particularity that characterizes moral action in the contemporary world. Although narrative literature as is exemplified in the canon of great novels can be seen to mirror the particularity of the moral life, the narrative structures of myths and of fairy stories do not appear to do so. Nor are they characterized by the subjunctivity and dialogical form which has been recognized as the other essential attribute to the moral force of the novel. Instead, the tales are either regarded as moral narratives in universal, essentialist terms, quite inappropriate to contemporary cultural perspectives, or as purveyors of an oppressive morality, which is itself equally inappropriate. The conclusion might be to abandon the narrative form of the fairy story altogether, at least for the purposes of moral education, and such conclusions are not unusual in educational circles (see Baird Saenger, 1993).

As a first step to refuting this conclusion, I would suggest that either/or thinking of this type is not our only option and can be replaced by a more inclusive perspective which rejects the quasi-religious universalism of Campbell and Bettelheim whilst respecting their sensitivity to the power of the symbolisms and narrative structures of the tales; and which seeks to combine this respect with a critical mistrust of distortedly inappropriate moral values that may have been layered into them. However, this does not address the apparent inability of the tales to portray the complexity and particularity of the moral life in an appropriate, dialogical form. To do this, we need to examine more fundament-ally the relationship of fairy tales to the two distinct traditions from which its early literary form emerged, namely the *mythic* tradition and the *oral* tradition. As a crucial and integral part of this relationship we find the narrative form of drama, which has, from its very origin, a tradition of engaging with and questioning the moral meanings of tales in the mythic tradition.

Note

1 Lucaks (1968) argues, in effect, that dialogism is characteristic of *any* great novel which, in his phrase, 'contains within itself the seeds of its own criticism', p. 61.

Chapter 3

Myth, Morality and Drama

In an early essay, Bruner explored the pedagogical power of myth and its situation in contemporary society. The form of myth, he argued, is principally that of drama, a fact which lies at the heart of its significance as a source of instruction. Myth has a dramatic shape because that, too, is the shape of the personality. To explain this he refers to Freud, who likened the personality to a cast of characters, which a playwright has the ability to decompose and project into the *dramatis personae* of the stage. The genius of the Greek dramatists lay precisely in their power to do this, to enter vividly into the feelings of the opposing parties in a conflict and to present them on stage in a fashion that was at once both mythic and realistic; that is, through the representation of preternatural forces and characters, they could describe a society which the audience could recognize as its own. But at the heart of the instructive power of myth Bruner locates the dramatic nature of the multiple self, within which our discordant impulses are bound and structured in a set of identities.

> Here myth becomes the tutor, the shaper of identities; it is here that personality imitates myth in as deep a sense as myth is an externalization of the vicissitudes of personality. (1960, p. 280)

Referring to Campbell's concept of the 'mythologically instructed community', he continues:

> the mythologically instructed community provides its members with a library of scripts upon which the individual may judge the internal drama of his multiple identities. For myth . . . serves not only as a pattern to which one aspires but also as a criterion for the self-critic. (ibid., p. 281)

Myth and identity, therefore, exist in a symbiotic relationship, the one with the other. Myths reflect the conflictual and various identities of the psyche which, in turn, finds explanations and models of behaviour from among the corpus of images and identities that myths provide.

> What is ultimately clear is that . . . myth must be a model for imitating, a programmatic drama to be tried on for a fit. (ibid., p. 284).

As drama is not only the principal form of myth but is also *a priori* the shape of the human personality, myths have particular significance; they form 'the treasure of an instructed community' (ibid., p. 286) as they enable individuals to understand the inner conflicts caused by their internal cast of identities. The implication is that we should view our lives not only as narrative but as enacted narrative, where the models we imitate are in enactive form and where much of the drama takes place within the psyche. If drama imitates life, it is because life is experienced not only as narrative but, more particularly, as *dramatic* narrative.

That is not all that Bruner is implying. Myths provide us not only with models to aspire to but with criteria for self-criticism. The psyche has a dialogical relationship with the myths which influence it, a critical awareness, a sense of judgment and choice of identity. And the prevailing myths need to be such that they fit the varieties of our plight and our aspirations so that choices are indeed viable; and this Bruner doubted to be the case in contemporary society.

> All that is certain is that we live in a period of mythic confusion that may provide the occasion for a new growth of myth, myth more suitable for our times. (ibid., p. 285)

Mythic confusion leads to frustration and 'a lonely search for internal identity'.

One might conclude form Bruner's thesis that myths which provide a dramatic fit are crucial to the moral health of a society as they provide individuals with an intelligible dramatic narrative and with roles with which they can identify. In MacIntyre's terms: 'Mythology, in its original sense, is at the heart of things' (1981, p. 216). Although his conclusions are expressed through the discourse of psychology, they resonate with MacIntyre's argument on how we learn the virtues through stories.

Bruner's particular usage of the term *myth* is undefined and embraces not only traditional mythological subject matter but also any idealized life patterns which control a community's visions. It is a definition influenced by Eliade and Campbell, which sees the pervasive influence of myth on the psyche as necessary and beneficial, a view contested, as we shall see, most notably by Roland Barthes. Bruner also has a very broad definition of drama which he conflates rather too easily with myth. Williams has contested this tendency:

> Drama is now so often associated with what are called myth and ritual that the general point is easily made. But the relation cannot be reduced to the usual loose association. Drama . . . is neither ritual which discloses the God, nor myth which requires and sustains repetition. (1975, p. 11)

In other words, where myths aspire to permanence, repeatability and Truth, drama deals in particularity and specificity. These are significant distinctions, which will be returned to later. Nevertheless, Bruner's three areas of interest — the close relationship between myth and drama; how this affects the moral identities of individuals in particular societies; and how myths need to change — will be central to this chapter, where I will argue for a concept of myths which accepts their social necessity but also the necessity for them to change; which recognizes their power to educate but also their power to distort; and which views their apparent universality as a potent stimulus to the imagination but, in the final analysis, as illusory and dependent upon mutability and translatability rather than any real state of permanence. Within these tensions, I believe, lies their potential for moral regeneration, a potential which needs to be tapped. For, if the quest for identity, the search for the good life, is at the heart of the moral process, when it is lonely and inward looking, when the communal narratives and the myths which inform them fail to make connections with individuals, then, to borrow MacIntyre's phrase, these individuals will become alienated, 'anxious stutterers in their actions as in their words' (op. cit., p. 216). And where we read myth in an adult context, so we should read fairy tale in a child's context, for fairy tales themselves are mythic constructs, collectively presenting models for children to 'judge the drama of their internal identities', dramatic roles embodying concepts of virtue for them to identify with and to imitate. But this latter claim — that, within these parameters, we can conflate fairy tale with myth — needs some arguing first.

Fairy Tale as Myth

If Bruner approaches the field of myth from a psychological perspective informed by Freudian theory, so too does Bettelheim; but, when comparing fairy tale with myth, Bettelheim's conclusions are typically orthodox and clear-cut.

> Mythical heroes offer excellent images for the development of the superego, but the demands they embody are so rigorous as to discourage the child in his fledgling strivings to achieve personality integration. While the mythical hero experiences a transfiguration into eternal life in heaven, the central figure of the fairy tale lives happily ever after on earth, right among the rest of us. Thus a happy though ordinary existence is projected by fairy tales as the outcome of the trials and tribulations involved in the normal growing-up process. (1976, p. 39)

According to Bettelheim, children know they can only emulate the virtues of the mythical hero to some small degree. These heroes, in fact, are there to fashion the conscience, to impose an idealistic set of goals for children to live up to — a view not unlike Walter Benjamin's, although Bettelheim sees the function of myth as healthy, not oppressive. For Bettelheim, then, fairy tales and not myths are the stories which offer role models 'with a dramatic fit', promising the possibility of future happiness on earth.

> Whatever strange events the fairy tale hero experiences they do not make him superhuman, as is true for the mythical hero. This real humanity suggests to

the child that, whatever the content of the fairy tale, it is but fanciful elaborations and exaggerations of the tasks he has to meet, and of his hopes and fears. (ibid., p. 40)

Bettelheim's distinction between myth and fairy tale suggests, paradoxically, that, in Bruner's sense of the term, fairy tale *is* myth. Jack Zipes has no doubts that the fairy tale is indeed myth, although his definition is more complex, his use of the word *myth* more expansive and the implications he draws more circumspect. His theories are drawn from an ideological standpoint which has a broad, social vision of myth but which mistrusts its political purposes. If Bettelheim sees myths as essentially pessimistic and Bruner sees them as mirroring the conflictual identities of the psyche, then Zipes sees them as deceptively oppressive.

What interests Zipes is how myths and fairy tales continue to exercise a hold over the western imagination. They appear to be natural, eternal, to contain universal truths; but this is, in fact, an illusion.

These myths and fairy tales are historically and culturally coded, and their ideological impact is great. Somehow they have become codified, authoritative and canonical. . . . They seem to have been with us for centuries, for eternity, but we neglect the manner in which we created gods and magic to hold our experiences and lives intact. (1994, p. 4)

This illusion is the result of an ideological mythicization of the tales and to describe how this has been effected, Zipes refers to the theories of Roland Barthes.

Myth consists in overturning culture into nature or, at least, the social, the cultural, the ideological, the historical into the 'natural'. (Barthes, 1977, p. 165)

If myth, according to Barthes, is 'a type of speech . . . frozen, purified, eternalized, made absent . . .' (Barthes, 1973, p. 123), then myths assume the look of generality but are laden with hidden, ideologically weighted values. That fairy tales appear to be natural, universal, ahistorical and therapeutic in fact disguises their historical origins as literary versions of tales which originated in oral peasant communities but which were appropriated in literary forms first of all by the eighteenth century French aristocracy and later, in the service of domesticating the imaginations of children, by the nineteenth century bourgeoisie. Zipes believes that perspectives such as Bettelheim's, which insist on regarding the tales as quasi-religious, sacred texts, serve only to perpetuate a bourgeois hegemony.

Worship of the fairy tale as holy scripture is more of a petrification of the fairy tale that is connected to the establishment of correct speech, values, and power more than anything else. (Zipes, 1994, p. 15)

Fairy tale is myth because none of this oppressiveness is immediately evident. The tales are revered as eternal and universal, when they are, in fact, ideologically constructed, historically situated, cultural artefacts that continue to fascinate; but the important point is that they *are* open to revision. Revisionist fairy tales are written to disturb the values of the classic tale in an attempt to demythicize the genre, 'to alter the reader's views of traditional patterns, images and codes' (ibid., p. 9).

Zipes' perception of the educative inadequacy of traditional fairy tales and his promotion of new, revised versions contrasts with Bettelheim's aggressive conservatism but is compatible with Bruner's call for a new growth of myth more suitable for our times. The revisions Zipes refers to, both here and in other works, are literary revisions — that is, ideologically motivated, individually authored, new, printed versions of fairy stories. Such versions tend to be monological, prioritizing the author's moral vision. What is more interesting for this study is his analysis of the oral folk tale, the historical precedent of the literary fairy tale, which was very different in its form and function. From this analysis we can begin to appreciate that there is another, more dialogical approach to revising fairy stories; for once the stories are readdressed in a communal, performative manner rather than as a private, printed endeavour, there can result a significant and transformative effect on their inherent values, approaching what Williams has called:

> a complex opening up of ritual to public and variable action; a moving beyond myth to dramatic *versions* of myth and of history. (1975, p. 11)

Oral folk-tales were told by gifted tellers, intended to explain natural occurrences such as the change in seasons, to celebrate the rites of harvesting or hunting, to amuse, and to offer possibilities of fantasy wish-fulfilment. Their social function, according to Zipes, was to bring members of a tribe or community closer together, to provide them with a sense of purpose or *telos*. It was a communal, not a private experience.

> The tale came directly from common experiences and beliefs. Told in person, directly, face to face, they were altered as the beliefs and behaviours of the members of a particular group changed. (op. cit., p. 10)[1]

There are three highly significant points here. First of all, the tales were related in versions which were locally determined, not universal in Bettelheim's sense, dealing with themes which were relevant to a particular community at a particular time; claims for the ephemeral, universal and timeless wisdom of fairy tales are very difficult to sustain when we appreciate that there was never any one, original, sacred version, acting as the bearer of psychic truths. Secondly, the tales were part of a shared, public process, more akin to a dramatic performance than a private, literary reading; and finally they were adaptable to change, historically and geographically, to address the needs and concerns of particular communities which constituted the audience. It is evident that herein lies a way of reappropriating the literary fairy tale; for the oral tradition offers, within its very form, a means whereby the literary tale can be communally redefined, repossessed or, as Zipes would have it, demythicized. Demythicization might be understood as a process akin to the raising of political awareness, its intention being to enable the members of a community to become critically aware of the stories *as myth*, to rehistoricize them and thus create a critical distance between the listeners and the tales in order to break their oppressive hold.[2] But such a communal sharing of a mythic story might also be deployed as the beginning of a process of mythic renewal, by which I mean the presentation of the story from a moral perspective which renders it problematic, brings conflictual elements to the fore and allows for the construction of new meanings relevant to a particular community. Such an approach might encourage, in turn, new perspectives to be shared on how the tale represents thick ethical concepts, thus working against the reifying tendency of myth, defined by Slotkin as: 'a . . . process through which metaphorical descriptions of reality come to substitute for an apprehension of reality' (1992, p. 73). In this way the tale could become demythicized in Zipes' sense whilst reclaiming something of its mythic function in Bruner's sense.

Such an approach to myth is not, in fact, new. In classical Athens, the tragic dramatists incorporated a variety of contemporary elements into their shared mythology in order publicly to problematize and play out the ethical and political issues of the time. By turning our attention briefly to these early dramatizations of Greek mythic tales, we find some illuminating analogies. For in the very origins of western drama one of its crucial functions was the process of mythic questioning and rejuvenation, a process which has always been fundamentally concerned with the moral health of a society, which, as we shall see, continues to be active in contemporary British theatre and which I shall propose can and should be active in today's primary school classrooms.

Myth and Morality in Classical Greek Drama

The same mythology was a language which served different masters long and well as the dynamics of thought. Its use in each period, however, was different and with each social advance its previous service was already done. The tribal kings used mythology to support their dynasties, the aristocracy to enhance their prestige, the tyrant perhaps to reconcile and appease, the democracy to express its conflicts. (Little, 1967, p. 9)

Little's description of the historically transient meanings derived from mythology within the ancient Greek world is succinct. He stresses the significance of the stories as bearers of shared meanings which were adapted, or rather translated, from era to era in order to legitimize the prevailing power structures. There is a danger, however, that the picture presented by the above quotation may appear rather too clear-cut and simplistic. For the stories were not simply reappropriated by the new controllers of each succeeding social structure;

rather there was a confusing period of transition, where the language of the virtues, contained and defined within the Homeric myths, became no longer sufficient to provide understanding and guidance for social action. By the time democracy had been established in Athens, this language had become a source of debate and the tales a means for exploring the ethical and political values of the *polis.*

MacIntyre (1967, 1981) has described this moral transition at length. For Homer, there was no distinction between social role and individual virtue. A man was deemed to be good if he possessed (i.e. performed) the virtue of his allotted social function; for the king, the ability to command, for a wife, fidelity and so on. There was no way of being good which lay outside the perform-ance of one's role and shame was felt by the person who failed to perform it successfully. Moral concepts were social facts but could only be applied to those for whom the social system had provided a vocabulary; slaves, for example, lay outside the moral order and were thus given the status of chattel rather than person. The poems of Homer presented an idealization of a par-ticular kind of social life which became problematic as soon as the idea of a single moral order broke down. One of the results of this breakdown was a change in the concept of the nature of virtue, which came to signify certain human qualities which could be divorced altogether from social function.

As post-Homeric Greece became more widely aware of radically different social orders — through the impact of the Persian invasion, colonization, increase in trade and travel — those philosophers who came to be known as *sophists* began to debate the relativity of certain moral concepts; for example, as different cities observed different customs and laws, was justice itself a relative concept, definable only within those laws and customs which differed from city to city? By the fifth century BC moral and political conservatives were still trying to retain the fixed, Homeric meanings of the received vocabulary which had defined the different virtues of friendship, courage, self-restraint, wisdom, justice and so on. A failure to achieve this stability of language and myth was seen by some as a major cause of moral degeneracy. Thucydides, for example, made the following indictment of revolutionaries in Corfu:

> The meaning of words no longer had the same relation to things, but was changed by them as they thought fit. Reckless doing was held to be loyal courage; prudent delay was the excuse of a coward; moderation was the disguise of manly weakness; to know everything was to do nothing. (cited in MacIntyre, 1967, p. 12)

These causes of moral confusion in pre-classical Greece are reminiscent of the postmodern condition which characterizes western society in our own age, a similar era of growing moral relativism where the prevailing myths are clung to by conservatives but have nonetheless, for many people, lost their moral cogency[3], and where there is wide-scale disagreement over the meanings held within the vocabulary of moral precepts. MacIntyre describes how, within this context, the philosophers of classical Athens attempted to redefine the virtues, not out of any clear sense of agreement but, in his words, 'as a response to incoherence' (1981, p. 135). And the dramatists, in a similar response to incoherence, reworked the stories which were the heritage of their mythologically instructed community and represented the conflicting views of political and moral virtue that existed within their democratic society. A brief look at how two of the great tragedians treated the same Homeric myth will provide an illustration of how new versions of the same myth could be presented to carry differing moral emphases.

In the *Oresteia* (transl. Vellacott, 1988) of Aeschylus, the story of Agamemnon's return from the Trojan Wars, his murder at the hands of his wife and her lover and the subsequent trail of matricide and revenge this engenders, is presented as a conflict of loyalties, between those demanded by kinship and those owed to the laws of state. Although no secure or facile solution to the conflict can be offered, the drama ends on a note of civil concord, emphasizing the rational power of justice embodied within the civil legislature of Athens. The final play of the cycle, *The Eum
inedes*, uses myth to extol the necessity of this new moral code, that embodied within civic law, as opposed to the pre-democratic and tribalistic code of family vendetta and vengeance, which still persisted in playing a disastrous role in Athenian society. The purification of Orestes' matricide at the conclusion of the play is an offer of hope and an affirmation of the rationality of the democratic legal system of the city. By contrast, the *Electra* of Euripides (transl. Vellacott, 1972), dealing with the same act of vengeance, portrays it as conceived and committed through fear and weakness. Whereas the command of the Oracle, that Orestes murder Clytemnestra and Aegisthus, is treated with sympathy by Aeschylus, it is portrayed by Euripides as a challenge which, if Orestes had the moral strength, he would resist. His compliance with the command is presented as an act of moral cowardice, the act of someone who prefers to obey authority, despite the wickedness of its orders, rather than face up to moral independence. Both plays use the myth to explore the same social evil but, whereas Aeschylus celebrates a political solution, Euripides condemns the moral weakness of individuals. As Williams comments in his own, brief commentary on the plays: 'it is not just detail that is altered; it is the dramatic meaning of the experience' (1968, p. 221). And, as a result, the *moral* meaning of the experience.[4]

Why did drama become the medium for the interrogation and revision of myth in classical Athens? Bruner of course would see the explanation partially in psychological terms — drama being the natural shape of myth because drama reflects the shape of the personality. But more convincing are those arguments which take into account the public, political function of drama and its direct linkage with earlier communal forms of storytelling in what was still essentially an oral culture. Green (1994), in tracing the emergence of Greek theatre, sees as seminal the fact that Attic society was in a state of transition from an oral to a literate society, where storytelling had the important social function argued by Zipes.

> It is typical of many societies that story-telling . . . has the effect of binding
> these societies or communities together. The common experience these stories
> represent reinforces the communal aspects of their life. . . . Theatre developed
> in a context where a level of 'public' performance was the norm, and where
> stories were heard rather than read. (1994, pp. 5, 6)

Storytelling in verse developed during shared ritual practices, where the people
met as a community during important times of the year and critical times of
life. Theatre, therefore, was 'a product and an aim of community activity' (ibid.,
p. 6), 'The performances belonged to the community. They were theirs' (ibid.,
p. 9).

Moreover, Green emphasizes that, although the Chorus came to act on
behalf of the audience, the dividing line between performers and audience
was never fully evolved and that consequently there was a much greater sense
of audience involvement than is current in contemporary western theatre.

This sense of general involvement Rush Reim (1994) locates within a
broader analysis of what he describes as the 'performance culture' which existed
in Athens. He sees at its heart the participatory democratic process itself, where
up to four times a month the freeborn citizens of Athens could meet to join
in directly with the governance of their city, having the right to speak and to
vote. This culture he defines as one which:

> played out its political and ethical concerns in an aggressively public and
> performative fashion. (1994, p. 74)

The Greeks' was a theatre with a powerful social function, for theirs was a
society, as MacIntyre points out, where the categories political, dramatic and
philosophical were much more intimately related than is generally accepted in
our society today.

> Politics and philosophy were shaped by dramatic form, the preoccupations of
> drama were philosophical and political, philosophy had to make its claims in
> the arena of the dramatic. . . . We lack, as they did not, any public, generally
> shared communal mode either for representing political conflict or for putting
> our politics to the philosophical question. (1981, p. 138)

This lack identified by MacIntyre has been criticized by contemporary practitioners such as Edward Bond and Peter Brook who see a central, moral role
for theatre in any healthy, democratic society.

> It is precisely here (in the theatre) that we find our need for justice and not
> merely for food and clothing — it is our need for the meaning to our life.
> (Bond, 1995)

MacIntyre sees the communal and political centrality of drama as inseparable
from the particular vision it embodies of ethical action in general. To adopt a

stance on the virtues is to adopt a stance on the narrative character of human life:

> the difference between the heroic account of the virtues and the Sophoclean amounts precisely to a difference over what narrative form captures best the characteristics of human life and agency. (op. cit., p. 144)

He provides an important clue as to what characterizes the dramatic narrative as opposed to other narrative forms when he describes as 'a Sophoclean insight: that it is through conflict and sometimes only through conflict that we learn what our ends and purposes are' (ibid., p. 164).

This understanding brings us full-circle, for both he and Bruner see the conflicts at the centre of mythic drama as educative of life as it is lived and experienced. In other words, just as morality is expressed through social action, drama is the artform that mirrors and is shaped from social action. In Athens, drama, the most performative and public of art forms, was an integral part of the democratic process; and the publicly shared reinterpretation of myth allowed for an open interrogation of moral and political values which could be manifestly celebrated, revealed as conflictual, challenged or reassessed.

Myth, Morality and Drama Today

When comparing drama with myth, Williams makes some crucial distinctions. Drama, he insists, is:

> specific, active, interactive composition . . . an open practice . . . a complex opening of ritual to public and variable action; a moving beyond myth to dramatic versions of myth. . . . (1975, p. 11)

Williams chooses his words carefully and, as usual, they are dense with meaning. The fact that drama is *specific* emphasizes its particularity; it is an *active*, not a passive experience; it is *interactive* — social, perhaps participatory; and it is a *composition*, constructed consciously with some specific meaning or function. Drama is an *open practice*, not closed and private but public and open-ended so that, through it, the closed narratives of myth and ritual become *variable* through *action*, action which mirrors the social and moral life. So, through drama, we *move beyond* the presentation of myths as narratives which aspire to carry universal meanings irrespective of time and culture to *versions* of these narratives, each exploring meanings dependent upon the contexts within which they were created. In other words, if myth demands assent, drama implies dissent and thus exposes myth to public reinterpretation and change.[5]

I am proposing that, historically, in western theatre, there has been an association between drama and myth which has been one of interrogation, revision and renewal and that this process has traditionally had a moral as well as a cultural function. O'Neill is surely right when she states:

> These ancient motifs and relationships are played out again and again through the ages and still speak freshly to us. (1995, p. 33)

Often these motifs have permeated what appeared to be new stories, as the Phaedra myth permeated Zola's *Thérèse Raquin*, for example; but often the myth has been addressed directly through a reinterpretation of previous dramatic versions of the myths. Gilbert Highet's theory to account for the persistence of mythic drama is blunter than most but characteristic of many:

> The central answer is that myths are permanent. They deal with the greatest of all problems, the problems which do not change, because men and women do not change. (1957, p. 540)

Dickinson (1969) accepts Highet's hypothesis and quotes Hawthorne in the introduction to his study;

> No epoch of time can claim a copyright on these immortal fables. They seem never to have been made; and certainly, so long as man exists, they can never perish; but, by their indestructibility itself, they are legitimate subjects for every age to clothe with its own garniture of manners and sentiments, and to imbue with its own morality. (cited in Dickinson, 1969, p. 1)

Permanent, indestructible, immortal. Such hyperbole will no longer hold. It implies that somewhere there lurks an ideal version of myth, whose meanings are universal, adaptations of which can only 'garnish' this thing of sacred significance which carries its own kernel of indestructible truth. An unhelpful nostalgia can be detected, the reverence for a gorgeous and thickly peopled past which overshadows the present. Kirk offers a more convincing argument for their endurance when he points to: 'the extraordinary literary qualities of the classical works they pervade' (1974, p. 110). It is the quality and age of the literary versions, so many of which are in dramatic form, that provides their awesome sense of permanence and which has led some critics to draw no distinction between myth and dramatized versions of myth. The fact is that there are no permanent versions. 'It is . . . not possible to abstract a single "orthodox" meaning of "the myth"' (1968, p. 221).

Williams' comment on the *Electra* myth is broadly applicable. But with literature, as Kirk has pointed out, comes 'the concept of the fixed text' and, with that, 'the concept of the correct text' (op. cit., p. 110). It is only one step further to the concept of the culturally sacred text.

> In the purely literary sources . . . the myths tend to be treated as something special, as a kind of self-contained wisdom received from the past. (Kirk, op. cit., p. 108)[6]

However, such reverence does not reflect the approach adopted by those twentieth century European playwrights who have chosen to rework the Greek myths, writers such as Giraudoux (1935), Anouilh (1951) and Sartre (1947) and more recent British theatre practitioners such as Edward Bond (1979) and Caryl Churchill (1990). Here there has been a renewed and vigorous interest in openly interrogating the classic versions of the myths. Feminist playwrights, in particular, have been willing to challenge directly the idea of the culturally sacred text and I have chosen to analyse a recent example of this — Timberlake Wertenbaker's play *The Love of the Nightingale* — as it highlights a number of issues of central concern to this study. Formally, it interrelates to myth through an adventurous intertextuality that offers a radical alternative to a more straight-forward re-working of the story. Thematically, it has at its heart the same concerns argued by Zipes, that literary versions of myths, being predominantly part of a male discourse, hold and hide patriarchal values which need to be challenged and demythicized. And, within its reflection on the cultural trans-mission of myth, it provides a critique of the social and moral functions of drama, with implications which are highly significant for the practice of edu-cational drama.

Notes

1 Kirk says very much the same thing as Zipes when he writes: '. . . tales told by story-tellers, or in less formal ways, have no absolutely fixed outline in a non-literate culture. The central themes remain fairly constant but the details and emphases change with the interests of teller and audience' (1974, p. 30).
2 See Zipes (1996) which details projects carried out with classes of children where this is his stated aim.
3 See, in particular, Bloom (1987) and Bennett (1993). These arguments were, of course, rehearsed in some detail in my introduction.
4 This perspective is supported by scholars of Greek Tragedy. See Kitto (1973) pp. 104–106 where he argues that tragic dramatists 'manhandled' the myths, stating that 'Aeschylus made the myth convey what *he* meant' (p. 106). See also Taplin (1985) p. 165, who emphasizes that 'Greek tragedy is entirely topical and the mirror of its own times. It was composed for the audience of fifth century Athenians, not for a Bronze Age audience; and its general preoccupations, moral, social and emotional are those of its age.'
5 I am, of course, writing from the perspective of western drama here. Asian theatre practices, on the contrary, allow for no such challenge or variation, as was graphic-ally illustrated in the case of Beijing Opera by the film *Farewell, My Concubine*.
6 The resonances here with Bettelheim's approach to the classic fairy tale texts are telling. Although he proposes that fairy tales are better told than read to allow for greater flexibility, his comments upon which versions should be related and why reveal that this flexibility is indeed limited. See 1976, pp. 150–156 on the telling of fairy tales; and pp. 166–183 on why, according to Bettelheim, the Grimms' *Little Red Cap* is preferable to Perrault's *Little Red Riding Hood*.

Chapter 4

Re-casting the Phaedra Syndrome: Myth and Morality in Timberlake Wertenbaker's *The Love of the Nightingale*

In a recently published study, Albert S. Gérard examines what he calls *The Phaedra Syndrome* in four major theatrical texts: *Hippolytos* by Euripides; *Phaedra* by Seneca; Lope de Vega's *El Castigo sin Venganza*; and *Phèdre* by Racine. The subtitle of his book — *Of Shame and Guilt in Drama* — indicates the nature of the preoccupations of his inquiry; not only is it an analysis which contrasts the way that several important playwrights have presented the character of Phaedra but, more interestingly, it is an investigation into how their treatment of her relates to the moral and intellectual climate of their times. The story of Phaedra's incestuous love for her stepson is, he argues, 'an archetypal situation of transgression' and his explanation of its persistent fascination as a source for drama is worth quoting in full.

> In the nutshell of the nuclear family the emergence of a sexual relationship between the husband's son and his stepmother offers a fascinating diversity of subversive trends, especially where the 'natural' phallocratic authority of the paterfamilias is sanctioned by public opinion and religious dogma. Such a situation compounds adultery with incest. It brings into play the fundamental psychological motivations of love and honour, sex and vengeance. It exemplifies the utter disruption of natural order and moral hierarchies. It almost inevitably compels author and reader alike to pass moral judgement and to take sides in the contest between natural impulses and ethical precepts. (1993, p. 3)

He concludes his essay with some interesting observations on postwar treatments of the Phaedra syndrome, which he sees as having resurfaced in films such as Ingmar Bergman's *Smiles of a Summer Night* (1956), Louis Malle's *Le Souffle au Coeur* (1971) and Bertolucci's *La Luna* (1979). What characterizes these treatments is their lack of moral outrage and even cheerful violation of one of the ultimate social taboos, direct mother-son incest. Such a 'trivialization of sex in art' he sees as directly spawned by the 'postwar permissive society, one of whose most conspicuous characteristics is the liberation of sex from ethical considerations' (ibid., p. 134) and he doubts whether the Phaedra syndrome can be regarded as a relevant topic for serious aesthetic treatment in contemporary society.

Gérard is no doubt right to speculate that Phaedra's agony of sexual guilt does not speak directly to the preoccupations of a contemporary audience but his diatribe against western society's 'so-called "liberalism" and hedonistic laxity' (ibid., p. 135) is critically unhelpful. Issues of sex and ethics remain very much at the heart of contemporary moral concern but there are now competing philosophical frames of experience through which they are viewed. In particular, Feminism has challenged the very phallocratic authority within which the Phaedra myth is firmly rooted. Whereas a stepmother's lust for her stepson may formerly have proved to be powerfully symbolic of a threat to the moral and social order, from a feminist perspective this order is one defined and described by men. This is particularly significant when the themes explored — sex, shame and guilt — are represented within the person of a female. In fact, Phaedra is one of many 'guilty' stepmothers within the western mythic tradition, stretching from Pharoah's wife in *Genesis* to the Queen in Disney's *Snow White*. As a part of this male discourse, the Phaedra syndrome can be seen as one of a number of potent cultural myths embodying hidden attitudes and values with regard to male and female sexuality which need to be exposed and challenged, as they distort social reality at the same time as they help shape social assumptions; for, enshrined as it is within major works of western theatre, the myth may be muted in our times but is by no means silent. I wish to suggest that such a challenge has, in fact, been raised in Timberlake Wertenbaker's play *The Love of the Nightingale*.

In order to interrogate the values of the Phaedra syndrome, Wertenbaker has chosen an alternative myth as the plot for her play, that of Philomele. It is a myth in which the incestuous lust is experienced by a King for his sister-in-law rather than by a Queen for her son-in-law and where the lust is consummated through rape rather than denied and repressed. It is a complex play which David Ian Rabey sees as:

> the culmination of Wertenbaker's questionings of the terms and conditions of using language, making moral judgments and being human. (1990, p. 527)

From this perspective its themes are indeed broad but it is through the play's dialogic relationship with the Phaedra myth that some of its more important meanings emerge. This relationship is engaged on more than one dramatic level and, through investigating it, we can see how Wertenbaker deprivileges the dominant discourse of the Phaedra syndrome by having it interanimate with a relatively unknown myth which treats the same themes of sex, guilt, shame and vengeance but with crucial underlying gender differences.[1] At the same time, it raises questions concerning the moral and educational function of mythic drama and, in particular, the ethical need for female voices to engage dialogically with the tradition in order to bring to it new moral understandings. As Adrienne Rich has written:

We need to know the writing of the past, and know it differently than we
have ever known it; not to pass on a tradition but to break its hold over us.
(cited in Hersh, 1992, p. 409)

The play itself is an adaptation of the myth of Philomele (Graves, 1960) and
is set in three distinct places; in a civilized Athens with its theatre and philosophy, in the darker northern Kingdom of Thrace, with its Dionysic rituals and
secrecy; and on the sea voyage between the two. It tells of how the Thracian
king, Tereus, as a reward for saving Athens, marries an Athenian princess,
Procne. Lonely within the very different cultural surroundings of Thrace, Procne
asks Tereus to bring her younger sister, Philomele, to be her companion.
While in Athens and later on the return voyage, Tereus lusts after Philomele
and, when she rejects his advances, deceives her into believing that her sister
is dead. In a fit of jealous rage, he kills the Captain of the ship whom she has
chosen to be her lover and later, he rapes her. As Philomele threatens to shame
him in public for his deed, he cuts out her tongue and keeps her secretly a
prisoner. Years later, Philomele is recognized in a Bacchic festival by her sister
as she performs a grotesque re-enactment of her rape and mutilation. Together
they kill Itys, the son of Procne and Tereus, and during their flight from him,
all three are transformed into birds; Procne into a swallow, Tereus into a
hoopoe and Philomele into a nightingale.

   The Phaedra myth interanimates the text of the play at two levels; by
direct allusion and through a subtler form of intertexuality. The former occurs
in two central scenes, the first in Athens when we are presented with frag-
ments of Euripides' *Hippolytos* as a play within a play, watched by the king's
court with Tereus as guest. Later, during the rape scene, Tereus explains and
excuses his lust and his rape by direct reference to the play. But it is the more
subtle structural interplay I wish to investigate first, by looking at how the
moral values normally represented through the actions of the two protagonists, Hippolytos and Phaedra, are displaced and redistributed from within the
frame of female experience. Although Wertenbaker's textual referencing is to
Euripides, she is not only contesting *his* representational authority but the
cultural centrality of the myth itself which, as Gérard correctly points out, is
dependent upon a public sanctioning of phallocratic authority.

   Hippolytos and Philomele, the victims of incestuous lust and violence, are
represented as virginal and virtuous. Virtue in Hippolytos is characterized largely
by his chastity, autonomy and disinterest in sexuality; he is among:

   . . . those whom modesty enters at birth
   the instinctively good (126) (Euripides, transl. Bagg, 1974)[2]

Philomele's virtues are very different. She warmly embraces her own sensuality and thrives on the warm companionship with her sister, whom she shocks
with her frank description of sexual desire:

   He's so handsome I want to wrap my legs around him. (p. 2)[3]

This positive, albeit comic presentation of female sexuality contrasts not only with Hippolytos' cold asceticism but also with its representation by Euripides as something both destructive and shameful. This is signalled by the vindictiveness of Aphrodite and the haggard, spiritually broken image of Phaedra on her first entrance and, significantly, Wertenbaker includes extracts from both of these scenes within her condensed presentation of the Euripidean text. The contest between natural impulses and ethical precepts, seen by Gérard to be at the heart of the moral dilemma posed by the Phaedra syndrome, is not cast by Wertenbaker within the person of the female. Philomele feels no such contest, no sense of guilt associated with her sexuality and is openly capable of enjoying and discussing it. By shifting the contest from within the female to within the person of Tereus, she refocuses it to include issues of gendered power relationships.

The Phaedra syndrome, in fact, when viewed from the perspective of female experience, is a distortion of social reality; sexually motivated violence and incestuous abuse are largely perpetrated by males against females through the act of rape. Wertenbaker's play immediately identifies the destructive forces within society as emanating not from expressions of female sexuality but from acts of male violence and the warped sexuality it engenders. The opening scene, which establishes the companionship of Philomele with her sister, is framed by one of graphic male violence as two soldiers exchange insults, notably of a sexual nature, before killing each other. If, in the Euripidean text, female jealousy and lust are identified as manipulative causes of violence and disorder in the world, in Wertenbaker's play, these conditions already underpin the very authoritarian, male world inhabited by Tereus. To quote René Girard:

> Violence . . . . . . is characteristically initiated and controlled by men — it is gendered power, aligned with the male, which is typically used to reify the stability of patriarchal structures. (cited in Hersh, op. cit., p. 416)

Social order is not synonymous with moral order within such a power system. Despite the moralistic contempt for Phaedra uttered by Tereus as he watches the play within a play, this moralizing is exposed as hypocrisy when, asked by Procne to explain his rape of her sister, the answer he gives presents a true picture of his moral vision: 'There are no rules' (p. 47).

In the Euripidean drama, Phaedra is never in any doubt of her guilt and her overriding concern is for her passion to remain undisclosed. The fragility of her honour is heightened by the fact that she is a woman:

> I knew that my passion, indulged or not,
> would make me repulsive to others, especially since
> I am a woman — our sex is a very disgrace. (625)

Her honourable reputation (eukleia) is everything and she fears shame (aidos) above all else. Of course, whether it is morally healthy for a society to control the ethical behaviour of its members in this way is one of the major themes of the Euripidean play. As Charles Segal has written:

> Through Phaedra's concern with appearance, reputation, the outside world, Euripides raises questions beginning to be asked in his time about the inadequacy of an ethic based entirely upon external, social sanctions. (cited in Gérard, op. cit., p. 16)

But whether they be internally felt or externally feared, shame and guilt go hand in hand in the person of Phaedra, despite the fact that she commits neither incest nor adultery. In *The Love of the Nightingale* the same elements of honour, shame and guilt are in play but they are structured differently into the text. Tereus' crimes include murder, mutilation, incest, adultery and rape and yet when asked by his wife if it was shame that kept him silent his answer is straightforward 'No' (p. 46). If Phaedra's response to her passion is to become consumed by guilt, Tereus has no response other than violence. As Philomele says:

> There's nothing inside you. You're only full when you're filled with violence. (p. 35)

Tereus' lack of shame is dramatically illustrated in the scene immediately after the rape when, with the blood of Philomele's ruptured virginity still on his hands, he returns home to embrace his wife. This is in notable ironic contrast to the words of Phaedra when she says:

> My hands are clean
> The stain is in my heart (477)

and later when she utters her contempt for the dissimulation of unfaithful wives:

> How can such frauds . . .
> Look quietly into the eyes of their husbands? (636)

The social reality of rape in a patriarchal society is that the stigma of shame will be attached to the woman. Niobe, Philomele's nurse, as the voice of conventional social attitudes, understands this:

> A cool cloth. On her cheeks first. That's where it hurts most. The shame. (p. 31)

Philomele too, has to confront the assumption that not only must she feel the shame but also accept the guilt.

> I was the cause, wasn't I? Was I? I said something. What did I do? (p. 34)

Her strength and her tragedy is to refuse to accept either and to demand that Tereus accept both:

> It was your act. It was you. I caused nothing (p. 34)

She pledges to publicly shame him by shouting out the truth to the people of Thrace. Like Phaedra, Tereus cannot tolerate the truth to be voiced; but, unlike her, he is a moral hypocrite and the silence of his accuser will suffice. So he cuts out Philomele's tongue.

Speech and silence are central issues in both plays. Speech will betray Phaedra's *aidos*, silence may preserve her *eukleia*.:

> How could I trust my tongue — which can set
> others right, but cannot even sense
> the damage it does to itself? (612)

From a feminist perspective, Phaedra's desire for silence may be construed as resulting from her unquestioning acceptance of a patriarchal moral order which uses shame as a means to oppress her; and we can interpret it as indicative of a political tendency throughout much of history for the voices of women to be silenced. Such an interpretation, however, can only be argued through a deconstruction of the Euripidean text. Wertenbaker's decision to make the silencing of Philomele dramatically the most shocking scene in the play, more shocking even than the rape, brings the whole issue of the silencing of women literally to the forefront of the action. It cannot be ignored and its political significance is stressed by the words of the Female Chorus which overtly link the silencing of Philomele with the silencing of oppressed people both today and throughout history.

> *Helen*: Why are races exterminated?
> *Hero*: Why do white people cut off the words of blacks?
> *Iris*: Why do people disappear? The ultimate silence.

Deprived of a voice, people will react with violence and this is true of both Philomele and Phaedra. The scene depicting Philomele's killing of Itys is preluded by the following words:

> *Iris*: Imprison the mind that asks.
> *Echo*: Cut out its tongue
> *Hero*: You will have this.

Allison Hersh's description of the representation of female violence in two other female re-workings of Euripides, Caryl Churchill's *A Mouthful of Birds* and Maureen Duffy's *Rites*, is equally applicable to *The Love of the Nightingale*. These plays, she writes:

dislodge the conventional belief in women's non-violence to propose a model
of female violence which is grounded in political resistance. (op. cit., p. 416)

Both Phaedra and Philomele are responsible for the deaths of young males
but, whereas Phaedra deceives and manipulates the male power structure to
mete out an act of personal revenge, Philomele is her own agent and her act,
committed while she is surrounded by her sister and the female Bacchantes,
is a representation of bloody political rebellion. It is, furthermore, a darkly
ironical reflection of Phaedra's fear that the shame of the mother will be transmitted to the children (640–650); the violence which Tereus has inflicted with
no sense of shame is transmitted back to his son and Procne forces him to
confront his own guilt:

You, Tereus. You bloodied the future. For all of us. (p. 47)

Phaedra's vengeance is achieved through a false accusation of rape. The assumption that women make such accusations when they are rejected by a man
is a persistent one in male discourse and has recently resurfaced in Michael
Crichton's film *Disclosure*. Philomele's rape, however, is horrifically real and
she achieves revenge through publicly communicating this. In order to manage it, she who has been deprived of a voice finds one through theatre. The
form and content of Philomele's theatrical language, with its grotesque manip-
ulation of life-sized puppets, is reminiscent of Artaud's *Theatre of Cruelty*.[4]
It communicates the Truth through shock but for her, as for Boal, theatre has
become a necessary and political act, having as its aim the engenderment of
social action to remove oppression. This is a very different theatre from the
one she knew in Athens, whose values indulged her preoccupations with the
vicissitudes of the human heart but tragically failed to prepare her for life, as
an analysis of the scene of the play within a play will show.

The whole scene is highly ironic as Wertenbaker toys with different audience responses to the Euripidean text in a fashion which is at once playful
and serious in its intent. In fact, the characters of the Queen, the King, Philomele
and Tereus present us with four contrasting responses to *theatre*. For the
Queen, Euripides' drama is like an episode from a popular soap and she comments throughout only on issues of plot, on who loves whom and what happens
next. The King has a more sophisticated view; for him the play shows 'the
uncomfortable folds of the human heart' (p. 10) and he believes that it can
help him reach a decision on whether to allow Philomele to make the journey
to Thrace in order to be with her sister. However, his approach is that of the
pedant who sees art as a source of mystical understanding, as a substitute
religion. He reacts superstitiously to the words of the chorus as they lament
Hippolytos' death and interprets them as a warning not to send Philomele
away from her father's lands. Ironically, this decision would have saved
Philomele. But such a view of theatre as a pseudo-religious touchstone rather
than as a stimulus for enlightened action and choice, is shown to be inadequate.

It is easily dismissed by Philomele and the king finds no words to rationally argue his decision when it meets with her objection.

'We have no theatre or even philosophers in Thrace,' says Tereus (p. 11). He expresses dislike for the theatre, ironically on moral grounds 'These plays condone vice' (p. 10) and yet he reacts strongly and directly to the play's moral discourse. He approves of Aphrodite's determination to bring low 'the proud heart which dares defy me' (p. 9); he pronounces Phaedra's passion as 'wrong' and her act of vengence as 'vile' (pp. 10, 12). But the heady mixture of the play's poetry, his growing attraction for Philomele and her justification of Phaedra's love has a profound effect on him. He is seduced by its sensorial potency and its fatalistic discourse and, not unlike King Pandion, he will use it to disclaim responsibility for his own actions.

Philomele reacts to the play in the manner of the culturally educated and artistically sensitized young girl. She understands the tragic injustice of Phaedra's passion and weeps at the end:

> It's the play. I am so sorry for them all. (p. 13)

She condones Phaedra's passion by blaming it on forces beyond her control; 'you must obey the gods,' she tells Tereus (p. 10) and excuses Phaedra's vengeance in fatalistic terms: 'Why destroy what you love? It's the god' (p. 12). More than this, Phaedra embodies for her a romantic view of intense female passion to which she aspires. 'How beautiful to love like that!' (p. 10) is her naive but ironic response to Phaedra's suffering. Her confused but intense emotional reactions remind us of the dangers which Brecht objected to in what he called 'Aristotelian' drama; Philomele sees the theatre as a place to indulge her emotions but fails to see how it is influencing her own life.

> But, Father, I'm not Hippolytos. You haven't cursed me. And Tereus isn't Phaedra. (p. 12)

Its discourse has taught her a fatalistic view of action into which she educates Tereus. What she sees as Art — beautiful and moving but distant and unreal — he absorbs as a set of values which will, at one and the same time, guide his actions and excuse his hypocrisy. The gods are presented as the personification of these values. Whereas the Phaedra of *Hippolytos* is an oppressed figure, suffering moral torment because she feels their force so strongly, Tereus the male oppressor, can manipulate them to excuse his violence. During the rape scene he says as much, quoting Philomele's words to imply her own complicity:

> Who can resist the gods? Those words are your words, Philomele. They convinced me, your words. (p. 29)

But — and this is the point — they are not really her words. They are the words which reflect, albeit distortedly, the values embedded within the fundamentally male discourse of the play. It is significant that Tereus finds within them a philosophy to justify his violence. In this sense, Philomele is betrayed by her upbringing and her education; hence the quote from Sophocles' lost tragedy which prologues *The Love of the Nightingale*:

We (women) are nothing; who in our fathers' house
Live, I suppose, the happiest, while young,
Of all mankind; for ever pleasantly
Does Folly nurture all. (p. xi)

This completes the irony within the words spoken to her father, quoted above: 'You haven't cursed me'. Deprived of the knowledge that will help her understand social reality by being exposed to stories which do not adequately reflect female experience, she has, indeed, been figuratively cursed by her father and the institutionalized discourse he is a part of.

Greek theatre, as much as any other theatre in western history, had an essentially moral purpose. In choosing Greek mythology as source material to treat the subject of rape and the silence imposed on the voices of its victims, Wertenbaker is overtly signalling that her drama, too, is a moral one. But if Greek tragic theatre, as Bakhtin would have it, was fundamentally an authoritarian discourse which 'monologized' moral experience, (Kelly, op. cit., p. 44) hers is dialogic in the sense argued by Helene Keyssar:

(here) we find the most deliberate and conscious assertions of polyphony, of refusals to assert or finalise dominant ideologies, of resistances to patriarchal authority and to a unified field of vision. (op. cit., p. 95)

It is a play in which more questions are posed than answers given and which has at its moral centre the dialogical interplay of two myths, the one voiced from within a tradition of male discourse, the other chosen to interrogate that myth in the different voice of a woman[5]. The ambivalence and non-resolution of the action at the end of the play gives further dramatic form to this dialogism.

Itys wants Philomele, now a nightingale, to sing but she will do so only if he will ask her questions. The scene concludes as follows:

Philomele:	Do you understand why it was wrong of Tereus to cut out my tongue?
Itys:	It hurt.
Philomele:	Yes, but why was it wrong?
Itys: *(Bored)*	I don't know. Why was it wrong?
Philomele:	It was wrong because —
Itys:	What does wrong mean?
Philomele:	It is what isn't right.
Itys:	What is right?
	(The Nightingale sings)
	Didn't you want me to ask questions?
	(Fade)
	(p. 49)

The elusiveness of moral certainty only emphasizes the need to keep asking the fundamental moral questions. The dramatic image is of a female encouraging a young male to keep asking them of her, to gain a female perspective on moral experience. But her voice utters no useful answers; rather do they reflect the circularity and impenetrability of myth, and eventually it is transformed into the song of the Nightingale, aesthetically beautiful but devoid of all rational moral content. Earlier in the play, the Male Chorus presented us with three definitions of myth, which resonate with the theories of Barthes; myth as 'public speech'; myth as 'the content of that speech'; myth as 'the oblique image of an unwanted truth, reverberating through time' (p. 19). Here we have a dramatic image which highlights the need to achieve moral understanding by interrogating the cultural values that resonate through time from the mythic dramas which help shape our actions. At the same time, it represents the historical absence of the voices of women in giving dramatic expression to their moral interpretations of these myths. By re-working and re-evaluating the Phaedra syndrome, Wertenbaker has sought to find such a voice and present us with a model for doing so that is as artistically innovative as it is socially necessary.

Notes

1   Cf Helen Keyssar's comments: 'The spectacle and dialogue of theatre mediate but do not resolve differences: the essential strategy . . . is to bring together diverse discourses in such a way that they interanimate each other and avoid any overarching authorial point of view' (1991, p. 95).
2   This and all subsequent quotes from the Euripidean text are from *Hippolytos*, translated by Robert Bagg, (1974). References provided are from the numbered lines of verse.
3   This and subsequent quotes from *The Love of the Nightingale* are from the Faber & Faber edition (1989). Quotes are provided with numbered page references.
4   '*L'action du théâtre . . . est bienfaisante car poussant les hommes à se voir tels qu'ils sont, elle fait tomber le masque, elle découvre le mensonge, la veulerie, la bassesse, la tartuferie*' Artaud (1964), p. 44.
5   Cf Gilligan: 'In the different voice of women lies the truth of an ethic of care, the tie between relationship and responsibility and the origins of aggression in the failure of connection' (1982, p. 173).

Chapter 5

Emotion, Reason and Moral Engagement in Drama

Wertenbaker's play is intended to have a strong emotional impact. Like Philomele watching the fate of Phaedra, we may well be moved to tears by her suffering. We will almost certainly be horrified and outraged by her rape and mutilation, angry at Tereus' violence and hypocrisy but perhaps shocked and confused at the form her vengeance takes. At the end of the play, we are left with questions which need to be addressed, not only with regard to our own emotional reactions to the events we have witnessed but also to issues of cruelty, injustice and revenge pertaining to our contemporary world, in par-ticular concerning acts of violence committed by men against women. The emotions are aroused to stimulate debate and argument; they are meant to disturb and provoke discord among the audience, so that the issues raised by the play do not disappear from consciousness once the audience leaves the auditorium.

The place of emotion and reason in the moral process, and the relation-ship between the two, have been at the heart of philosophical debate over the nature of morality since the time of Plato and Aristotle. Unsurprisingly, this relationship has also preoccupied those theorists and practitioners who believe that drama has a moral function, the most influential twentieth century exponent being Bertolt Brecht.

> We need a type of theatre which not only releases the feelings, insights and impulses possible within the particular historical field of human relations in which the action takes place, but employs and encourages those thoughts and feelings which help transform the field itself. (Brecht, in Willett, 1974, p. 190)

For Brecht, theatre was a forum to promote a socialist worldview, where moral questions were of paramount consideration but seen as inextricably linked to political and economic processes. 'I would like to be good but how can I pay my rent?' Shen-Te's plea to the Gods in *The Good Person of Setzuan* is indicat-ive of Brecht's belief that goodness is natural to human kind but social struc-tures, when unjust, militate against it. Brecht, particularly in his early writings, saw emotion as the potential enemy of reason in the theatre; and he objected to what he termed non-epic, Aristotelian drama because of the way it used emotion to draw the audience into a total identification with the sufferings of a protagonist. In Brecht's mind, this kind of abandonment to sensation led an audience to ignore the moral decisions which motivated the action,[1] to learn nothing about how human forces produce injustice and how this can be remedied. More damningly, it led them to pity such suffering but to sense it as inevitable. His own epic theatre was intended, therefore, to address primarily the intellect rather than the emotions in order to encourage transformative, political action.

> For the epic theatre is a process of 'demystification' of those hitherto nameless, anonymous forces: To give them name and place, remove from them their inscrutable 'mythology', de-Satanize them and de-mythologize them. The essence of the new theatre is to de-alienate man, restore him to a consciousness of active power . . . to provoke him into seeing that change is possible. (Ewen, 1970, p. 222)

It has been strongly argued that, to an extent, Brecht's best plays work despite rather than because of his theories:[2] that, in a play such as *The Life of Galileo*, he allowed the sensuousness of the man to predominate, for emotions to play a much larger part in his practice than was argued in his theory. But Brecht never in fact objected to emotion *per se*, rather to its potentially numbing effect on the intellect. Wertenbaker's play is Brechtian in its emotional effect because the victim of the action is clearly identifiable as representative of a social group of victims, not as an isolated, unique case; and the suffering is seen as the effect of male violence, not the divine hand of Fate or of some unavoidable, uncontrollable force. Brecht's theories emphasize that emotions *can* be harnessed in the service of moral action but that they must challenge, arouse and provoke the audience, not simply move them to pity.

A more recent and influential critique of Aristotle has been mounted by Augusto Boal. Boal's argument is long and complex and draws not only upon the *Poetics* but also the *Nichomachean Ethics* and the *Politics* (Boal, 1979, Part 1). In brief, Boal argues that Aristotle, equating the virtues with the good life, concluded that the highest virtue of all was justice and that justice was enshrined within the constitution of the *polis*. Laws are therefore, according to Aristotle, the maximum expression of justice; and, as happiness is achieved through being virtuous, the necessary conclusion is that happiness consists in obeying those laws. Such a vision is elitist, being all very well for those who have framed the laws to sustain their power, argues Boal — in the case of ancient Greece, the free, male, aristocratic classes — but only for those classes. As a population cannot be uniformly content or satisfied, it must be rendered uniformly passive through repression. One of the most effective means of oppression, according to Boal, is Greek tragedy which 'exists as a function of the effect it seeks, catharsis' (1979, p. 27). Catharsis is defined by Boal as a form of correction and purification; pity and fear are the means, not the ends of this process. What tragedy seeks to do — and succeeds in doing most effectively — is to purge the spectator of any anti-social elements, any urge to disobey or overthrow the laws; for Aristotle, such urges are vices, errors or weaknesses which need to be destroyed.

> This system (of tragedy) functions to placate, satisfy, eliminate all that can break the balance — all, including the revolutionary transforming impetus . . . it is designed to bridle the individual, to adjust him to what pre-exists. (ibid., p. 47)

Boal argues that this poetic-political system for intimidating the spectator, for eliminating bad or illegal tendencies, is still in operation today in such popular cultural forms as westerns and soaps.[3] In Boal's own *Theatre of the Oppressed*, emotion has the opposite function; rather than acting as the means by which revolutionary impulses are purged, it is the means by which they are aroused. By becoming involved in the action, by experiencing an oppression through dramatic participation and attempting to resolve it, spect-actors are provoked, cajoled and hopefully empowered into an understanding of the nature of a particular oppression and the ways it might be redressed:

> It is not the place of the theatre to show the correct path, but only to offer the means by which all possible paths may be examined. (ibid., p. 141)

Individuals themselves must be free to choose the path they see as appropriate. Boal's theatre, in many ways, is the heir to Brecht's, where emotion is supposed to serve reason in a theatre which is designed to act as a rehearsal for the revolution; and where moral and political action are inseparable.

The influence of Boal has been marked on British drama teachers, both at primary and secondary level, and *forum theatre* is now a standard strategy in the classroom.[4] With this influence, and the influence of Brecht, has come an accompanying neglect of Aristotle among established theorists, most of whom identify themselves with the political left.[5] This strikes a discordant note with those areas of moral philosophy and research theory which have had a strong influence on this study, elaborated in other chapters, by no means dominated by figures on the right and where there has been a marked, resurgent interest in Aristotle's ethical theories.[6] It also jars with theories of the democratic function of theatre in Athens, described in Chapter 3, and smacks of a simplistic attempt to judge the politics and culture of Ancient Greece from a contemporary left/right perspective. In fact, to accept the theories of Brecht and Boal without closer scrutiny is to close our eyes to other possible understandings of Aristotle's theory of the moral purposes of the emotions, understandings which, I would argue, can assist us in the planning of dramatic experiences for children and which are not at odds with the empowerment to action urged by both his antagonists.

Aristotelian theatre stands condemned for its oppressive or coercive use of emotion, principally through the process of catharsis, because it prevents rational thinking and obfuscates moral understanding. This conclusion, however, hinges upon two assumptions, both of which are debatable: that there is a stable, agreed definition of catharsis, despite the fact that this has eluded scholars for centuries; and that there is a strong dichotomy between emotion and rationality, with rational cognition being the qualitatively superior of the two. To approach the latter point, it is evident that the rationalist position embraced by Brecht in his early writings is the philosophical heir to a perspective pervasive in western thought since the Enlightenment. When David Hume, for example, concluded that morality needed to be explained and justified with reference to the passions, he did so after having first concluded that it could not be the work of reason. In response, Kant based morality firmly within the domain of reason, as he concluded the converse — that it could not be placed within the emotions (MacIntyre, 1981, p. 49). Such either/or conceptual paradigms which are the legacy of the Enlightenment are, however, inadequate to describe the complex interactions of cognition, emotion, sensory feeling and rationality which characterize much of human activity. The concept of 'irrational fear', for example, is voiced often enough. Such a concept implies that the emotion of fear can, and at times ought to be, rational. It is also clear that children can *learn* fear — of strangers, for example, or of unsafe sex. The important thing is that the emotion, in this case fear, has an object in relation to which it is suitable; and that fear is understood as rational when felt in appropriate contexts. As Inglis has written:

> Feelings themselves are . . . intimate and central to cognition and recognition of the social and public world. (1986, p. 73)[7]

And Scheffler has commented:

> The life of reason . . . requires suitable emotional dispositions. It demands, for example, a love of truth and a contempt for lying . . . revulsion at distortion, disgust at evasion, admiration at theoretical achievement . . . The wonder is not that rational character is related to the emotions but that anyone should ever have supposed it to be the exception to the general rule. (1991, pp. 4, 5)

This argument over the nature of the relationship between reason and emotion was at the heart of the debate in moral educational theory discussed in Chapter 1, where Kohlberg's Kantian rationalism was seen to be wanting in comparison to those theories which recognize the fusion of emotional and rational cognition in the moral life. A theory which emphasizes the paramount importance of one over the other for the purposes of moral learning in the theatre must be similarly suspect and Brecht's most widely admired plays — *The Caucasian Chalk Circle, Mother Courage and Her Children, The Life of Galileo* — all work by negating such a dichotomy rather than by illustrating it. So, for example, when Grusha hears the cry of the child, this is narrated by the storyteller in a way supposed to keep our emotions in check; yet it can be a moment of great and focused emotion in a way which illuminates how emotion and cognition are inseparable. For to understand her plight is to feel it; we know it in terms of the emotions, not in spite of them.

David Best's arguments in support of the rationality of feeling within the Arts add further weight to this claim; that:

> emotional feelings are not separate from or opposed to cognition and under-standing, but, on the contrary, emotional feelings are cognitive in kind, in that they are expressions of a certain understanding of their objects. (Best, 1992, p. 9)

He is particularly at pains to denounce the subjectivist conception of emo-tional feeling, which construes emotions on the model of sensations, as 'radic-ally oversimple' (ibid., p. 6). Sensorial response — pain if I am hit with a hammer, irritation if I am stung by a nettle — is independent of cognition, as we feel it whether we know about the source or not. Emotional response, by contrast — fear of the stick, annoyance with the nettles — is dependent upon cognition. As Best points out:

> it is precisely the crucial role of cognition which distinguishes emotional-feelings from sensation-feelings. (ibid., p. 6)

Boal, by contrast, makes no distinction between the two when he describes art as 'a sensorial way of transmitting knowledge' (op. cit., p. 53). This failure is a theoretical flaw in both artistic and educational terms, for it is the very cognitive aspect of the emotions which renders them susceptible to growth, development and change.

The cognitive function of emotion is of equal importance when investigat-ing the other, related objection to Aristotle, the nature and purpose of cathar-sis. Both Brecht and Boal accept the definition of catharsis based upon medical analogy, as a purgative process intended to maintain the emotional balance of the individual. Thus, while Brecht emphasizes its obfuscatory qualities, Boal stresses the oppressive function of the feelings it arouses. Neither refers to sources or theorists to support their understanding of the term, arguing it from within their own interpretations of Aristotle's intentions. However, Martha Nussbaum, a classical scholar and philosopher, has recently challenged this definition of catharsis through an analysis of its linguistic roots. Examining its word family, she argues that:

> the primary, ongoing, central meaning is roughly one of 'clearing up' or 'clari-fication' i.e. of the removal of some obstacle . . . that makes the item in question less clear than it is in its proper state. (1986, p. 389)

Analysing various contexts within which it is used in pre-Platonic texts, she explains how catharsis often signifies speech that is not marred by some obscurity. She sees the medical context, used to designate purgation and, by analogy, spiritual purification as a special application of this more general sense. For Plato, cognition which is *katharos* is obtainable when the soul is not impeded by bodily obstacles.

> Catharsis is the clearing up of the vision of the soul by the removal of these obstacles; thus the katharon becomes associated with the true or truly knowable, the being who has achieved catharsis with the truly or correctly knowing. (ibid., p. 389)

This was the meaning of catharsis which Aristotle inherited from his mentor. Nussbaum argues that his use of the term in the *Poetics* describes a particular type of clarification provoked by the emotions of pity and fear, which act, in this case, as sources of illumination.

> Emotions can sometimes mislead and distort judgment . . . But they can also . . . give us access to a truer and deeper level of ourselves, to values and commitments that have been concealed beneath defensive ambition and rationalization. (ibid., p. 390)

Far from obfuscation, then, the aim of catharsis is clarification, learning through emotion about those things that matter most to us. This interpretation is in line with Best's argument, inasmuch as it recognizes emotion as having a cognitive energy, and with accepted interpretations of Aristotle's ethical theory:

> For Aristotle, feelings themselves can be the embodiment of reason. It is not just a matter of reason controlling and guiding the feelings. Rather, the feelings can themselves be more or less rational. Reason can be present in them. (Norman, 1983, p. 52)

The reason for the popularity of the theories of Brecht and Boal among those who have written about drama in education are partially, I would argue, pedagogical and partially political. Politically, many theorists and drama practitioners feel sympathy toward Brechtian values and admiration for the extraordinary and innovative work of Boal.[8] Pedagogically, both theorists are attractive as they see the purposes of drama as instructive and empowering, validating a particular type of content for the drama lesson often popular with those who lean toward the left; topics such as male violence, unemployment, homelessness, documented by David Hornbrook and evidenced within the pages of *2D*.[9] The idea of catharsis, on the other hand, in its more traditional interpretation as a purgative process, has been associated in drama teaching with the now discarded vision of drama as the lesson where emotional energy is channelled and discharged in an orgy of noisy, ill-disciplined self-expression (Robinson, 1981, pp. 152–55).

Catharsis as interpreted by Nussbaum, however, has much more in common with what has for a long time been seen as a mainstream function of drama teaching; it stresses the cognitive aspect of emotion and suggests that drama's educational potential centres around its capacity for illumination, thus calling to mind Heathcote's famous maxim that drama is about revealing to children what they already know but don't yet know they know. This function of drama in education has been succinctly expressed by Robinson:

The use of drama in schools to engage the expressive actions of children is one of the ways of enabling them to confirm (their) personal responsibilities by investigating what their beliefs, ideas, attitudes and feelings actually are. (Robinson, 1980, p. 161)

Aristotle specified that, in tragedy, this clarification should be actualized through pity and fear but, following Nussbaum's definition, it is hard to see why other emotions should not have such potential in a broader schema of educational drama; anger, indignation, repulsion, admiration, sympathy, or the 'fruits of the spirit', such as joy and communal well-being; all might be harnessed for educational purposes, to clarify our understandings of the virtues as *thick concepts* and thus inform our moral values.

Nussbaum's conclusions would doubtless be criticized by some Feminists for assuming the existence of an essentialist self and for ignoring the issue of the power and the hegemony of moral discourse.[10] In this light, the clarification might serve only to reaffirm as true the ideologically dominant values we have culturally absorbed. We would do well, for example, to remember the fate of Philomele, who saw in the figure of Phaedra a confirmation of her vision of romantic love. These are Boal's objections voiced from a different critical perspective but, in response, we may postulate that not all ideologically dominant values are necessarily wrong or malevolent; and that cathartic experience in itself is non-ideological. For, whatever my ideology — Christian, liberal humanist, Feminist, Marxist or a hybrid of these or of others — there can be little doubt that, in the humdrum, petty irritations and messy confusions of everyday life, values, including moral values, can become confused, clouded, contradictory, not to say inarticulate or ill-informed. This is particularly the case in contemporary western society, in what David Hornbrook has described as 'the densely textured political ethnography of post-imperial liberal democracy' (1989, p. 50). When we clarify this confusion in some small way, we become better able to articulate and understand what our values actually are. In this sense, the insights we acquire through cathartic clarification are equivalent to the acquisition of emotional knowledge. They are:

> ... sources of illumination or clarification, as the agent, responding or attending to his or her responses, develops a richer self-understanding concerning the attachments and values that support the responses. (Nussbaum, 1986, p. 388)

But they are potentially more than this. With emotional knowledge can come moral knowledge for to learn the virtues is to learn particular feelings and particular emotional responses.

> Virtues are dispositions not only to act in particular ways but to feel in particular ways. ... Moral education is an 'éducation sentimentale' (MacIntyre, 1981, p. 149)

In the final analysis, catharsis itself is non-ideological and amoral. Moral responsibility lies with dramatists and teachers, with those who harness its energy to explore or explain or create particular cathartic experiences in particular dramatic contexts. What matters is the *wisdom* and appropriateness of what is learned through catharsis, sadly lacking in Philomele's case and serving to remind us of these very responsibilities.

Nussbaum's interpretation of catharsis is not dependent upon the existence or otherwise of universal values or an essentialist self. There can be no one universal clarification or emotional response within a drama, of course; it is patently evident to any teacher or practitioner that a drama has no *single* effect, predictable or otherwise, upon an audience or a group of children. Responses can depend upon a number of variations within the individuals watching or participating: their personal cultural baggage, their past narratives and future aspirations; the social nature of the group who share the drama; or, as Robinson insists, whichever 'self' happens to be prominent at this moment in time.

> None of us consists of a unique sense of self . . . Personal consciousness is a maelstrom of competing self-images which shuffle and blend continuously according to past experiences, immediate events and the subject states they produce. (Robinson, 1980, p. 155)

However, to concentrate our educational argument on the self, as critics of drama-in-education have tended to do (Hornbrook, 1989, Chapter 5; Nicholson, 1995, p. 28), would be rather to miss the point, for the emphasis in drama is never primarily on the self but on the self *in relation to others*. As an audience in drama, we watch other people; as participants, we role play or interact with or act as other people and it is for or as someone else that we feel. The emotions stirred in drama, some of which are listed above, are *other-regarding*;[11] and stimulated by our potential for human attachment. This is what Aristotle described as our *orectic* potential, our innate capacity to reach out to others, one of the givens of our social nature, particularly evident in childhood and similarly emphasized by feminist moral theorists such as Carol Gilligan and Nell Noddings (Gilligan, 1982; Noddings, 1984; Nussbaum, 1986, p. 264). We learn about the moral actions of others and speculate upon why they do as they do; about possibilities and alternatives where we are engaged to draw from our own moral resources but which stretch us and make us reflect precisely because they are not our personal stories but situated in a world of otherness. Clarification of why others might act as they do, and the effect of these actions, is our primary focus of attention. Of course, such clarification is inextricably bound up with our own moral identities, as these actions are viewed and apprehended through the perspective of our own values. But these values, culturally and ideologically shaped though they may be, are, as Robinson emphasizes 'capable of change' (ibid., p. 160).

The nature of moral response to drama has been approached from a different theoretical perspective, one which takes account of ideology but which, unlike the theories of Brecht and Boal, is not driven by ideological commitment. The conceptual framework provided by Bernard Beckerman provides a model to explain how drama can either reinforce or challenge our values.

Beckerman argues that there are two types of performance, the *iconic* and the *dialectic*. The iconic performance celebrates and confirms audience values by concentrating and embodying social values and images, its point being to 'prove' what the audience already believes. He points to pageants and parades as the most extreme examples of iconic action and describes how, in the field of drama, both comedy and melodrama are essentially iconic as they leave the audience's values undisturbed. Interestingly, he comments that most political theatre, such as agitprop, can be categorized as iconic as 'it does not change people's minds. Rather does it confirm the opinion of believers' (1990, p. 81). In contrast to this, Beckerman proposes that dialectic action subjects values to challenge. It works through subversion, by creating an appealing but oppositional claim on an audience's allegiances, and is thus able to disturb its moral sensibilities through tugging at its emotions in oppositional directions simultaneously and thus forcing it into reflection. As a clear example of this, he refers to the final scene of Gavin Richards' London production of Dario Fo's *Accidental Death of an Anarchist*, where the audience is shown two alternative endings. In the first, the journalist leaves the corrupt police officers to be blown up. But this, Beckerman comments, affronts the liberal sensitivities of the western theatre-going public; so another ending is staged, only to show how it leads to her murder at the hands of these officers. In both cases, the consequences are devastating.

> Through this device the production sets different sides of our liberal sensitivity into conflict with one another. We have to confront our own allegiances. It is in this way, through dialectic action, that Fo achieves what Brecht advocated: simultaneous engagement and detachment that force the audience to resolve emotional disjunction through thinking about the implications of the play. (ibid., p. 87)

But dialectic action is not just the prerogative of Brechtian theatre. In the case of Shakespeare's *Macbeth*, we are confronted with a man who commits actions which are abhorrent to us but who is presented as a vulnerable human being with a moral conscience:

> To the extent that the actor seduces us into sharing his mental action and allowing our empathic nerves to vibrate with his emotions, we are on his side. One set of values, our horror of murder and tyranny, is juxtaposed against another set of values, our sympathy for an anguished human being. (ibid., p. 86)

Beckerman argues that all western drama will be either iconic or dialectic as it is practically impossible for it to unfold in a value-free context. This is the result of two processes unique to drama; the fact that drama is a human medium, where the audience cannot fail to make human attachments; and through the actualization of conflict, or, in Beckerman's terms, the 'interaction and contrast with one person straining against another' (ibid., p. 83). As he comments:

> The human attachment we have for one or another person calls upon us to make choices, which in turn involve a context of values. (ibid., p. 83)

This, I believe, is a concept which serves to connect the theories of Brecht, Boal *and* Aristotle and its implications for educational drama are worth examining. Dramatic action, whether iconic or dialectic, works by stimulating our innate sense of human attachment, our *orectic* potential, and it does this through the immediacy of human representation. In other words, for drama to work, we have to be morally engaged, to care in either a positive or negative sense about the people being fictionally represented and what is happening to them. This is the case for both iconic and dialectic action. In this sense, consciously or unconsciously, we make choices, deciding where our attachments lie and these choices are value-related. The emotions we feel and the moral choices they lead us into making are *other-regarding* and happen during the dramatic action. Beckerman points out that in iconic action the alignment of values is between characters — between the stock heroes and villains of comedy and melodrama, for example; in dialectic action, however, this alignment is divided *within* characters, as with Macbeth. This is what is largely responsible for what he describes as a *moral risk* for the audience, a process which has been commented upon indirectly by Goldberg in relation to Shakespeare's *Antony and Cleopatra*:

> ... it explores and questions, in the very process of presenting him (Antony), what nobleness of life might appear to be as he is seen by this and that character's eyes ... and what it might be to us, who see the life in this and that way of seeing. (1993, p. 41)

These considerations of drama's moral educational potential emphasize the twin elements of observation and response to actual human representation. For young children, this underlines the value of appropriate Theatre in Education programmes and offers strong support for the inclusion of Responding to Drama as a key element within the drama curriculum (Arts Council of Great Britain, 1992). It also points to the potential within the concept of the *actor-teacher*, where the teacher not only takes on a dramatic role but, in addition, consciously uses other theatrical conventions and sign-systems open to the actor — such as gesture, costume, gait, tone of voice, symbolic objects — as resources to engage the children's value attachments (Lawrence, 1981; Oddie,

1984). In this way, the actor-teacher can harness the moral cognitive energy integral to other-regarding emotions and dispositions such as pity, sympathy, indignation, solidarity, gentleness and charity, not to mention their darker companions such as contempt, antipathy and guilt. But the onus is not entirely on the teacher in role, of course. Beckerman writes from the perspective of conventional, western theatre, which has evolved clear boundaries to demarcate the roles of performer and audience, whereas in process drama these roles become far more fluid. At first, it might appear that this form of participatory drama promotes the role of the active participant at the expense of the reflective audience. However, O'Neill, in particular, has argued that 'participants in process drama can be changed into observers without abandoning involvement' (1995, p. 120). Her understanding is that:

> where the participants' sense of being both actors and audience is actively promoted, the dramatic world will be built on a powerful and effective combination of dramatic action and active contemplation. (ibid., p. 130)

Hence the children's responses, which are integral to the moral learning, can become both active and pro-active through the participatory form of process drama.

We can now speculate on how such classroom practices might relate to work with fairy stories, in the light of the theoretical points discussed so far. It is clear that Zipes' project has much in common with Brecht's. Brecht's mistrust of Aristotelian drama and Zipes' critical stance toward classic fairy tales are similar in concern, and Brecht's theory of distancing, the *Verfremdungseffekt*, had a similar purpose to Zipes' own theory of disturbance. Both Brecht and Zipes, influenced by Marxist theory, wish for empowerment through knowledge of the historical and political forces which shape our lives. Both tend toward seeing emotion and reason as distinct, mistrusting the potential of the one to render the other blind; and Boal's revolutionary theatre, seeking to identify and empower people to overcome oppression, has a similar political agenda. The theatre of Brecht and Boal seeks to challenge and provoke, to contextualize and historicize action and Boal, in particular, wishes to open up problems, suggest possibilities but leave resolutions open-ended so that participants can decide upon them for themselves. Their approaches would suggest a use of dramatic action dialectic in its intention, perhaps playful, certainly subversive, challenging or openly interrogating the values within a tale by introducing an oppositional empathic alignment. An approach which sought the kind of clarification which Nussbaum sees as characteristic of catharsis could, on the other hand, lead to either iconic or dialectic action. The difference here for the teacher will, I suggest, lie in the intensity, the sustained seriousness of the drama, less playful than the former approach; perhaps more subtle in its structure and more poetic in its form.

Such hypotheses need to be explored in the light of the points argued here and in the previous chapters. I have argued that stories best convey the nature of the moral life to children but that those in the mythic tradition pose problems within the area of values. These problems emerge from the lack of subjunctivity and particularity in their narrative structures and from the historical, literary tamperings which have often provided a monological, didactic overlay to their story lines. If, as I have argued, there is historical evidence for regarding drama as an art form capable of actively interrogating, reinterpreting and renewing the values in mythic tales, then it does so through establishing a level of personal engagement with these values which is at once emotional and cognitive in nature and moral in its focus. The challenge now — and it is a substantial one — is to see how such theory can enlighten our understanding of classroom practice in this area. This I propose to do through case studies, where any generalizations can be argued, as Aristotle would have preferred it, from within the context of particular cases, which are themselves the determining factors of experience.[12] It is to a fuller consideration of the form such classroom practice and such research methodology should take that I now turn.

Notes

1 See *A Dialogue about Acting* (Willett, 1974, pp. 26–29) in which Brecht comments upon the performance of Helene Weigel as Jocasta's servant in *Oedipus Rex*. He saw her performance as a conscious but unsuccessful attempt to involve the audience, to get them 'to take part in the moral decisions of which the plot is made up' (ibid., p. 28). Her failure was not due to her ability as an actress but to the audience's mindset, who saw drama as 'an opportunity for new sensation' (ibid., p. 28) 'For this audience hangs its brains up in the cloakroom along with its coat' (ibid., p. 27).

2 See, for example, Esslin, (1984); Ewen, (1970); and Gray (1976). The accepted wisdom of these critics has more recently come under attack. See Brooker (1988). Brooker argues that Brecht saw *The Life of Galileo* as 'a big step backwards' (p. 185) and points to his last play *Days of the Commune* as mainstream Marxist, epic, dialectic theatre. Brecht had never betrayed or revised his project, he concludes.

3 Brecht's comments on the film *Gunga Din* are an interesting complement to Boal's argument. He explains how the film touched him, how he laughed at all the right places; but how, fundamentally, he knew that the worldview presented by the film was distorted, despite its artistic success. See Willett, p. 151.

4 See Hornbrook (1989) pp. 47–51. Two of the latest drama manuals for primary teachers each present depoliticized forms of *forum theatre* as drama strategies, alongside freeze frame, teacher-in-role et al. See Readman and Lamont (1994) and Woolland, (1993).

5 See Hornbrook, op. cit., p. 50. Sometimes this neglect is replaced by open disapproval. See Neelands (1994), in particular, n. 16, p. 14. For an example of how closely and openly influential figures within drama in education identify with the political left, see Lawrence (ed.) (1993). Here, articles by Heathcote, Bolton and Neelands are accompanied by extracts from, among others, Brecht.

6 Carr (1986, 1987) draws heavily upon Aristotle's ethics, both directly and indirectly via MacIntyre, when proposing that education be viewed specifically as a professional *practice* and when describing a critical paradigm for educational action research.

7 I am indebted to this article for much of the previous analysis of fear.

8 See once again Hornbrook (1989) pp. 47–51 for a brief sociology of this alliance between the educational drama establishment and the Left.

9 See, for example, Joyce (1987); Hall (1988); and Edmiston (1995) where the author details a drama about social prejudice. See also Hornbrook (1989), n. 38, p. 173.

10 See Hekman (1995), p. 40. She notes such objections to Nussbaum's overall neo-Aristotelian stance.

11 Interestingly, Carr suggests that the virtues might be seen as belonging to one of two categories: those of self-control and those of attachment. The virtues of attachment he defines as '*other-regarding attitudes*' (1991, p. 200), including sympathy, benevolence, generosity etc. These are explored in more detail in a subsequent case study.

12 Cf Nussbaum (op. cit., p. 317) on the relationship in Aristotelian philosophy between the particular and the general. 'The situation is a source of illumination; the illumination becomes the source of a new general account.'

Part 2

Theory and Practice in the Classroom

Chapter 6

Drama for Moral Education: Potential Features and Problematic Aspects

Drama, to quote the words of Raymond Williams again, moves 'beyond myth to dramatic versions of myth'. In proposing a historical relationship between drama and myth where drama interrogates, revises and renews the moral values within the myth, I analysed Wertenbaker's play principally to illustrate how this relationship is still vigorous in contemporary theatre rather than to propound her particular feminist vision. It is evident that Wertenbaker sees that the *form* of drama is as crucial to its moral purpose as is its content and that this form should aim to empower rather than to indulge its audience emotionally. I will now argue that, if fairy stories are to undergo a similar process of moral exploration in the classroom, then the form of drama we use for this purpose is crucial to the project; and that this form should be dialogical in nature, harnessing the performative characterisitics of the oral tradition from which the tales originate but enhancing them to become participatory in nature. Such a form of drama, in fact, as exists within the current traditions of drama in education.

There is a rich and complex history to educational drama within Britain, spanning the length of the twentieth century. This has been well-documented by Cox (1970) and Robinson (1981) and usefully critiqued and summarized by Bolton (1984) and more recently by O'Hara (1996). From early pioneers such as Harriet Finlay-Johnson and Caldwell Cook, writers and practitioners within the field — Peter Slade, Brian Way, Richard Courtney and John Allen, for example — have emphasized drama as a practice and as a process for learning rather than as a body of texts for passive reception. This approach, of course, shares much in common with the child-centred, progressive philosophies inspired by the writings of Rousseau and Froebel; but opinions as to what exactly constitutes the nature of learning through drama have always been fluid and open to argument, as have any specific views on the moral benefits of drama for children. In the case of Peter Slade, for example, (1954) the form of Child Drama was in itself a source for good in an essentially therapeutic sense, characterized as it was by intense activity, spontaneous play and the qualities of Absorption and Sincerity.[1] Issues of content were practically irrelevant for Slade, who saw dramatic meaning as inherently symbolic and private to the children involved.

> The child creates theatre in its own way, own form, own kind. It is original art of high creative quality. Most adults are stubbornly blind to the loveliness they will not see. (op. cit., p. 183)

Elsewhere he writes:

> The constant repetitions and use of symbols in the realm of child behaviour, also the acting out of situations before they can have been experienced, is entirely in line with the Jungian conception of the collective unconscious. (ibid., p. 48)

Such language and sentiments are reminiscent of Bettelheim, stressing as they do the importance of the subconscious, the autonomy and preciousness of a child's experience, and portraying adult interference as an unwelcome intrusion.

Slade's influence was considerable but its emphasis on form as opposed to content was radically challenged in the 1970s by the work of Dorothy Heathcote, arguably the most influential exponent of educational drama this century.[2] Like Harriet Finlay-Johnson, Heathcote was interested primarily in how drama could be harnessed as a learning medium for subjects across the curriculum such as history and literature; but unlike her predecessor, she was not interested in how it could assist children in the learning of facts so much as how it could facilitate an understanding of what Bolton calls 'the universal implications of any particular topic' (1984, p. 52). Heathcote's work was characterized by a number of revolutionary features, most prominent being her use of *teacher-in-role*, a strategy which enabled her to influence the dramatic action, and hence the children's learning, from within, as a fellow participant.[3] Although her own writings have been few, those of Gavin Bolton (1979, 1984, 1992) did much to spread the philosophy and practices of her particular style of drama, as did the numerous workshops and demonstration lessons taught by herself and Bolton throughout the UK, Australia and North America. It was in North America, with articles by Wolfe (1978) and Colby (1982) that theoretical studies into the area of moral education through drama began to advocate the practices of Bolton and Heathcote.

Wolfe focused directly on the work of Kohlberg, suggesting that significant moral dilemmas, approached through drama, could stimulate moral development according to the Kohlberg taxonomy. Colby — whose work constitutes the most thorough and focused examination published to date of drama's potential for moral learning — built on Wolfe's ideas but took them further. Embracing Kohlberg's theory of moral stages, Colby (1982) constructed an argument which proposed that drama of the type taught by Heathcote and Bolton could encourage moral growth by pressing children into reasoning one stage above their current level. He cited unpublished research by Johnson and Bauer (Colby, ibid., p. 26) which, although failing to prove that drama could achieve such growth, nevertheless drew conclusions which Colby found to be significant. With detailed reference to two Heathcote-style dramas, Colby argued that, when such dramas are clearly focused on moral developmental objectives, significant growth in moral reasoning becomes possible due to drama's ability to yoke the realms of the affective, the visual and the kinesthetic to the moral reasoning process. He proposed that this style of drama provided room for rational refection, in line with Kohlberg's stage theory, to work alongside the emotional ethic of care and responsibility developed by Gilligan, which combination could move children's moral reasoning up a stage.[4] In a later article, Colby (1987) developed his argument further, concentrating on published research which illustrated the shortcomings of developmental analysis and classroom role plays when used to encourage moral growth. He was particularly struck by the work of Oliver and Bane (1971) and their argument for teachers to recognize the importance of those non-rational, moral sensitivities which remain unaddressed when the concentration is upon the processes of moral reasoning alone. They asserted that moral controversy is: '. . . more powerfully described through the metaphors of the dramatist which transcend public language' (Oliver and Bane, cited in Colby, 1987, p. 73).

Particularly in Gilligan — but also in the later Kohlberg (1981) — Colby saw support for such a broader and more ambivalent understanding of moral development. The strength of drama, Colby concluded, lies in its potential to encourage children to think metaphorically as well as analytically, and in the opportunities it offers for children to experience and reflect upon the 'truth of metaphor'.

It is significant, I think, that Kohlberg's theory of moral stages and the pedagogy of dilemma analysis are muted in the later article, indicating a shift in Colby's perspective to one which more closely matches the argument developed in Chapter 2 of this thesis. Even if we reject his earlier theoretical dependence upon Kohlberg, however, Colby's work remains lucid and informative and I refer to it in further detail to help illuminate my own practice in Chapter 8. This practice belongs to the tradition fostered by Heathcote and advocated by Colby, but in a form developed, altered and disseminated by other practitioners such as Cecily O'Neill (1976, 1982, 1995), David Booth (1994) and Jonothan Neelands (1984, 1992). The term *process drama* is used currently to describe this type of educational, improvisatory drama, emphasizing its concern with significant, dramatic learning experiences sought through the creative processes rather than from within received and distant dramatic products. Its features have been usefully listed by Taylor as follows:[5]

- Separate scenic units linked in an organic manner
- Thematic exploration rather than isolated or random skit or sketch
- A happening and an experience which does not depend upon a written script
- A concern with participants' change in outlook
- Improvisational activity
- Outcomes not predetermined but discovered in process
- A script generated through action
- The leader actively working both within and outside the drama

These characteristics are indicative of its open-ended, participatory nature and would appear to be ideally suited to the communal storybuilding which is integral to the fieldwork of this research project. However, since the late 1980s, the validity of this form of educational drama has come under vociferous attack from various academic theorists within the field of drama education. The ensuing debate has raised important issues about aesthetic and cultural practices beyond the parameters of this book, but some of their criticisms are central to its concerns and need to be addressed before proceeding further.

Foremost among these critics is David Hornbrook. His influential book, *Education and Dramatic Art* (1989) is a strong, often vitriolic attack directed against the epistemological claims made by Heathcote, Bolton and their followers for the type of drama they practice. One of his key criticisms is that they locate learning in drama within the area of psychology rather than culture, having as their major aim the apprehension of certain absolutes or universals, which, on analysis, turn out to be nothing more than bland, liberal humanist platitudes. Thus Gavin Bolton's list of the universals revealed through drama — 'protecting one's family, journeying home, facing death, recording for posterity, passing on wisdom, making tools etc' (cited in Hornbrook, 1989, p. 66) — are quoted only to be subjected to ridicule.[6] Significantly, Hornbrook points disparagingly to Heathcote's predilection for 'primitivism' in many of her dramas, where students are requested to 'play out the inter-cultural dilemmas of tribal communities'. He goes on to comment:

> Underlying this simple, noble savage view of primitive societies are the phenomological assumptions . . . that there are certain realities, or essences, which form the common features of all human consciousness. (ibid., p. 66)

Hornbrook rejects this universalist view of the self and favours an education in *dramatic art*, by which he means, in effect, the traditional cultural practices of the western theatre. Heathcote's form of drama, he argues, has dislocated drama from its roots within the arts and, through this, from its cultural history and moral and political purposes. The result he sees is a moral vacuum:

> (an) existential and narcissistic wilderness in which we circle in search of truth, value and meaning but in which all the so-called social learning of the drama class, however conscientiously engineered, must in the end be condemned to wander aimlessly. (ibid., p. 67)

Only through a re-engagement with the historical, performance practices of drama and the political and social meanings within our heritage of playtexts does Hornbrook believe that drama can leave this wilderness and re-enter the world of collective, critical judgment.

An earlier critic of Heathcote was, in fact, a Marxist practitioner from within this theatrical tradition. Nicholas Wright (1980) saw her preoccupation with 'dropping from the particular into the universal' as in direct opposition to the nature and purpose of theatre.

The argument of the play is not ideal; it might be true only in the specific set of social, economic and cultural circumstances revealed and implied in the play. . . . It is, if you like, particular. But it is not universal. (Robinson (Ed), 1980, p. 104)

The danger he saw in Heathcote's practice was:

the temptation of inventing pseudo-facts, statements generally of a moral nature, which, though mere matters of opinion, products of a particular ideo-logical context, are presented as though they were of absolute and permanent value. (ibid., p. 100)

For Wright, Heathcote's universal truths are neither true nor universal. His Marxist critique of her practice, equating the moral with the political, foreshad-owed that of Hornbrook and raised squarely the problem of value hegemony within the person and power of the drama teacher: 'At what point may (the student) decide that what is universal, say, for the teacher is not universal for him?' (ibid., p. 102).

These concerns have found an echo in the feminist voices which have recently raised some pertinent questions concerning the aims and practices of process drama (see also Fletcher, 1995). Helen Nicholson has challenged Heathcote's belief in universal truths and in an essentialist, authentic self, argu-ing that: 'the notion of universality is exclusive, and reveals through deconstruc-tion, the dominant concerns of a hegemonic culture' (1995, p. 28). She has attacked the same universals listed by Bolton and criticized by Hornbrook for their phallocentric preoccupations and has queried Bolton's description of the 'essential goal in drama teaching', namely

that the central learning . . . involves some kind of change in subjective mean-ing, a change in felt value . . .

My question is concerned with whose values are they? and why are they better than the students' own? Here we see in operation the will-to-power of the practitioner, who has eliminated diversity in favour of the perceived rational-ity or wisdom of his or her own moral code. (Bolton, cited by Nicholson, ibid., p. 31)

At the heart of these criticisms there is a shared mistrust of hegemonic values masquerading as universal truths. The objections to Heathcote's primitivism and to her belief that drama is ultimately concerned with universals emanates from this mistrust. Such concerns have been pre-eminent throughout this study and echo my own within the fields of moral theory, theories of meaning in traditional stories and the relationship between myth and drama. To put for-ward process drama as the form able to deal with precisely what it has been accused of fostering might therefore appear at best misguided, at worst per-verse. So to what extent are these criticisms valid?

A cursory look at the literature on or by Heathcote supports to some extent the view propounded by Hornbrook regarding her fascination for primitivism. Whether in a tomb drama with 12 year-olds or in a drama based on the Hawaiian goddess Pele, Heathcote was evidently taken not only with primitivism but, more especially, with the springboard it presented to explore the concept of myth as a bearer of a special kind of truth.[7] In her essay *Drama and the Mentally Handicapped*, she writes:

> I have evidence of some rather earth-shattering explorations which seem almost Jungian in their manifestation. As if myth were tapped and universals perceived during the action. (Johnson and O'Neill, 1984, p. 150)

Her belief in the relationship between myth and universal truth is similar to that expressed by Joseph Campbell and Mircea Eliade, who believed that the purpose of all myth was to re-establish the 'creative era':

> . . . magical, in a sense, since by reconstituting that era one can revive some of its unique, creative power. (Kirk, 1974, p. 63)

In flirting with such sentiment Heathcote was in danger of investing the form of myth with a special kind of mystical truth, which could serve both to mystify the nature of learning through drama and, mistakenly, to conflate drama with myth. For example, in an essay entitled *Drama as Challenge* she writes:

> When the Greeks on the hillsides watched the stories they knew, 'lived through', yet again, who knows what strength was given to them by this re-acquaintance with their myths? (Johnson and O'Neill, 1984, p. 83)

The quote from Williams which opened this chapter reminds us that each dramatization of a myth changed its moral and political significance and effectively contextualized it, politically and historically, hence opening it up to argument. Neither Aeschylus, Sophocles nor Euripides regarded the myths as mystical sources of strength for the population of Athens but used them to convey particular meanings relevant to the society of the time. What the Greeks gained from a reacquaintance with their myths is a question more fruitfully approached by critical and historical analysis rather than mere wonder. We know, for example, that in *The Trojan Women* Euripides was using the myth to expose the political and moral hypocrisy of those conducting the war with Sparta, using the Greeks' treatment of the vanquished women of Troy as a direct analogy for the brutal treatment meted out to the inhabitants of Melos for having refused to side with Athens. His dramatic intention was to move away from the unchanging remoteness of myth into the particularity of history, not vice-versa, and is a clear illustration of Nicholas Wright's proposition.

Criticisms of Heathcote, in this respect at least, may be seen as valid; and there is no doubt that her perspective on primitivism and myth has had some influence on the work of subsequent practitioners.[8] However, Hornbrook appears to conflate the work of Heathcote and Bolton with *all* practice in the field of drama in education; for he has in his sights not only these influential practitioners but the very form of process drama itself (Hornbrook, 1995). Nicholson, too, extends her criticism to other prominent practitioners of process drama and postulates an alternative model for the drama curriculum which builds upon Hornbrook's definition of dramatic art (Nicholson, 1995, p. 35). Paradoxically, while criticizing essentialist and exclusive practices, she expounds a view of drama-in-education which could in itself be seen as essentialist in nature and, whilst exhorting the necessity to embrace difference and diversity within our practice, she voices no recognition of the differences that exist between the aims and values of particular practitioners of process drama.[9] It is as if all Greek dramatists were to be equated with Aeschylus. In order to respond to the critics, the central questions that need to be addressed within the parameters of this book are to do with whether, as a practitioner of process drama, I am necessarily condemned to mythic primitivism when working with mythic stories; to a misguided quest for universal truths when working within the field of moral education; and to be always an unwitting agent of hegemony within the field of values.

The first two questions are much easier to dismiss than the third. My own approach to and use of myth in drama lessons is self-evidently very different from those attacked by Hornbrook. Myth, for me, is not a dramatic form to harness for the purposes of primitivism or spiritual enlightenment; it is a story from which to begin a drama. To use Cecily O'Neill's term, it is a *pre-text* for drama, which operates: 'by framing the participants effectively and economically in a firm relationship to the potential action' (O'Neill, op. cit., p. 22).

This potential action is strongly contextualized and made particular through role and frame. The use of mythic stories catalogued in the work of David Booth and O'Neill herself give ample evidence of how this can be done. Furthermore, it is again quite clear from the literature on process drama that, for quite some time, universal truths have not been on the agenda. For Heathcote, these universals were not, in fact, moral absolutes but common human experiences, emotions linked to examples of when they are typically felt. Indeed, her practice as described in Wagner (1979) illustrates how able she was at problematizing moral assumptions. Despite Hornbrook's accusations, the search for universals does not preoccupy the recent work of O'Neill (1995), Booth (1995) or Neelands (1994, 1995). As I trust my case studies will illustrate, it is quite possible to work through process drama in order to dwell within and explore the particularity of a situation just as it is possible to write stories or poems which may or may not aspire directly to the universal. If the particular situation is reflected upon to seek analogies or make evaluations, this is not the same as 'dropping into the universal'. As I have previously argued, particularity is not the semantic equivalent of unique and a generalization need not aspire to the universal. Furthermore, if all generalizations are necessarily influenced by the dominant concerns of a hegemonic culture, then this must be the case for those who critique this culture as well as those who are supposedly duped by it. To frame our arguments in this way is to fall victim to the fruitless circularity of assertion and counter-assertion which MacIntyre sees as so harmful to contemporary moral debate.

Nevertheless, the question of how values and ideology shape our teaching, whether in drama or in any other academic discipline, is a difficult one to negotiate. It is important to admit that, within the conventions of process drama, and particularly through the use of teacher in role, teachers have the option to operate from within the drama, which provides them with a great opportunity to manipulate its value agenda in ways that they may be only partially aware of. Furthermore, the literature of drama-in-education does contain some dubious claims made by practitioners about the efficacy of their dramas for bringing about change in children's values. A brief analysis of a recent article by Brian Edmiston (1995), I believe, can usefully illustrate both of these dangers, thus shedding some light on the problematic nature not only of moral education through process drama but also the difficulties of evaluating one's own practice in the field.

Edmiston is a practitioner of process drama who has a number of articles published in academic journals and a chapter in a book on research in drama education. His work is of particular relevance to my own interests as it consists largely of reflective accounts of his own practice and is often concerned with moral education through drama. In fact, he is one of the very few practitioner researchers to have attempted a comprehensive theory for understanding the moral dimensions of process drama, drawing specifically upon Bakhtin's theory of dialogism to suggest a model for developing such understandings. However, problems occur in the way he relates this theory to his own practice and in the claims he makes for a drama referred to as the *Space Traders Drama*, which had as its educational agenda the theme of prejudice. In his initial contact with a class of 13 year-olds, Edmiston informs us that he detected widespread prejudice against people on welfare and this led him to adapt a story for drama which, in effect, was intended to challenge and change the children's attitudes. The drama evolved around a futuristic scenario in which aliens visit an America on the verge of bankruptcy and offer the government all the gold they need in exchange for all Americans in receipt of welfare. By the end of the drama, Edmiston believes that children who had previously been dismissing those on welfare as lazy and worthless have changed their attitudes and this he puts down to the way the drama helped the children dialogize their experience. By this he means that, built into the structure of the work, there were opportunities for the children to listen to, evaluate and internalize a variety of perspectives which led them to revise their initial ethical standpoints. He concludes:

> As a drama teacher I have come to recognize the awe-ful power which we have to enter into deep and significant conversations with students which change the ways they view the world and their selves. (ibid., p. 123)

I perceive several problems with Edmiston's overall argument. First of all, the generalized claims he makes for the class's change of attitude are backed up by reference to written and spoken evidence taken from only two or three pupils. As such, these claims fail to convince. Nor must the children's changed attitudes necessarily be interpreted in the ways Edmiston suggests. For example, in his conclusion, he describes how the classteacher asked the children to write about whether there had been anything fair or unfair within the drama. One girl, Jenny, who had previously argued that if people on welfare were unemployed then it was their own fault, now wrote with far more sensitivity and compassion. 'You can't put a price on someone's life. . . . Maybe they couldn't help not getting a job. We were all being too selfish' (ibid., p. 123). Edmiston argues that this change of heart came about due to Jenny's own work within the drama. 'In the drama work', he writes, 'Jenny had not only constructed ethical positions, she critiqued them'. There is a simpler interpretation, however. Children can be very adept at detecting what it is that the teacher wants to hear and the socially well-adjusted among them are often happy to respond accordingly. It is difficult to see the teacher being satisfied with such a drama without soliciting and consequently finding responses such as this from sensitive children who might soon grasp the message of the drama without having to construct and critique their own ethical positions within it. From the article, we have no indication as to how, exactly, the final writing session was introduced by the teacher, whether there were, for example, any leading questions or nuances of expression which might have further indicated to the children the type of written response which would earn his praise.

For the teacher's value agenda is crucial here. It is clear that this drama had an overarching intention, to achieve a specific and predetermined change of understanding which the teacher saw as morally desirable. This essentially monological approach is at odds with his dialogical intentions. And Bakhtin himself was aware of this tendency in drama, seeing it as a monological art form, an anomaly which Edmiston fails to engage with (Pechey, 1989, pp. 57–62). There is therefore something of a theoretical muddle in Edmiston's position, or at best a paradox at its heart. He presents his own ethical understandings as in no need of the kind of dialogical critique he has urged upon the children's. Although advocating, with Bakhtin, that 'each person, adult or child, has a unique perspective on the world and on every interaction' (ibid., p. 116) he has devised a drama in which only one perspective is ethically tenable; namely, the one he has decided upon in advance.[10]

Although I have proposed that Edmiston's intention was to change children's attitudes, his stated agenda was more open-ended, namely 'to enable them to explore such ethical concerns as justice, fairness, prejudice and tolerance' (ibid., p. 114). Elsewhere he states that process drama can 'enable students to create their own ethical understandings about issues of importance to them' (ibid., p. 115). The warm, child-centred language of enablement and exploration, together with verbs such as *construct* and *critique* also used in the opening sentences, suggest an open-ended teaching agenda which places the emphasis on the students' autonomy. Yet all the specific examples from the drama which Edmiston refers to suggest a more precise and closed agenda, namely that of radically changing their perspectives, notably from prejudiced to unprejudiced.[11] This is hinted at in his understanding of the advantages of dialogic as opposed to monologic thinking:

> If we resist dialogue then we tend to minimize our sense of responsibility and ossify our thinking. Our morality becomes more 'monologic', static, fixed and judgmental rather than dynamic and open to change. (ibid., p. 117)

The problem here is twofold; there appears to be a contradiction between Edmiston's stated and actual intentions; and the concept of 'change in understanding' as radical and observable, which he advocates through his deeds as opposed to in his words, is open to challenge. Edmiston is, not surprisingly, most pleased with those children whom he interprets as having changed from one state of mind (prejudiced) to another (unprejudiced). But there is more than a hint in this article that change *per se* is morally more desirable than resistance to change, whereas the obverse might well be true in, say, a drama set in 1930s Germany, where a doctor was being pressurised to no longer treat a Jewish patient. Moreover, 'change in understanding' need not mean coming to a different position but could involve the deepening of an existing position. It might take the form of a deepening of compassion, or of a deepening of one's commitment to egalitarianism which had recently begun to waver.

I have critiqued Edmiston's article at some length not as an attack upon the substance of the drama nor upon the aims of the teacher but in order to show that the scepticism of critics such as Hornbrook and Nicholson within the area of values and process drama does have some justification in observable practice; and to illustrate some of the dangers which need to be negotiated by a research project such as mine, similar as it is to Edmiston's. To illustrate the dangers is not to be defeated by them, however. As I argued in Chapter 5, values are brought to drama lessons by teachers and students and no particular values are inherent to the form of drama itself. As in every classroom, drama teachers are in a position of authority, which means their values matter. They choose the starting point for the drama and make choices as to what form learning through drama will take. Even the most progressive will choose how the pre-text is to be chosen and how the decisions which will shape the drama are to be made, as clear an imposition of a value agenda as any other. This is really the point. As a teacher, it would be misguided, even irresponsible of me, to suggest that my value agenda is either as neutral or as significant or insignificant as that of anyone else in the classroom. However, if we are conscious and aware of our values; are willing to be open about them and justify them; and — most importantly — critically scrutinize them in practice, then we approach our teaching reflectively, maturely and with intellectual integrity.

Notes

1 Slade wrote as recently as 1993 advocating the moral worth of the drama he practised with delinquents in Birmingham during the 1960s. 'I believed children ought to go through the cathartic spitting out of fears and experiences,' he commented and described how 'we would set them jumping from rostrum block to rostrum block to the sound of hot jazz and, when they were exhausted, we would deal with them'.

2 Writings by Heathcote are included by Drain (1995) alongside those by such eminent practitioners as Brecht, Dario Fo, Craig and Artaud.

3 For extensive theoretical analysis of aspects of teacher in role, see Morgan N. and Saxton J. (1987), Chapter 3.

4 Colby makes brief mention here of the work of Courtney (1980, pp. 39–60) and Martin L. Hoffman (1976) whose work is worth a little closer examination within the context of this study. Courtney's theory of *Dramatic Age Stages*, drew heavily upon Piaget, Erikson and Kohlberg but was also influenced by Hoffman's list of 'Empathic Stages' of moral growth in terms which, although dissimilar to those proposed by Gilligan, nevertheless stress, as she did, the importance of connectedness and sympathy. Courtney sees in Hoffman's stage theory 'the kernel elements of dramatic growth' (ibid., p. 43) and writes: 'moral growth hinges upon the ability to experience the inner state of others, and this relates directly to impersonation' (ibid., p. 41). Hoffman's stage theory can be criticized for the same reasons as those of Kohlberg and Erikson (see Chapter 1) but his description of the characteristics of an 'Empathic Sympathy' stage resonates interestingly with the self-other continuum I argued to be at the core of moral engagement through drama in Chapter 5. 'He (sic) can act out in his own mind the emotions and experiences of others, while all the time maintaining that the other is a separate person from himself' (Courtney, op. cit., p. 43).

5 From Taylor, P. (1995). The term process drama is generally attributed to O'Neill. See O'Neill (1995) and also O'Toole, J. (1993).

6 Hornbrook comments: 'This simple primitivism is always mystifying because it denies contemporary experience. How often, I wonder, do we make tools? Would a visit to a DIY hypermarket be counted as a "universal" for today's young people?' (op. cit., p. 175).

7 For accounts of the Egyptian drama see Wagner, 1979, pp. 206–208. For the Goddess Pele drama, see Johnson and O'Neill (Eds), 1984, p. 91. Primitivism was also a characteristic feature of many of Bolton's dramas. Bolton provides details of one example when a group of children were playing the members of a primitive tribe and found two sweatbands which belonged to boys absent from the class. He describes how they were '. . . ceremoniously carried back to the cave . . . we sat round them and . . . deciding our fellow tribesmen had met their deaths, we buried the bands' (quoted in O'Toole, 1992, p. 221).

8 Interesting examples of primitivism pepper Morgan N., and Saxton, J. (1987). Here is their example of symbolization: 'The empty bowl in the centre of the circle signifies the hunger of the tribe. And for one it represents suffering for her children; for another it represents his failure as a provider; for another it represents the anger of the Gods . . .' (p. 5).

9 I would agree with her proposition that: '. . . difference is to be celebrated and valued, and oppressive categorisations are to be binned forever as ownership of

a negative will-to-power' (1995, p. 30). However, her argument seems geared to exclude practitioners of process drama. It is also worth noting that the practice of Heathcote and Bolton was never static and primitivism was only one aspect of it. In their latest, joint publication, there is nothing mythic or Jungian about any of the work analysed. See Heathcote D. and Bolton G. (1995).

10   See Edmiston (1994) for an example of a drama in which he avoids this by not approaching it with such a predetermined agenda.

11   For example, he opens his article with two sentences uttered by the same boy, one at the beginning of the drama, one towards its conclusion: 'What should we do with the prisoners? Should they go off in the spaceship? It doesn't matter if they die, they're worthless anyway.' 'I've changed my mind. You can't decide for people. Even if we need the money we can't make them go — they're people too' (op. cit., 1995, p. 114). This is a similar transformation to Jenny's. A further problem, of course, is how to equate children's utterances in role with their actual beliefs. Edmiston blurs this distinction.

Chapter 7

Researching Drama in the Classroom

The case studies which form the bulk of the second part of this book explore in practice how classroom drama with fairy tales as pre-text can engage children in moral processes and encourage them to explore and articulate ethical concepts. I have taken as my starting point that, historically, one of the cultural functions of drama in western civilization has been to open moral debate by poblematizing accepted social and moral values expressed within a society's shared mythology; and have chosen to focus on my own teaching to explore the issues involved. However, in my critique of Edmiston's account, I focused upon issues of value bias, indicative of the dangers inherent to such reflexive analyses of one's own practice. There are other research models available, of course, and my reasons for rejecting them need to be explored.

A recent, large-scale project led by John Somers of Exeter University is an example of research in educational drama which has consciously adopted procedures to ensure value-neutrality and provide objective proof of its findings. It took as its starting point the implicit belief of many drama teachers that learning in drama lessons can effect substantial change in children's social and moral attitudes. In Somers' words, the research attempted:

> ... to discover whether exposure to particular circumstances experienced by students in drama affects their attitudes to issues embedded in those circumstances. (1996, p. 109)

This is a position argued by Edmiston, of course, but, significantly, Somers adds that his research report is written: '... in the knowledge that there is little supporting evidence in the field that would stand up to rigorous scrutiny by psychologists or sociologists' (op. cit., p. 109).

On reading the report, this qualification can be seen to have shaped the entire project design for, unlike Edmiston's account, it seeks to provide evidence in the form of quantifiable, statistical data as well as documentary, qualitative comment. A drama entitled *Simon*, at the centre of the report, exemplifies this. It was aimed at encouraging children to feel greater empathy for children with Down's Syndrome by creating a drama, set in a youth club, in which a boy with Down's Syndrome called Simon becomes a member.[1] The research was undertaken in thirty schools across the UK and teachers were asked to apply a six-point Lickert scale to measure children's attitudes as demonstrated in a questionnaire administered before and after the drama; and to apply a social distance scale to quantify children's attitudes towards Simon at different points in the drama. These figures were computed and compared to the attitudes of children in a control group who did the same topic with no drama input. Somers claims that the statistical evidence points to significantly increased attitudinal change in children who took part in the drama sessions.

It is evident from Somers' reference above to 'rigorous scrutiny' that he has planned this research partly in response to perceived shortcomings in personal accounts of practice; and partly in response to the current political climate and the resultant pressures it has placed upon educationalists and educational researchers. Taylor has recently described this climate as an era of neo-positivism, which seeks to provide 'the secure framework upon which curriculum action must flow' (1996, p. 4).[2] It is an era, as argued in the introduction, in search of certainty and quantifiable results, mistrustful and dismissive of those who would see education as complex and problematic and characterized by the language of testing, performance indicators and measurable outcomes. Somers' research design is an impressively robust response to the current educational climate and is one which would have been supported by Troyna (1994) who argued against 'soft' (i.e. reflective) research precisely because it will always be marginalized in the current political climate. But it is nonetheless a response which brings with it its own problems.

There is a tendency within positivist research design to conflate objectivity with measurement and to equate both with Truth; to view objectivity as impersonal and subjectivity as *only* personal. Yet the distinction between subjective and objective observations is as false a dichotomy as that between emotion and cognition, examined in Chapter 5. A more accurate understanding of objective statements would see them as interpersonal, where two or more observers of the same event come to similar conclusions. Such statements are, of necessity, interpretations of events, based upon evidence, but still open to disagreement and misunderstanding. And underlying value positions inform such observations, even in the scientific world, where, we must remember, evidence pointed incontrovertibly to the earth circling the sun for many centuries. If scientists can — and do — disagree over their interpretations of evidence, this must be even more the case with regard to those who would investigate the social and the moral world. As Guba and Lincoln have pointed out, research paradigms:

> . . . are all inventions of the human mind and hence subject to human error. No construction is or can be incontrovertibly right. (cited in Taylor, op. cit., p. 18)

Positivist research design does not ensure the triumph of value-neutrality and objectivity. As Bernstein has asserted, the replacement of political theory by scientific empiricism in the social world would only ensure that:

. . . primary questions about what men are would no longer be seriously asked; instead, there would be the uncritical acceptance of ideological biases. (1976, p. 62)

One of the dangers, then, in researchers playing by the current rules is that they may be uncritically accepting the ideological biases of those who have made the rules. The values are still there but they are at best obfuscated and at worst denied.[3]

Positivist research models do not, then, remove values from the research equation. Furthermore, they aspire to a modernist vision of truth, one which is, perhaps, congruent with a worldview such as we find in Kohlberg's theories of moral development but not with the perspective adopted in this study.[4] As a result, they will tend to conform to an *objectives model* of rational curriculum planning, described by Elliott as: '. . . guided by quite clear and specific statements of intended learning outcomes, defined in terms of measurable changes in student behaviour' (1991, p. 135).

If located within such a model, drama's effectiveness will be determined by measurable and objective performance indicators, even when operating within the most elusive areas of learning. However, in his presentation of this model of curriculum design, Stenhouse (1975) saw its uses as situated within the areas of skills and information and not within those of knowledge and understanding. He proposed that there are, in fact, four educational processes which include not only *training* and *instruction* but also *initiation* and *induction*.[5] While initiation is concerned with securing commitment and conformity to certain social norms and values, often embodied in the ethos of the school, induction is the most elusive and, in many ways, the most crucial process, for it is concerned with giving access to *knowledge*, defined by Stenhouse as 'a structure to sustain creative thought and provide frameworks for judgment'. He goes on to add: '*Education as induction to knowledge is successful to the extent that it makes the behavioural outcomes of the students unpredictable*' (op. cit., p. 85, author's emphasis).

Stenhouse's distinctions are broadly similar to those proposed by Eisner (1985), who distinguished between *instructional* and *expressive* objectives, the former referring to skills and content, the latter to questions in need of exploration and issues to be engaged with. Expressive objectives, by their nature, cannot be specified in advance. Both Somers and Edmiston, in searching to measure predictable outcomes, focus their research attention upon instructional objectives, presenting drama as a means of training and initiating children into certain moral attitudes. Somers might justify this approach by arguing that his purpose is to provide drama teachers with evidence to argue their cause with policy makers outside the drama community. My own research, in contrast, focuses on a use of drama with expressive objectives, for the purposes of induction into moral knowledge, hence aspiring to what Stenhouse saw as complementary to the objectives curriculum model, namely the *process model*. This recognizes that:

... the key procedures, concepts and criteria in any subject — cause, form, experiment, tragedy — are, and are important precisely because they are, problematic within the subject. They are the focus of speculation, not the object of mastery. (1975, p. 85)

I would argue that the thick concepts through which we grasp and understand the virtues which constitute ethical behaviour, and the moral dilemmas which inevitably permeate social life, form the substance of moral knowledge in a process curriculum model. Here, teachers will not set out to measure whether attitudes have been changed or to gauge whether children have been turned into morally better people in a relatively straightforward cause and effect continuum. They will attempt to induct them into an understanding of the moral life; to use Stenhouse's words again, they will seek to provide them with frameworks for judgment and structures to sustain creative thought. Consequently, my research focus is different from that of Somers. It sets out to illuminate how drama engages children in significant moral processes of thought, feeling and representation. Technical rational or positivist research procedures are unsuitable for evaluating or researching into such areas which, as Stenhouse points out, are problematic by definition and whose outcomes are necessarily unpredictable; and yet it is precisely in these areas where practical deliberation is needed, for they are what make education a social practice rather than a technical process.

This view of education as a social practice is central to Schön's concept of reflective practitioner research. Schön sees everyday, professional practice as characterized by 'messy, confusing problems which defy technical solution' (1987, p. 3) — the paradox being that within this swamp, as he calls it, lie the problems of greatest human concern. These 'indeterminate zones of practice' escape the canons of technical rationality because they are characterized by 'uncertainty, uniqueness and value conflict' (ibid., p. 6). Good practice in such a field has at its heart 'a core of artistry':

> Artistry is an exercise of intelligence, a kind of knowing ... It is not inherently mysterious; it is rigorous in its own terms; and we can learn a great deal about it by carefully studying the performance of unusually competent performers. (ibid., p. 13)

Schön's vision of practice as an art has a parallel in Eisner's model of *educational connoisseurship*. Eisner (1985) sees educational practice as an 'inordinately complicated affair, filled with contingencies that are extremely difficult to predict, let alone control'. He goes on: 'Connoisseurship in education, as in other areas, is that art of perception that makes the appreciation of such complexity possible' (1985, p. 104).

Both Eisner and Schön shift the emphasis in researching educational practice away from the measurement of quantifiable outcomes into a more detailed, qualitative appreciation of the practitioner's art. And Schön is very clear that the audience for such work is ideally other practitioners, who can learn from the practice of fellow professionals through becoming part of a discourse community.

Such a concept of educational practice is congruent with the view of learning presented in the earlier chapters of this thesis, inasmuch as it is consistent with MacIntyre's interpretation of the Aristotelian tradition and sees a central role for storytelling in the development and dissemination of professional knowledge. According to Aristotle, there are two forms of rationality, *techne* and *phronesis*.

> Technical rationality is the form of reasoning appropriate to making products; practical deliberation or *phronesis* is the form of reasoning appropriate to doing something well. (Elliott, 1991, p. 138)

Social practices are made up of skills but are always more than an aggregate of those skills as they need to have regard to ends and values which define those practices and develop phronesis, which Carr translates as 'practical wisdom' (1987, p. 171). The virtues are definable as goods internal to particular practices and are distinguishable from external goods — such as wealth or good health — as they benefit communities of practitioners rather than individuals. There is a danger when education and educational research are understood in technical terms only, in that those ethical issues or underlying values, central to the concerns of a practice, become discounted or ignored. As Carr expresses it:

> Without practical wisdom, deliberation degenerates into an intellectual exercise, and 'good practice' becomes indistinguishable from instrumental cleverness. The man who lacks phronesis may be technically accountable but he can never be morally answerable. (1987, p. 172)

The fact that, as teachers, we are morally answerable for what we do implies that we are liable to be called to account, which means we should be prepared to give an account of the actions we have taken. Such accounts as I refer to here are those we render to our fellow practitioners who are best placed to critically evaluate them. They are, first and foremost stories and they are profoundly ethical in their concerns.[6]

The Case for Case Study

I have argued that, in the absence of grand theory, stories afford us our best hold on the moral life, charting as they do the vicissitudes of human intentions and actions, contextualized in culturally and socially specific situations. The same holds true of educational practice, for reasons which are largely similar and this has been evidenced by the recent growth of interest in ethnographic research and case study throughout the human sciences. At the cutting edge has been the work of Clifford Geertz within the field of anthropology. He argues that we take anthropologists seriously not because of the facts they produce but when they manage to convince us 'of having, in one way or another, truly "been there"' (1988, p. 4). Citing Foucault's *What is an Author?* he points out that the writings of an ethnographer or anthropologist have more in common with literary than scientific discourse, with the author-function described by Foucault (ibid., p. 7). In an earlier work, he uses the phrase 'thick description' to characterize the hermeneutic art, which aims to describe and explain the meaning and significance of actions and behaviour as they occur 'in a cultural network saturated with meanings' (Eisner, op. cit., p. 112). Recognizing as he does the importance of writing well, 'where giving reasons for people's actions is the same thing as describing them more fully and more vividly' (Inglis, 1993, p. 164). Geertz's own work provides a model for the literary, narrative case study whose purpose is to construct an accurate, convincing picture of social reality.

Case studies have traditionally been in use in such disciplines as anthropology, sociology or organizational behaviour and only more recently within the field of education. Adelman and Jenkins (1976) define case study as: 'an umbrella term for a family of research methods having in common the decision to focus an inquiry around an instance of action' (p. 140).

Kenny and Grotelueschen (1984) see them typically as:

> intensive investigations of single cases which serve both to identify and describe basic phenomena, as well as provide the basis for subsequent theory development. (p. 37)

These points are important. Case studies are stories — contextualized, single instances — but they are focused and rigorous and are intended to contribute toward theory. Importantly, they generate theory that is grounded in practice[7] but the research methodologies they employ and the shape the research can take are not rigidly defined. Like the cases they inquire into, case studies themselves, in their design and in their conclusions, are problematic. Truth, with a capital T, or measurable certainty, are not their objectives but illumination and a broadening of understanding most certainly are. In the words of Eisner: 'Their generalizing qualities are not so much located in Truth as in their ability to refine perception and to deepen conversation' (1991, p. 205). Such is the aim of this research, however problematic and value-laden its area of investigation and the methodology through which the inquiry was conducted might have been. It is to an analysis of this methodology that I now turn.

The fieldwork was conducted with three overriding, practical concerns. Firstly, it embraced the principle of *openness*. In Carroll's words, this means: 'there is no restriction that can . . . direct the research into predetermined goals or paths of action' (1996, p. 78). Although I had a clear overall research focus,

I was not setting out to *prove* but to *explore* and I never knew what the exact focus of each case study would be until the data was being analysed. As Levi-Strauss wrote: 'Exploration is not so much a matter of covering ground as of digging beneath the surface' (cited in Geertz, 1988, p. 43).

Secondly, I wished to work as far as possible under the same constraints of curriculum, time and space as faced the classteachers with whom I was working in their everyday, professional lives. This I saw as important if the work is ever to speak directly to primary school teachers. It would also act as a sober reminder to myself of the realities of classroom life faced by the students whom I teach, a point which leads on to my third overriding concern. I needed to ensure that the research supplemented and enriched my own, everyday professional practice and did not become too much of an additional burden to it. This was meant to aid the crystallization of my own understanding of the fieldwork as much as it was intended as a necessary coping strategy.

There were five stages to the fieldwork, namely

- selecting the tales and the focus for the dramas
- selecting the schools and the classes with whom I would work[8]
- teaching the lessons and gathering the data
- analysing the data
- presenting the findings

The case studies were not construed as an action research cycle; in other words, the findings of one were not intended to influence the design of another. Consequently, they sometimes overlapped and, although they each went through the five listed stages in ways which were broadly similar, they progressed at different rates and were open and responsive to different influences at each stage, in particular from my reading or my professional conversations with colleagues.

Selecting the Tales and the Focus for the Dramas

My initial thought was to concentrate on one source, either tales from the Hindu or the British tradition, but I eventually dismissed this as an artificial constraint, untypical of how I would act as a classteacher and one which would quite probably limit the problems I could explore through drama. In the end, I decided to work with five tales from a variety of cultural sources, each of which appealed to me as a teacher while suggesting a different moral focus for children of different age ranges. I have drawn from the entire experience of this work but have used the sequence of lessons with just three of the tales to analyse in considerable detail and provide the basis for the ensuing case studies.

'Jack and the Beanstalk' (Years 1 and 2)

This was the focus of a half-term topic chosen by a teacher with whom I had worked before. I was drawn by the morally ambiguous figure of Jack, the evident didacticism in some of its many versions and the potential to explore concepts such as promise-keeping, stealing, obedience, loyalty and bullying. In the end, it was the comic elements of the drama which most fascinated me and upon which I decided to concentrate my analysis.

'The Brahmin, the Thief and the Ogre' (Years 3 and 4)

A Hindu tale, originally from the *Panchatantra* but, in the version I used, adapted for children to take on a form similar to the Victorian fairy tale. This was another story with a strident, moralistic tone and it offered potential to explore the role of violence in such tales. The drama sessions I evaluated as reasonably successful but in no way outstanding and I chose to analyse them for this very reason.

'The Star Maiden' (Year 5)

Originally a tale from the Ojibway people of North America, and related by Barbara Juster Esbensen. I was attracted by the poetry, the symbolism and the moral force of its environmental message. However, I was aware of its representation of the Native American as 'Noble Savage' and I was interested in how drama might both deepen children's responses to the story and offer a different representation of Native American people. The drama left me with more ambivalent feelings than any of the others, feelings which I hoped the analysis would clarify.

Selecting Schools and Classes

I decided to work with children from a variety of local primary schools who had little or no experience in educational drama. This, I hoped, would help inform my understanding of the experiences faced by most of the students whom I teach and most of the teachers to whom I provide In-Service courses. It was my hunch, too, based upon professional experience, that a skilful use of teacher in role and a careful selection of dramatic conventions would enable young children, inexperienced in drama, to explore moral issues successfully within the art form. As Colby commented:

> if . . . skills are perceived as necessary pre-requisites for drama, then students
> are in danger of becoming 'exercised away' from meaningful engagement in

drama. Children learn to be better swimmers in the water, not by practising their strokes on dry land. (1982, p. 22)

I initially intended to work through each story with two contrasting classes of children and to use both as sources for evidence. However, although this worked well for the story of the *Brahmin*, with the other tales it quickly became clear that I had sufficient material for analysis after work with just one class. Of the four classes whose work is analysed in the three case studies, two were from village schools and two from schools in a large, industrialized city. All were state-funded but two had religious affiliations, one being Church of England and one Roman Catholic. One of the classes whose work is not analysed here was made up of 50 per cent Moslem and Hindu children. In the event, race and multiculturalism did not become ethnographic focal points for the three studies here, but the socio-cultural and religious contexts of each school did inform the analyses.

Teaching the Lessons and Gathering Evidence

Given that I wished to work under the same conditions as classteachers, and that I had to fit in with their own, densely-packed time-tables, no session was ever much longer than an hour in length; hall time was limited and the space was prone to be used by children or staff as a corridor; individual children were occasionally extracted or arrived late from special support or individual tuition; children who were absent one week were present the next or vice-versa; and work in the classroom was often limited by restricted space. The important point for me, however, was that the work reflected the social reality of the everyday primary school classroom for teachers coping with the pressures of the National Curriculum.

Gathering evidence was the most problematic of all areas of the fieldwork but the uncertainty was a necessary feature of a project where the focus of each study would be emergent rather than predetermined. Given that the attention would, however, always be on the lessons themselves, upon what the teacher and the children did within them, I was able to limit what I gathered to evidence which would capture this experience and make it intelligible and susceptible to subsequent analysis and argument. The data at the point at which it was gathered can be roughly categorized as either *raw* or *interpretive*, and as either *immediate* or *interim*. By raw data I mean evidence with no specific interpretive focus at the time it was collected, whereas interpretive data was, from the outset, concerned with evaluative judgments. *Immediate* data is that which was gathered at the time the lessons were prepared and taught, whilst *interim* data was gathered over a period of time between the teaching and the final written analysis. The *raw data* can therefore be listed as follows:

1 *The texts of the stories* used directly to inform the lessons and the *historical sources* of these texts.

2 *Lesson plans*

3 *Video and audio recordings of the lessons taught.* These were the most crucial records for subsequent analysis but only for the final case study was I able to secure the help of a university technician. On the other occasions the lessons were recorded by the classteachers and on audio tape as back-up. The children were evidently used to video cameras, either at home or in the classroom, and very quickly began to ignore its presence. It successfully captured whole class work in role; whole class discussions out of role; both teacher's and children's facial expressions, movements and use of gesture; and group work presented to the class. It did not capture the substance of children's talk when they worked simultaneously in small groups.

4 *Children's writing or drawing* from the sessions I took or follow up sessions led by the teacher. It is common in this kind of research for children to be requested to keep journals or to record their written responses at the end of a lesson (Edmiston, 1995; Somers, op. cit.). I have discussed some of the limitations of such evidence in the previous chapter and saw it as particularly problematic in my case for a number of additional reasons. None of the children were used to journal-keeping; some were very inexperienced, poor or very young writers; and the pressures on the drama time I had with each class were acute. I decided, again, to have them write in ways they were used to and in ways I would use, as a classteacher, to develop the drama ideas in separate sessions — through straightforward written questions, story writing, simple poetry, and drawing. These proved to be of limited value when I eventually found the focus for each case study and were most useful as sources of evidence in ways I would never have predicted, particularly in the case of *The Star Maiden*. In the end, the best sources of information about individual children's reflections and responses were the whole class discussions recorded on video and audio tape.

5 *Relevant school documentation.* None of the schools had a policy statement on drama, other than some very general statements subsumed within English documents, and the particular area of moral education was strongly associated with RE. I consulted each school's general statements of aims with regard to children's moral and behavioural development but I was concerned about the ethics of seeking permission to see individual children's records and was unsure whether this would be granted or would indeed by necessary. I decided to refrain from requesting such access unless an individual child unexpectedly became a particular focus of interest in ways which stretched beyond the information teachers could informally provide me with. In the event, this did not happen.

Most of the above evidence was gathered immediately, with the significant exception being the historical sources of the tale of *The Star Maiden*. The realization that this source was closer in tone and imagery to Esbensen's re-telling than I had thought it would be subsequently helped determine the focus for the analysis of the drama.

The *interpretive data* consisted of

1   *Teachers' comments and responses.* Most of these were immediate to the time of teaching and were gathered informally and recorded by myself in note form. I initially floated the idea to one or two teachers of their keeping a written journal of responses but this was given a neg-ative reception, mainly due to perceived demands upon teacher time, so I dropped the idea. In two cases, I contacted teachers for interim comments on specific issues. All teachers were asked to respond to initial written analyses of the drama sessions, though only one re-sponded in written form.

2   *Lesson evaluations.* These were my immediate responses to each session, recorded soon after it was taught.

3   *Journal.* This was on-going and loosely structured, in a loose leaf folder. It was a record of ideas, insights, doubts, responses to things I had read as they might impinge upon my understanding of the drama lessons, and to conversations with my colleagues and students. It was kept in note form throughout all five stages of the research process.

Analysing the Data

I have indicated that the principal problem associated with reflective practi-tioner research is concerned with ensuring sufficient critical distance between oneself and one's practice in order to analyse it fairly and with integrity. The process whereby a variety of perspectives are solicited to inform the research analysis is known as *triangulation*. Recently, however, Taylor has put forward the alternative concept of *crystallization*. This, he argues:

> rejects positivist and neo-positivist ideas of truth, validity and falsification, and confirms the importance of struggle, ambiguity and contradiction, all noted features of the reflective practitioner's journey. (1996, p. 44)

The metaphor of crystallization, he argues 'beautifully captures how our per-spectives are shaped by our "angle of repose"' (ibid., p. 44) and it is the concept which most accurately explains how I achieved critical distance from my teach-ing. One of the chief aids to this process of crystallization was time. Time distanced me from the immediacies of the experience and provided a gap wherein different experiences, thoughts, readings and conversations were given the conceptual space to inform my critical responses before beginning the formal analysis. In addition to the data gathered and listed above, each analysis was therefore informed by further sources of interim evidence, all noted in journal form. These were:

- a historical and critical literary analysis of the tale which had formed the pre-text to the drama;
- use of the drama structures developed during the sessions, and/or videoed extracts from the sessions themselves, as material for work with students and teachers. This provided the opportunity for further reflection upon the material and allowed my own perceptions to be informed by those of interested practitioners;
- the sharing of specific perceptions, ideas, doubts and insights with colleagues for discussion or feedback.

The visual and oral records provided by the videoed material were then transcribed in detail and studied for aspects which could illuminate what had by this time emerged as the points of particular interest for each case study. They were written in the form of performance records, with dramatic dialogue recorded in scripted form, together with detailed notes of relevant movements, gestures, facial expression and tone of voice. The transcriptions were kept in a loose leaf folder and made on one side only of A4 paper, with the adjacent blank sheet being used for notes and commentary.[9] This detailed record, when analysed, was to show, in Geertz's words, how 'the very small signals can carry very big messages' (1988, p. 59). I used coloured highlighter pens to denote different themes and used the skills of close textual analysis to make sense of the transcriptions, regarding them as artistic as well as historical documents. In this way the process of writing itself became a crucial part of the analytical process, a struggle to find a suitable form and an authentic voice, to do justice to what Geertz has described as the purpose of ethnographic texts.

> Ethnographers need to convince us . . . not merely that they themselves have truly 'been there' but . . . that had we been there we should have seen what they saw, felt what they felt, concluded what they concluded. (1988, p. 16)

The initial draft of each case study was submitted to colleagues and to the classteachers involved. Their comments and critical feedback informed the subsequent redrafts and helped deepen the process of crystallization.

Presenting the Findings

Each of the following case studies consists of:

- a summary of the tale in the version I used for the drama and an analysis of the moral values embedded within this text and in those historical sources which have influenced it;

- an explanation of the focus of the case study;
- a narrative summary of the lessons with relevant contextual details about the school, the children, the conditions under which the sessions were taught and the reasons behind the choice of focus for the drama;
- detailed analyses of selected parts of the lessons, intended to illuminate the particular focus of each case study.

Notes

1   The representation of Simon is evidently problematic in such a drama and was sensitively managed by the use of photographic material, by teacher in role as one of Simon's parents and by the use of an empty chair (op. cit., p. 110).

2   Taylor provides a brief description of the aims and values of positivism and neo-positivism and attempts a detailed refutation of its claims, particularly within the Arts. See pp. 4–16. For a further, more general account of positivism see Carr and Kemmis, 1986, pp. 61–70.

3   The attempts to universalize the evidence to make it count as proof involved the participation of 74 teachers, selected by LEAs and advisors as *good*, using the material which a group of five teachers had developed and saw as their best. Obviously issues of value were at the heart of the project from its commencement and Somers lists a series of thirteen bullet points where he detects need for further research, many of which are concerned with further objectifying the findings. Thus, at the completion of the project, he is well aware that issues of subjective value still remain unresolved (op. cit., pp. 117–118).

4   Significantly, Somers refers to the developmental models of Piaget, Kohlberg and Courtney on the first page of his report (op. cit., p. 108).

5   See Stenhouse, 1975, Chapter 6, pp. 70–83; and p. 97 for his comments on the comparative suitabilities of the objectives and process models of curriculum design.

6   For a detailed analysis of professional accountability and the nature of accounts, see Langford, 1985, Chapter 4.

7   See Glaser, B.G. and Strauss, A.L. (1967) for a full analysis of the concept of grounded theory.

8   For the purposes of this research, I normally began by finding a particular story I wished to work with, rather than attempting to find a story to suit a particular group of children.

9   The transcriptions did not record every interruption and every individual word spoken. They followed the development of the dialogue and recorded all salient contributions.

Chapter 8

The Brahmin, the Thief and the Ogre: Drama as Pedagogy for Moral Education

The Story: *The Brahmin, the Thief and the Ogre*

This story tells of a Brahmin who, though poor, always remained good, honest and humble and who regularly prayed to the Gods. Because of this, the Gods decide to reward him and a kindly person makes him the gift of two calves which he takes great care of. However, a Thief sees the calves and decides to steal them. That night, on his journey to the Brahmin's cottage, he is accosted by an Ogre who, on learning of the Thief's purpose, decides to accompany him in order to eat the Brahmin. Once in the cottage, however, they begin to argue over whether the Thief should steal the calves first or the Ogre eat the Brahmin first. Their arguments awaken the Brahmin who prays to the Gods and they promptly respond by getting rid of the Ogre; whereupon the Brahmin reaches for a stick and puts the Thief to flight by clubbing him over the head.

I found this English language version of the story in a volume entitled *More stories from Panchatantra* (1981). The *Panchatantra* is an ancient text, dating from between 100BC and 500AD and its frame story explains the purpose of the tales it contains. These are purported to be the stories through which a wise old Brahmin taught three stupid young princes the practical wisdom they would need to be successful rulers of the kingdoms they were due to inherit. As such, their lessons are about understanding and manipulating people and circumstances pragmatically rather than according to any ethical code. In this way, the tales are 'moral' only in the same sense as *Aesop's Fables*.

The Hemkunt Press is not stocked in English bookshops but is widely circulated in India, geared toward a reading audience of young children. It is a Sikh owned institution, but it packages as children's literature the stories from the entire variety of India's cultural and religious backgrounds.[1] Although a fable in its original form, the retelling of this particular story, by Vernon Thomas, reads like the sort of tale favoured by those nineteenth century writers who used fairy stories for morally didactic purposes.[2] It is interesting, therefore, to compare this version with a translation of the original (Edgerton, 1965). Here, the Brahmin does not strike the Thief but frightens him away by brandishing his club. The original also states clearly the moral of the tale: 'Even enemies may be useful when they fall out with each other.' This particular moral — a practical lesson for the Machiavellian prince — is not printed in the Hemkunt version and is, in fact, totally obscured by a number of didactic lessons implicit within the narrative.

In both versions, the protagonists remain *archetypal*, by which I mean that they conform to what Northrop Frye calls 'associative clusters' able to convey:

> a large number of specific learned associations which are communicable because a large number of people in a given culture happen to be familiar with them. (Frye, 1965)[3]

Although a child in an ethnically white area of Britain may be unfamiliar with the term 'Brahmin', this term becomes sufficiently communicable for an understanding of the tale when he is explained as a 'holy man'. The Brahmin and the Thief, therefore, convey Good and Evil on the human plane whilst the Gods and the Ogre do so on a supernatural plane. But whereas, in the initial tale, this symmetry was merely functional, in the children's version it is moralistic.

The original tale is a stark, short piece of storytelling, true to the oral tradition, with no literary embellishments. The gift of the calves, for example, is narrated without comment. It is not a moral reward but simply reflects the reality of Hindu society, where such gifts to a Brahmin are common and part of the social fabric of the caste system. The original listener to the tale would have recognized this as such, without any need for further comment. The important narrative point is factual, not moral, that the Brahmin possessed the cows, not that he deserved to have them.

In the child's version, however, the Brahmin's good fortune is portrayed as a reward for his virtue, described as follows:

> Once upon a time there lived a Brahmin who was so poor that he went about in rags, and had hardly anything to eat. But though he faced so much hardship, the Brahmin was good and honest. Daily he would pray, and accept without grumbling whatever fate had in store for him.

Goodness is, therefore, portrayed in terms of meekness, passivity, honesty and religious piety — model behaviour for a child reared on Victorian values, in fact, a model satirized, as we saw, in Saki's *The Story Teller* and one whose residue still persists in many primary classrooms today, in both Britain and India. That the child should identify with this model of goodness is reinforced by the description of the Brahmin's attitude to the calves he is given:

> He began to take great care of the calves. Daily he saw to it that they had enough grass to eat and water to drink.

He is kind to animals and they are described as his pets. Again, this is an interesting deviation from the original, where the calves are already grown and fattened and no mention is made of the Brahmin's care for them. The reality of life in Hindu society is that these calves are religiously symbolic of purity and prosperity but also economically very useful, likely to provide the Brahmin with milk, if female, or the force to pull his plough, if male. However, most of the Indian children who read the Hemkunt Press are urban and middle-class and many are not Hindu; and this revised portrayal of the calves creates an image of cuddly baby animals, accessible to any child reared in a culture where the liberal western tradition of childhood is dominant.[4]

The Brahmin's violence at the end of the story provides an ethical jolt in the narrative. When he clubs the Thief, it is not to protect the calves from harm, but his property from theft. The implied moral messages at this point seem to be that violence is justifiable when defending one's property and that thieves will be punished for their crimes. As with those Victorian fairy tales criticized by Tatar, the level of violence re-enforces the lesson; just as Mr. Miacca will chop your leg off if you disobey your parents, you will be beaten with a stick if you steal. Nevertheless, the Brahmin's use of violence sits uneasily alongside the model of passive goodness that he previously appeared to embody.

Here we have an example, therefore, of how, with the literary retelling of fairy stories, we get different and often contradictory values layered into their fabric creating moral anomalies which are difficult to resolve. Indeed, the issues connected with the use of violence raised unintentionally by the story are very relevant for a child in contemporary British society:

- Are children influenced by the exposure to violence in fiction? (witness the furore over violent videos such as *Child's Play 3* which accompanied two murder cases in 1993)[5]
- Is violence justifiable when defending one's property and if so, what level of violence?
- Can one be good *and* violent?

I have proposed that process drama provides a methodology which allows for the communal investigation and interrogation of the values within such tales. The literary form is as capable as the dramatic form for creating new moral meanings in stories, of course; and, as we saw in Chapter 6, process drama can become as didactic and monological as a literary text. In the sessions described below, my intention was to create a drama which dialogized Thomas' tale, seeking to illuminate how the children intepreted its moral agenda and then, through drama, to explore this agenda through problematizing it.

I wish to now move on to analyse aspects of the sessions I taught around this story. I refer to the different classes as *Sophie's class*, with whom I spent three sessions, each one hour in length, and *Martin's class* with whom I spent two fifty-minute sessions. With both classes, there was a week in between each lesson. Sophie's class was a group of 8 and 9 year-old children from a village Church of England school in Warwickshire. They were described by their teacher as a 'nice class' with a 'fairly typical social mix and spread of academic abilities'. Martin's class, aged between 7 and 9, were from a school situated in the centre of a socially deprived housing estate on the outskirts of a large city. Six of the children were statemented for particular learning and behavioural difficulties but, according to the classteacher, roughly half the class were in need of additional, learning support. I present the lessons below as narrative summaries, emphasizing the story which the drama developed.

The Lessons in Summary

Lesson 1:

This was essentially the same for both classes. I informed the children that the tale I was going to tell was from India and explained that Hinduism was one of the religions in India and that a Brahmin was a Hindu priest or Holy man. Other cultural or religious aspects which needed explanation I incorporated into the narrative of the tale, which I related orally and dramatically; that is, I took on the characteristics of all the characters and allowed them to speak directly when possible. After this, I explained the source of the tale via the frame story of the *Panchatantra* and asked the children to help me decide what the moral of the story might be, presenting them with a number of possibilities. After collecting their ideas, I then asked them to suggest examples of good ethical conduct and bad ethical conduct in the story,[6] and noted these down. With both classes, children volunteered that the Brahmin's hitting the Thief over the head was an example of bad ethics. Picking up on this idea, I asked if they thought this story was a good one for children of their age or younger and whether they thought the ending ought to be changed? All thought the ending should, indeed, be changed. I put Sophie's class in groups to work out possible different endings for the tale, suitable for children of their age, which they presented in dramatic form. With Martin's class, I did the same exercise via *forum theatre*, in which I played the Brahmin and different children took on the role of the Thief. I spoke and acted only as the children suggested.

In subsequent sessions with both classes, we invented, through drama, a new story as a sequel to the first, leaving the violent ending intact.

Lesson 2 (Sophie's Class)

I cast the children initially as local villagers and narrated a new section of the story, entering in role as a poor neighbour, recently moved into the village, the mother of three children. I told them how I was worried about my husband who had returned home late last night with his head bleeding and muttering something about going back to sort things out with a certain Brahmin. Under questioning, it emerged that my husband had been a thief, stealing food, gifts for me and toys for the children. He had been caught, however, and had subsequently made a promise to me to stop thieving. We had moved to this village to try to start a new life where he would not be known as a thief. The children soon told me that they, as villagers, knew what had happened and agreed to help me prevent my husband from doing anything wrong, also promising to ensure that he wouldn't come to any further harm. They set off through the woods and hid near the Brahmin's cottage. I approached as the Thief. They surrounded me and led me in to confess to the Brahmin. Children now took on the *collective role* of the Brahmin, whereupon I informed him that I had not come to steal his calves but to demand one from him; as he was supposed to be a good man, and in the best interests of my wife and children, he ought to comply with this request. A discussion ensued as the children tried to make sense of this unexpected turn and no resolution was achieved. I stopped the drama with the question: 'I wonder what Lord Vishnu is thinking?' and recast the children as the Gods, whereupon they discussed what they felt ought to happen. The lesson ended before this was concluded.

Lesson 3

After recapping the last session, the children returned to their roles as Gods and questioned me in role as the Thief as to my motives in returning and demanding that the Brahmin give me a calf. They eventually resolved that the quarrel must be a matter for the Brahmin and the Thief to decide amongst themselves, that divine intervention was inappropriate. I then cast half of the class in collective role as the Thief, the other half as the Brahmin and they argued the matter further. In small groups, the children then decided upon and acted out an appropriate ending to this new story.

Lesson 2 (Martin's Class)

The two drama sessions with Sophie's class were only partially successful, inasmuch as there was too much role changing which, in turn, added very little to the dramatic tension. There was, too, an overemphasis on talk and the changes of role did not achieve the variety of perspective I had intended and certainly did not deepen the children's involvement. Martin's class was more volatile and difficult to control. For these reasons I simplified the drama and kept the children in role as villagers throughout. This increased the drama's fluidity and created a simpler but more coherent structure. When the children apprehended the Thief (teacher-in-role), they sat him down and interrogated him. They began to sympathize with his case and went to the Brahmin (again, teacher in role) to try and convince him that he ought to give the Thief one of the calves. As with Sophie's class, these strategies were used to explore the dilemma, not resolve it and, in small groups, the children ended the session by acting out what they saw as an appropriate ending for the story.

Analysing Children's Ethical Thinking

Colby (1982) has analysed in some detail an extract from a justifiably famous videoed drama session led by Tom Stabler, *Elijah*, on the video *Three Looms Waiting*. It is a remarkable piece of improvised drama, but when Colby uses it to show how the moral reasoning of a group of 10 year-olds in role, within the space of a few minutes, shows evidence of moving from Stage 3 to Stage 5 of Kohlberg's Stages of Moral Development, we may well regard his conclusions with some scepticism (Colby, 1982, pp. 16–20). Stage 5 moral reasoning is in the post-conventional level and is often not achieved in mature adults, according to Kohlberg.

In the subsequent analysis, I make no similar claims. This is not simply because this particular drama was inferior but also because I see Kohlberg's schema as open to question, for reasons discussed in Chapter 1, and find the language of the virtues as expressed through social roles more in tune with the nature of dramatic narrative than the language of universal moral precepts. Within the context of my own research, the claims I make are far less ambitious than those made by Colby. Nevertheless, I think that, even within ordinary lessons such as these, which do not produce remarkable results, there is enough evidence to explore how children can and do engage with ethical thinking and express moral meaning through the art form of process drama.

The Children's Perceptions of the Values in the Story

I presented a list of seven statements and asked the children each to choose as many as three of them as the most likely morals to the story. The reasons for presenting options which I had previously thought out myself were twofold: to avoid the simple *do's* and *don'ts* I would have expected from children so young; and to ensure that the moral of the original story was unobtrusively among those open to choice.[7] Forty-three children were involved in all and I present their opinions below:[8]

- If you steal, you will be punished — 20
- If you pray, God will look after you — 35
- If you are kind, you will be rewarded — 38
- Even your enemies can help you if they quarrel with one another — 4
- Be careful of the friends you choose, as they might get you into trouble — 22
- Thieves are bad people — 24
- No matter how poor you are, you must not steal — 38

These responses appear to support the interpretation of the values implicit to the story which I offered earlier. It is also quite clear that the children picked up these values, rather than the intended moral of the original tale and that they were used to stories carrying didactic messages. This exercise helped determine the focus of subsequent sessions, which took the last statement on the list as its starting point.

The children suggested the following as examples of good and bad ethical action. Unlike the previous responses, these suggestions were entirely their own:

Good Ethics:
The farmer gave the Brahmin the calves (both classes)
The Brahmin prayed to Vishnu
The Brahmin was always helpful and good
The Brahmin looked after the calves (both classes)
Vishnu influenced the farmer to be generous (both classes)

Bad Ethics:
The Ogre wanted to eat the Brahmin (both classes)
The Thief tried to steal the calves
The Ogre and the Thief quarrelled
The Brahmin hit the Thief on the head (both classes)
Two teamed up against one (both classes)

The children, then, although not capable of presenting a satisfactory moral for the story in their own words, were nonetheless capable of recognizing a wide variety of good and bad ethical behaviour within the context of the story. Perhaps they would not have been able to define them as such, but they had no trouble in articulating manifestations of generosity; religious piety; helpfulness; care for living things; the benevolent exercise of authority; selfishness; quarrelsomeness; violence and bullying. These were the virtues and vices they implicitly understood, examples of the thick concepts through which they grasped and made sense of the moral universe and Williams recognizes that this implicitness is, in part, characteristic of how these concepts influence action.

> The benevolent or kindhearted person does benevolent things, but does them under other descriptions, such as 'she needs it', 'it will cheer him up', 'it will stop the pain'. The description of the virtue is not itself the description that appears in the consideration. (1985, p. 10)

So, if the first of these exercises enabled the children to *de*construct the ethical values embedded in the narrative, this latter exercise allowed them to begin to *re*construct the ethics of the story in the light of the sense they made of the characters' actions.

Drama Pedagogy as Pedagogy for Moral Education

At the time I taught these lessons, there had been much reporting on the television and in the press on crime and violence, particularly committed by youths. Such waves of moral panic[9] sweep the media at regular intervals and the reporting, in particular in the tabloids, tends to sensationalize the issues, turning complex problems into simplistic headlines. Reporting on his research into the sources of children's information, Cullingford comments that 'Items (of news) remain part of an inventory of attitudes rather than the construction of clear principles' (1992, p. 28). He goes on to point out: 'The images experienced on television might not always be understood but they nevertheless contain an impact that remains' (ibid., p. 30).

The choice of focus for the drama was, therefore, intended to provide a platform for the exploration of a current moral debate through a situation which acted as a metaphor for these issues. The drama was intended to work dialogically against the story but I did not wish to replace one over-simplified message with another. My aim was to create a more morally ambiguous instance of stealing, to raise questions and not provide answers. By creating a believable social background for the Thief, I created a moral dilemma that I did not have any answers to myself and no agenda as to how I wanted it to end. My sympathies were split between two characters and this I felt was essential for the drama to be both honest and effective.

In the analysis which follows, I have chosen to focus not on any meanings which children might have expressed outside of the drama, but on their work within it. My intention is not to present drama as a vehicle whose efficacy we judge only in a child's responses outside the art form but to illuminate how drama can enable children to make moral meanings in ways which are distinctive to it. As drama is a multi-dimensional activity, I have addressed this analysis according to six frames of reference which emerged as the most apposite lenses through which to view this particular case study. I believe they could be transitional toward a more general model but am not presenting them as such here.

1. Archetypes and the Brotherhood Code

Archetypal characters within fairy tales have a strong narrative function as they impact immediately upon children, providing clear and instant recognition patterns. This contrasts with the gradual and complex way in which the characters of the more literary novel are conveyed to the reader. The figures in fairy tales share more in common with the stock characters of popular fiction and also, importantly, with those of popular drama. This link has been emphasized by O'Neill who writes:

> Valuable pre-texts for process drama occur in folk-tales, fairytales, myths and historical incidents . . . Myth and archetype never merely reside in remote and seemingly irrelevant tales of long ago. Their powerful echoes still wait to wake us through the pre-texts we employ. These archetypal and essentially dramatic threads in the work will connect it with a wider theatre heritage and the

> literary, mythic and dramatic legacy of other cultures as well as with the soap
> operas and popular movies, where archetypes clearly persist. (1995, p. 43)

The archetypal characters in the original story carried morally simplistic meanings, serving to define the moral reference points of the tale; a holy man is
good, a thief and an ogre are bad. Such simplicity is similar to the formulaic
nature of the characters in B movies and Turner, in analysing the appropriateness of Propp's morphology of the folk-tale to popular films such as *Star Wars*,
draws comparisons similar in implication to the points made by O'Neill. He
speculates that: '. . . the modern feature film and the primitive fairy tale serve
similar functions to their respective audiences' (1993, p. 71).

It is worth lingering for a while to consider the archetypal B movie character and the moral impact he or she makes. Such figures are, of course,
associated with particular genres of film. In such films — the western, the
thriller, or the police drama, for example — the villains, heroines and heroes
are as readily identifiable as the ogres, witches and princesses of fairy tales but
the immediacy of their impact is due to the visual and aural signalling conveyed by their physical presence — costume, posture, facial expression, tone
of voice. In a classic *film noir*, too, one such as *The Maltese Falcon* or *The Big
Sleep*, our recognition of the stock characters of the private eye and the *femme
fatale* are made similarly immediate through visual and aural means: her black
dress, his distinctive hat and suit; her lingering gaze and sensuality, his cynical
wise-cracking and hard-boiled exterior. However, with these images come
moral expectations equally immediate but at once more ambivalent. Both
characters will be flawed and will generate sexual heat which resonates with
a more general sense of moral danger. He will operate on the margins of the
law administering his own rough justice, will be surrounded by corruption but
will remain untainted by it. She will tempt him and, though his pride and
decency will prevail, it will not do so without emphasizing his loneliness, a
loneliness which signifies the difficulty of retaining a moral position in a corrupt
society.

Polanski's *Chinatown* sets up these ambivalent moral expectations only to
undermine and frustrate them. In many ways, Jake Giddis appears to be the
archetypal private eye in the mould of Philip Marlow. He wisecracks, is single-
minded in his search for truth, and his work brings him into conflict with the
local police, who are professionally and intellectually his inferiors. The plot of
the film appears to closely follow those typical of the genre. Giddis becomes
sexually involved with his client, a wealthy widow, who is hiding a dark secret
which he manages to expose in the film's dénouement. But the comparisons
are misleading for, although Giddis might look like Philip Marlow, he is his
moral inferior. The plot is set in motion through Giddis' predilection for hand-
ling cases of adultery, which Marlow makes clear he will never touch. Evelyn
Mulray might have the appearance of a *femme fatale* but she is not hard and
scheming, but a vulnerable and courageous woman. Her secret is, indeed, a
guilty one but the guilt is her father's, not her own. In the end, Giddis' pride

does not morally save him, it leads to disaster and, though he proves to be Mrs Mulray's nemesis, this marks the triumph of evil and error, not of justice and truth, and there is no moral redemption in the final images of loneliness and loss. In this film, the archetypes, and hence the genre, are transformed and this disturbance leads to a deepening of their moral resonance.

Archetypal characters such as the private eye, like the genres in which they are embodied, are culturally learned, of course. The figure of the Brahmin was, however, culturally distant for both these classes of children but, through dramatic storytelling, I was able to endow him with the stock characteristics of goodness and piety which they could immediately recognize. I knelt and prayed, seriously and with humility, to thank Lord Vishnu for his generosity; I smiled at the calves and mimed petting them. The Thief I portrayed in a neutral light in the initial story. The fact that he was described as (and only as) a thief, that he set out to steal and that he struck up a nefarious deal with an ogre was sufficient to establish his archetypal characteristics which I later, within the drama, wished to undermine. Children's comments within the drama showed that these simple impressions of good versus bad, embodied within the two oppositional characters, were very persistent. 'You were going to steal! Stealing is bad!' was the unsurprising and emphatic denunciation made by one girl in role as the Brahmin during the second lesson with Sophie's class. The following short section is also taken from this lesson. I was in role as the Brahmin and the children had come to warn me that the Thief was returning to my cottage:

Brahmin: I'm not sure I need your help. I've got this big stick. That frightened him away last time. Why can't I use this again?

Vill 1: Because you hit him on the head and his head was bleeding.

Vill 2: He was only trying to steal because he was poor and he hasn't got any food.

Vill 3: He doesn't have any money.

Brahmin: Well I was poor and I didn't have any food and I didn't steal anything.

Vill 2: Well you're good, aren't you?

Brahmin: Well he should be good!

Vill 4: That's because you've got Lord Vishnu and he hasn't.

The Brahmin is still seen as essentially good, despite his violent action which the children had condemned; but the Thief, although his intentions were bad, is no longer seen as a bad person. This is a simple but important point. The drama of *The Brahmin and the Thief* had begun with two archetypal figures representing good and bad but their simplistic moral meanings had been quickly undermined through a combination of visual signalling (analysed in the next section), and by a change in the frame through which the Thief was presented. At the heart of the drama there remained a tension, however, between the moral restrictiveness of the archetypes and their moral reassessment, which the events of the drama had set in motion. This was a process dramatically far less sophisticated than in the film *Chinatown*, of course, but notably similar in its intention and moral purpose and it can be illuminated by reference to Dorothy Heathcote's theory of the *brotherhood code*.

If archetypal figures help children make connections between the particular and the general, then, within process drama, the *brotherhood code* helps children make similar connections but in a way which is morally expansive and thus able to transform and deepen the archetype. Wagner has described this essential feature of the brotherhood code as follows:

> The new situation on the outside might look far removed from the child's own experience. Yet because the people in that situation are in the same brotherhood as those who are familiar, the child can focus on the common element long enough to identify. (Wagner, 1979, p. 52)

So, for the purposes of this drama, the Brahmin was in the brotherhood of all those who are envied for their good fortune; who face personal danger through this envy: who use violence to defend their property; who are challenged to examine their moral consciences. Although the children could not articulate this understanding in such terms, their actions in, for example, coming to protect the Brahmin, and their words in role, such as those quoted above, indicate that this is how they came to view him and his situation. The Thief, on the other hand, came to belong to the brotherhood of all those who resort to crime due, in large measure, to social circumstances; who try to reform their moral actions but fail; who suffer as a consequence of their misdeeds; who come to believe in the social justice of wealth redistribution.

Through the brotherhood code, culturally distant figures such as the Brahmin and the Thief came to carry ambivalent and conflicting moral meanings in a conflict which was nonetheless comprehensible to these young children. Furthermore, the expansive quality of the brotherhood code helped prepare the way for a redefinition of the moral sympathies evoked by the narrative and hence continued the redefinition of the children's moral perspectives, begun with the initial deconstruction of the story's values in the first session. These perspectives were anchored in particularity and were articulated through the language of drama.

2. The Moral Force of the Dramatic Image

Colby (1987) has argued cogently that classroom simulations and role plays provide only limited opportunities for moral growth, arguing that visual dramatic metaphors provide a much fuller moral experience. He illustrates his argument with reference to the closing image from David Edgar's adaptation of *The Life and Adventures of Nicholas Nickleby*.

Nicholas, now happy and successful, stands before another wretchedly poor cripple in the streets of London. . . . Nicholas reaches down, picks up the boy and stands with him in his arms. His eyes look anguishedly heavenward as the teeming, indifferent populace of the city swarms around him. As an image, it resists a facile translation into language, yet it evokes in an immediate, eloquent and visceral way a range of meanings from the realm of ethics and religion. (1987, p. 78)

As with the moment in *Julius Caesar*, when Brutus strikes Caesar with the knife, presenting a visual metaphor of the betrayal of a friendship in the interests of political freedom, the moral metaphor is here contained in a dramatic image. Colby refers to a moment in an educational drama session described by Gavin Bolton, where a handshake between a black South African and a white South African journalist contained great dramatic power and moral significance. He explains:

These significant experiences are similar to the notion of catharsis . . . a notion of practical wisdom or moral insight promoted through the 'temporary alignment of passion, emotion and desire with right principle.' (1987, p. 11)

Such images gain their power through their location in time and space; that is, through their place within the dramatic narrative and via the semiotic communication of their visual signs — one human being holding another, a look of anguish, a handshake. Such *moments of awe*, as Heathcote and Bolton somewhat unhelpfully describe them, are analogous to the concept of catharsis theorized in Chapter 5.[10] They are, of course, difficult to achieve in a one-hour session in a primary classroom but the use of visual signalling to create significant metaphorical associations does happen readily in drama; and when these metaphors have moral meaning, this meaning is rendered both deeper and more accessible for the participants.

For example, when telling the story dramatically in the initial session, I deliberately ended it with a physical representation of the Thief cowering and protecting his head from the blows of the stick; later, in role as his wife, I spoke softly and held a small bundle representing a baby; when I reappeared as the Thief, I held a bandage to my forehead. All of these signalled that the Thief and his family were victims, thus stirring the children's orectic capacity for pity and deepening the dilemma for them (they had already seen me represent the Brahmin as a smiling, kindly person). In Beckerman's terms, the action became *dialectic*. Noddings, in particular, has emphasized the importance of visual signals for women when making moral decisions:

Faced with a hypothetical moral dilemma, women often ask for more information . . . Ideally, we need to talk to participants, to see their eyes and facial expressions, to receive what they are feeling. (1984, p. 2)

The fact that Noddings is focusing on women here is, in itself, metaphorical; women she sees as representatives of a morality based upon caring and compassion. Visual signs evoke these human sympathies and also allow for other processes apart from the linguistic to become engaged in the moral reasoning task. Referring to work done by Howard Gardner's research into the domains of intellectual competency, Colby writes:

> Drama by its very nature has the power to 'yoke' the competencies of the other domains to the moral reasoning task, thus allowing those with greater visual/spatial or kinaesthetic intelligence to bring their talents to bear on the problem. (1982, p. 24)

In order to see how children can create simple dramatic images which resonate moral meaning, it is interesting to look briefly at how three girls and two boys from Martin's class decided to conclude the drama.

1 *Brahmin*: I'm sorry I hit you on the head. *(Hands the thief and his wife a calf. All smile and hug each other)*

2 *Brahmin*: I'm sorry I hit you over the head with the stick.
 Thief: That's OK. *(Suddenly brandishes a small stick at him)* I've still got half of it! *(Pauses, looks at the stick, then back at the Brahmin)* No! *(Drops the stick)* Thanks! *(Offers his hand to the Brahmin. They shake)*.

However blurred the distinction between child-in-role and child-working-with-friend, these dramatic images were strongly defined, moral metaphors which rejected violence while celebrating generosity of spirit and friendship. Through the particularity of story and the language of drama, the children had the means to explore and express their understandings of these thick, ethical concepts.

3. Moral Argument as Dramatic Dialogue

In the penultimate scene of *Top Girls* by Caryl Churchill, two sisters confront each other in a heated argument, representing together a political and moral dilemma faced by women in the 1980s: whether to achieve independence by adopting the socially dominant male values of ruthlessness and competitiveness or to adopt the traditional role of woman as carer, here portrayed potentially as unrewarding drudgery. Churchill herself is a committed feminist and socialist but the action is constructed dialectically, so as not to deliver a simple, didactic condemnation of the Thatcherite elder sister, Marlene. Both protagonists argue with passion; the moral situation is complex and is presented as such.

Moral discussion as dramatic dialogue differs from other forms of moral discussion in the classroom. Colby (op. cit., 1987) provides a comprehensive discussion of the formal weaknesses of debates, role plays and classroom simulations. Essentially his argument is that all mitigate against 'a real involvement in the predicament under study' (ibid., p. 76) by either encouraging entrenched argument or by concentrating exclusively on logic and problem solving. Citing a late essay by Kohlberg, he argues that: 'the personality is unitary; cognition and affect join in single structures rather than being divided into separate organs of impulse and cognition' (ibid., p. 74). If the passions are not harnessed, or if the problem is morally too clear-cut and lacks ambiguity, then discussion in role will fail to take on the power of dramatic dialogue. But there is a third and important constituent to dramatic dialogue which distinguishes it from discussion or debate; in Esslin's words: 'the verbal element in drama must function primarily as **action**' (1987, p. 83). What matters more than what is said is what the words do to the characters to whom they are spoken or who speak them; what counts is their effect on the way they see their situation and how this vision defines or will redefine their subsequent actions.

Below, I present two extracts, one from each of the classes, which go some way toward illustrating that improvised dialogue in process drama can attain these three characteristics of dramatic dialogue. Both extracts will be recognized as readily achievable within classroom drama by experienced practitioners. The first is taken from the final session with Sophie's class. The children were in collective role at this point, with half of the class taking the part of the Thief and the other half the Brahmin. I was outside the action and did not speak:

Thief:	How would you feel? If we hadn't stolen, then we wouldn't have had anything for my family and all of my family would be dead.
Thief:	If you give us a calf then we'll stop stealing.
Brahm:	The villagers manage all right don't they and they don't steal. The villagers are poor.
Thief:	Yeah, but they've got calves.
Thief:	And we can't afford it.
Brahm:	Why don't you go and find one?
Thief:	Because cows are sacred, you don't find them wandering around everywhere.
Thief:	You're not saying. . . . that we don't have to steal from you. . . . .you mean we can go and steal from. . . . .?
Brahm:	Well. . . . . .
Brahm:	(muted) No . . . no . . .
Brahm:	I'll give it you for a day . . .
Thief:	Oh, come on . . .
Brahm:	Plough your fields yeah, and I'll come over, yeah, and see how you're doing . . . and we'll decide about it then.

This was the section of the drama which had most influence on how the children in this class decided to conclude it. Throughout this discussion, the

moral ambiguity was constant and was responsible for holding the dramatic
tension. All arguments put forward were essentially valid (apart from the sug-
gestion to go out and find a calf). The overall flow of argument was logical,
with the children listening and responding to one another; but it wasn't a logic
detached from emotional concern. The section opened with a request from the
Thief for the Brahmin to empathize with his family's situation; the argument
which finally moved the Brahmin amounted to another appeal for him to look
beyond his own good fortune. But the Brahmin would not forget the previous
injustice he had endured at the hands of the Thief. His sense of indignation did
not disappear when he began the process which eventually led to the Thief
keeping the calf for a period of time in order to prove that he could be trusted
by the Brahmin to mend his ways. So the words led to an action agreed by the
children in role which embodied their cautious reassessment of what might
pass for justice in this particular situation.

The following extract, somewhat longer, is from the second session with
Martin's class. Here, I was in role as the Brahmin with the children as the
villagers.

Brahm:	So is he threatening me? Is he saying, 'Give me a calf or else I'm going to steal something?' Why should I listen to that? That's not good.
Vill:	No!
Vill:	He only wants to be your friend.
Brahm:	He only wants to be my friend? So he comes round and tries to steal things from me! Is that the way to be friendly to somebody?
Vill:	No, he wants to start a new life.
Vill:	He wants you to help him as well.
Brahm:	Well look, I don't know. . . . .
Vill:	Well, you're being a bit greedy with two. Why don't you give him just one?
Brahm:	I'm not being greedy with two! They're mine!
Vill:	You shouldn't have two! You should have one!
Brahm:	Why should I only have one?
Vill:	You're too greedy!
Vill:	'Cos if you give him one, you'll still have one left, won't you?
Brahm:	Do you think that's fair?
Vill:	Yeah! We're only trying to help him!
Vill:	Give him a calf!
Brahm:	Is that going to help him be a better person?
Vills:	Yeah!
Vill:	He'll be happy if you did that.
Brahm:	He'll be happy and a better person?
Vill:	He's got three children and he can't get a job and he needs food.
Vill:	And he can't get any money.
Brahm:	Will I be a better person if I give him a calf?
Vills:	Yeah!
Brahm:	Why will I be a better person if I give him a calf?

Vill:	'Cos you'll be sharing.
Vill:	You could share with him.
Brahm:	If you were me, would you give him a calf?
Vill:	Of course I would!
Vills:	Yeah!
Brahm:	But I'll have to work harder with just one calf!
Vill:	But if you have one calf and he has one calf then everyone will be happy.

The children had argued with quite some passion and their logic was driven by their desire for the Brahmin to take into account the feelings and desires of the Thief (he *wants* to be your friend; he *wants* to start a new life; he'll *be happy* if you did that). The moral ambiguity and hence the dramatic tension was different from that which found expression in the previous extract. As Brahmin, I began by forcefully stating my case but the children's accusations of greed led me to steer the conversation into an interrogation of their view of fairness. They could see that the questions I began to pose might be indicative of a nascent change of mind on my part. This intensified the tension, and I held it for as long as I could. The sense of moral ambiguity had, therefore, shifted its focal point to within the Brahmin himself. This the children were both witness to and could act upon through the persuasive power of their words which, once again, were anchored and enhanced by the amount of contextual detail they were able to draw upon.

4. Drama, Moral Education and the Practice of Virtue

In which of Kohlberg's stages of moral development is this latter extract best understood? Consistently, the children are arguing for the ethical principle that it is right for those who have to help those in need. Does this mean that they have reached Stage 6, the 'Ethical Principle Stage'? Conversely, is the whole discussion best seen as fostering an idealistic and naive view of human affairs, even one which is subversive, socialist and typical of trendy Marxist education lecturers? Both viewpoints are, I would argue, erroneous. The moral value and educational validity of the discussion is best appreciated in modest language and within the children's real social context. This group of 8 year-old children live in a deprived inner-city area where crime is common. At least half of the class has been diagnosed as having special educational needs and many exhibit behavioural problems and social difficulties. The school works very hard at providing a caring and tolerant atmosphere, however, and at fostering good communal relations among the children. This discussion allowed the children to apply, albeit in a fictional context, the virtue of conflict mediation and to argue for the virtues of generosity, fairness, forgiveness and compassion, all of which are emphasized by the school. In Aristotelian terms, they were being encouraged to *practice the virtues*.

> Just as musicians. . . . become musicians by practising on the lyre and the
> flute, so, says Aristotle, men learn the moral virtues by the practice of courage
> and justice. (Carr, 1991, p. 50)

The roles children are given and the acts, including the *speech* acts which
these roles generate, hold the potential for this practice.

With Martin's class, for example, the children remained as villagers for
most of the drama but, as villagers, they listened with sympathy to the wife,
disarmed the Thief whom they thought was about to commit a violent act;
offered gifts for his children; and pleaded for justice to be done to someone
other than themselves. When in role as Thief and Brahmin, they patched up
a quarrel; apologised for past wrong-doings; and gave and accepted gifts gra-
ciously. The various roles played by Sophie's class took them through a variety
of situations where similar demands were made of them to demonstrate the
virtues of unselfishness, sympathy, benevolence, kindness, generosity and
charity. And the nature of these virtues is, in itself, of interest. They are among
those cited by Carr to illustrate what he defines as '*the virtues of attachment*'
(1991, p. 200). These are virtues where an emotion or feeling or passion is not
engaged in a struggle with reason but is joined in alliance with it: 'The correct
attitudes consist of believing and caring for the right things in respect of the
good and well-being of others' (ibid., p. 201). Once again, the fusion of thought
with feeling, reason with care, lay at the heart of both the moral and the
dramatic process.

In his book *The Saturated Self,* Kenneth Gergen undertakes an analysis of
contemporary postmodern society and proposes that we need to reinterpret
much of what we take for granted as reality. Amongst his arguments, he
postulates that our emotions are something we learn to enact on appropriate
occasions. Drawing upon the work of psychologist James Averill (1985), he
describes emotions as 'cultural performances' and writes: 'We are not driven
by forces bottled up within us; rather we perform emotions much as we would
act a part on stage' (1991, p. 165). This argument is a development of the
cognitive analysis of emotion rehearsed in Chapter 5, where it was emphasized that emotions such as fear and love have known objects of attachment
and are quite distinct from mere sensation. To emphasize the culturally learned
nature of the performative aspects of emotion is to indicate that children need
to learn appropriate ways of expressing emotion in particular circumstances.
If we accept this argument, the case for moral education through drama gains
added validity. Learning how to practise the virtues, how and when to display
the emotions associated with them within a *fictional* context, is simply a reflection of how children learn the virtues in their social and cultural environments.
This is a point similar to Lipman's, who, in his influential work on teaching
philosophy to children, emphasized that ethical actions preceded ethical states;
in other words, that ethical actions tend to develop care and concern in those
who perform them. In his words:

> We cannot expect children to be considerate if we do not give them oppor-
> tunities to learn what 'being considerate' is through allowing them to practice
> in engaging in such conduct. (Lipman et al., 1980, p. 175)

This does not mean that children will automatically transfer virtuous behaviour
represented in drama into parallel situations in their real lives; but it does
indicate that they need the space and the opportunities to rehearse them if
they are to understand them. The value for both children and teacher, I would
argue, is the opportunity drama offers for exploring how virtues such as those
listed above can be appropriately manifested in particular contexts and under
specific circumstances. The practice of the virtues described here took place
in a possible world which the children helped create. In the drama there
evolved a story which became a shared, communal experience. And just as
tales in an oral culture provide a community with a stock of stories which
embody shared cultural and moral values, so can stories developed in this way
become shared reference points against which a classroom community of
children can, with the aid of the teacher, gauge their own actions and those
of others whenever such references are needed on future occasions.

5. The Force and Moral Ambiguity of Symbolic Objects

I can recall watching a programme back in 1980 in which Francis Ford Coppola
discussed the making of his film *Apocalypse Now*. He explained how he had
put a gun in his coat pocket and walked down a busy New York street to
experience what it was like to carry a weapon. The feeling of power which
surged through him he described as awesome and frightening. It is a truism
to remark upon Hollywood's fascination for weapons in general and for guns
in particular, certain of which have become mythologized, such as the Mag-
num 44 in *Dirty Harry* and the famous automatic rifle in *Winchester 73*. As
dispensers of destruction and violent justice in the hands of men who live by
violence, they are powerful, uncomfortably fascinating, morally ambiguous
symbols. The moral perspective they offer us is best summed up by the words
of Alan Ladd in *Shane* 'A gun is as good or as bad as the man who uses it'.

Allen Ahlberg has written a delightfully comic poem for primary school
children called *The Cane* (Ahlberg, 1984). Within its irony, it reveals a similar
fascination exercised over children by this symbol of violent justice, particular
to the mythology of the classroom. We had no guns in this drama, but we did
have a stick. A real one. A big one. As the Brahmin in the opening story-telling
session, I swung it back over my head as I prepared to club the Thief with it.
Later, with Martin's class, when acting the part of the Thief, I approached the
Brahmin's cottage holding it, to create the tension that I might be about to use
it. I knew this was risky and it was. As the children/villagers surrounded me,
some boys grabbed the stick and disarmed me. The fear I then expressed as
the Thief was very convincing as the metaxis at this point was so acute; there

was little to distinguish the fear of the Thief from the fear of the teacher. And when the boys broke it, albeit accidentally, this event became a powerful moral symbol that permeated the rest of the session and resonated throughout the images they created to conclude the drama. For example, the boy/Thief who brandished the stick, gleefully telling the boy/Brahmin 'I've still got half of it!' was experiencing something of the vicarious sense of power described by Coppola. He was also enjoying the tension of metaxis. But, after revelling in this heady mixture, he dropped the stick. Within the dramatic context, he had chosen to reject the creation of an image of rough justice in favour of one of reconciliation; within the classroom context, he played with the subversive energy of the stick but displayed self-control and an understanding of the moral code of the classroom. In both contexts, the reality of the stick heightened the tension and hence the force of the moral metaphor signified by its rejection. To express the meaning of this metaphor, I am tempted to paraphrase the earlier quote from *Shane*: 'A stick is as good or as bad as the boy who refuses it'.

6. 'Happy Ever After?': The Moral Resonance of an Ending

The ending of a story drama is as significant as the ending of a story for the values resonated will linger within us. Colby's reference to the closing image of *The Life and Adventures of Nicholas Nickleby* draws its moral meaning from Aristotle's idea of catharsis and leaves us with an image which embodies questions rather than answers, about the extent of human suffering caused by social inequalities and the apparently unending struggle of those who would attempt to remedy this state of affairs. Caryl Churchill's *Top Girls* leaves us with an unresolved argument about political and social values followed by the image of a frightened girl seeking comfort from the mother who has effectively disowned her. Again, it is an image which poses questions, in this case about the contradictory social and moral pressures facing women in contemporary western society as traditional female roles and values are reassessed within a social and economic structure which must inevitably produce winners and losers.

Drama is essentially about problem finding, not problem solving. The action must *finish* but, in Bakhtinian terms, false attempts to *finalize* it should be avoided. However, there is an obvious tension here between the requirements of a dialogical approach and the 'happy ever after' convention of the fairy tale which demands resolution in some utopian form. Moreover, if we accept that empowerment is a major aim of education, then one of the aims of moral education must surely be to help children grow into a sense of responsibility by convincing them that their ethical decisions can make a difference and that some are more justifiable than others. In moral issues there are no pat answers but, from an Aristotelian perspective, there are better and worse ways of living. And MacIntyre sees this approach to moral understanding to be at the heart of tragic drama when he writes:

There may be better or worse ways for individuals to live through the tragic confrontation of good with good. And. . . . to know what the good life for man is may require knowing what are the better and what are the worse ways of living in and through such situations. (1981, p. 224)

The confrontation between the Brahmin and the Thief was, of course, not a tragic one but it did bring opposing viewpoints of what constituted good action into conflict. Through the drama, both the Brahmin and Thief, and hence the children, could learn that there were better and worse ways of living through this particular conflict. Moral learning, in this sense, was not dependent upon how the problem was finalized, nor upon how the thought processes which informed this resolution fitted alongside a hierarchy of moral principles; rather it depended upon the opportunity it presented for the children to become increasingly responsive to the particularities of individual cases, to move forward despite the moral ambivalence of the situation.

I have, however, received some astute criticism on this particular aspect of the case study, which I quote in full below.[11]

What is the 'morality' of art? It lies, not in upholding apriori beliefs about how people should behave but in the integrity of being true to how people do and would in certain circumstances behave. Hence, it seemed to me that many of the alternative endings to the Brahmin/Thief story were false to the central morality of the story itself, in that they were 'unbelievable'. The Thief must needs be punished (presumably), otherwise thieving becomes acceptable, the Brahmin needs to act to defend himself and his property — after all, the Thief had 'agreed' that the Ogre could eat the Brahmin. It is there that the moral dilemma lies — and more deeply how should/could 'good art' handle such matters — have political correctness or conventional morality anything to do with it at all?

Did these endings constitute 'bad art' and is bad art incompatible with good morality? This view begs the important question of what constitutes the social function of drama and its intended audiences. The story used here offered a pre-text for dramatic transformation, not a moral blueprint for aesthetic emulation, and in the drama the children were devisers, performers and, of course, audience. In fact, the question might be more precisely phrased as: in what sense was this drama meant to be good art and who was it meant to be good for? Nor should the *unbelievable* nature of the children's endings be automatically depicted in a negative light; for unbelievable, utopian endings are what help define the fairy tale as a genre. Jack Zipes has written:

More than any other oral or literary genre, the fairy tale embodies the utopian gestus of our lives through the wish. By gestus I mean the way our behaviour, actions and thinking gesticulate toward one goal, and this goal is a place that we do not know concretely. It is no place and yet a better place. It is a place we know intuitively and we call it utopia. (1995, p. 165)

It is doubtless true that the endings devised by the children showed an optimistic vision of conflict resolution atypical of the world as we know it; but they were nonetheless true to the spirit of 'happy ever after' which the children knew to be characteristic of the genre in which they had been working. And, in their depiction of utopian conclusions to the tale, they expressed a vision where individual happiness was dependent upon communal happiness. It is important to remember, too, that the children were given both the experience of the tale *and* the experience of the drama. The conclusion of the drama did not replace the ending of the initial tale but constituted a dialogical alternative to it, working against the inevitability my critic implies as integral to the structure of the story. Nor did this resolution necessarily lead the children to see the problem as any the less complex. In response to a question I posed at the end of the drama: 'If you were Lord Vishnu, what advice would you now offer the Brahmin and/or the Thief?' one child wrote: 'If I were Lord Vishnu I would say to the Brahmin, "Think about what the Thief did and why he did it" '. The simplicity of this statement belies its wisdom. This 9 year-old child appears to understand that the moral meanings in stories are not simple and didactic, that we appreciate them through reflection and eventually must find them within ourselves.

In our postmodern society, children face a saturation of stories in all kinds of genres and no one, dominant cultural source can be said to provide them. This confusion can only be exacerbated by the fact that television, video and audio cassettes, comics, magazines and books do not provide any opportunities for children to engage in active discourse with their meanings, and hence with their values. As such, rather than being instructive, they are potentially so many 'invitations to incoherence', a phrase applied by Gergen to the postmodern technologies of social saturation (1991, p. 173). In contrast, Kirin Narayan has written of a Hindu Swamiji who teaches through stories chosen for their relevance to particular audiences at particular times. 'The text,' she comments, 'Like all folk narratives, was malleable to the teller's concerns and perceptions of his audience' (1991, p. 121). Working with story through drama, the values by which children are learning to live their lives in the present can be informed, clarified or guided by engaging with and, in this case, transforming the stories we share from the past. And in the communality of this process, we are practising what Gergen sees as 'the basis for a post-modern, relational view of morality, in which decisions are viewed not as products of individual minds, but the outcome of interchange among persons' (1991, p. 168).

Notes

1 I am grateful to my colleague Eleanor Nesbitt at the Institute of Education in Warwick for providing me with this and other information on Indian society and

Hindu culture which informs this case study. Dr Nesbitt is a member of the University of Warwick Religion and Research Unit and a recognized international expert within this field.

2   This is explored in depth in Chapter 8 of the thesis.

3   I am aware that the concept of *archetypes* is contentious and will use the term throughout this thesis in accordance with the meaning offered here by Northrop Frye; and with that proposed by Cecily O'Neill who refers, simply but clearly, to their 'generalizing resonance' (1995, p. 36). Jung, from whom we derive the term, saw them as something much more fundamental and universal. For him they were: 'psychic residua of numberless experiences of the same type, experiences which have happened not to the individual but to his ancestors, of which the results are inherited in the structure of the brain, a priori determinants of individual experience' (Brodkin, 1934, p. 1). I do not deploy the term in any such invariable or universalist sense but accept Frye's thesis that archetypes are culturally learned. Annis Pratt, in her work on women's fiction, provides a definition of archetypal literary criticism which reflects my own understanding of the term and a similarly pragmatic approach to its use. She writes: 'one must not deduce categories down into a body of material but induce them from images, symbols and narrative patterns observed in a significantly various selection of literary works. I conceive of archetypal criticism thus, as inductive rather than deductive, Aristotelian in its concern with things as they are rather than Platonic in suggesting them as derivatives from absolute, universal concepts' (1982, p. 5). This pragmatic approach within the context of folk and fairy tales would appear to be supported by the work of Thompson (1977) who shows how archetypal patterns, in this sense of the term, are detectable in folk-tales across cultures.

4   This development of childhood as a distinct phase of life in the liberal western tradition has been thoroughly examined by Aries (1979) and is supported by Hoyles (1989). Hoyles insists that childhood is '*a social construction, not a natural state*'. He sees this as having begun in the European towns of the late Middle Ages, with the change from feudalism to capitalism and the accompanying growth and institutionalization of schooling. The eighteenth century, in particular, witnessed a change in the concept of childhood as a state characterized chiefly by original sin to one of weakness which needed protection and of innocence which needed to be preserved. Rousseau's *Emile* was the literary work which did most to institutionalize this view which, of course, persists in many twentieth century infant classrooms. See also Walvin (1982).

5   The murder of toddler Jamie Bolger in Liverpool by two children, aged 10 years-old, was thought by some to have possibly been influenced by this video, as was the murder of Suzanne Capper in Stockport, Gr. Manchester, in December, 1992.

6   This is an approach developed by Baird Saenger (1993).

7   With Sophie's class, I did, in fact, ask them for their ideas first. I was provided with six responses: don't steal; don't be greedy; don't eat people; don't be selfish; learn how to be kind to people; don't be bad or, in the end, it'll be the worse for you.

8   The maths, of course doesn't add up, there being far more recorded responses than if each child *had* only responded three times. This is unimportant. I was not looking for statistical accuracy, simply an impression of which morals the children thought they could detect. By asking them to limit themselves to three, I was encouraging the children to make choices and not respond to all of them.

9 The expression *moral panic* was first used by Stan Cohen in 1972 to define a process where 'a condition, episode, person or group . . . emerges to become defined as a threat to societal values or interests'. See Branston and Stafford, 1996, p. 312.

10 O'Toole (1992, pp. 232–235) analyses this moment very thoroughly and argues that its particular significance was dependent upon the meaning the drama achieved due to its real context, of a white and a black student making this moment happen in South Africa in 1980. He comments: 'The boy was making and participants and onlookers were actively accepting, an ethical statement of significance in their real world, highlighting what should be by presenting what could not be, within the permission granted by fiction' (op. cit., p. 234).

11 These comments were received from an anonymous reviewer of a summary of this case study. See Winston (1995).

Chapter 9

Jack and the Beanstalk: Ethical Exploration and the Risks of Carnival Humour

The Story of *Jack and the Beanstalk*: Carnivalesque or Moral Quest?

Jack and the Beanstalk is one of the most popular and widely known British fairy tales, with scores of versions currently in print, as single volumes and as part of more general anthologies[1]. Its origin in folklore is thought to be ancient but is very unclear. As Peter and Iona Opie point out, a beanstalk reaching to the heavens is reminiscent of Jacob's ladder in the *Old Testament* and of the World-tree Yggdrasil in the Norse *Prose Edda* (1974, p. 163). Despite this, the earliest known printed version is Benjamin Tabart's *History of Jack and the Beanstalk, Printed from the Original Manuscript, Never Before Published*, which appeared in a sixpenny booklet in 1807[2]. The Opies see this as the source of all subsequent retellings, and this claim is supported by Neil Philip (1992) with one important exception. Joseph Jacobs' version, published in 1890, was claimed by the author to originate from an oral narration which he had heard some thirty years earlier in Australia. Having compared it with other oral versions from North America, Philip concludes that it is 'a lively, funny, supple telling', much closer to the spirit of the original, oral tradition than is Tabart's and 'the stiff, chapbook texts' which emulated it (1992, p. 8). This claim is significant as stories within the oral tradition tend to carry very different moral meanings from their literary counterparts.

Jacobs' version has, indeed, the wit, lightness of touch and jocular rhythms shared by many oral folk-tales and, importantly, it resembles them in its general tone of optimism and fantasy wish-fulfilment. There is a lack of psychological comment in the narrative which, in true oral fashion, concentrates on action, peppered with lively banter and brisk dialogue. From this we divine the nature of the characters. Jack is very much the trickster figure, to be found in such tales as *Jack the Giant Killer* and similar to such anthropomorphic characters as *Ananse* in the Afro-Caribbean tradition and *Brer Rabbit* from the Southern United States. He is cheerful and quick-witted throughout the tale, quick to propose ways of helping his mother and witty in his response to the old man with the beans:

'I wonder if you know how many beans make five?'
'Two in each hand and one in your mouth,' says Jack, sharp as a needle.
(1993, p. 66)

When the beanstalk appears, he climbs it without reflection or hesitation; nor does he show any hesitation in stealing from the Ogre or returning for a second time up the beanstalk 'to try his luck' (ibid., p. 69). He is 'bold as brass' when he meets the Ogre's wife for the second time, undaunted when she asks him if he is the boy who stole from her husband.

'I dare say I could tell you something about that but I'm so hungry I can't speak till I've had something to eat.' (ibid., p. 70)

On his third return, he shows a good deal of cunning, hiding outside the castle until the Ogre's wife appears, then slipping in through the open door and, unnoticed, on into the kitchen. This time he hides in the copper, not the oven, thus evading discovery when the Ogre and his wife later search for him. At the end of the story, the Ogre is dispatched swiftly, with a witty reference to the nursery rhyme *Jack and Gill*:

'Then the ogre fell down and broke his crown and the beanstalk came tumbling after.' (ibid., p. 72)

Jack and his mother become very rich, he marries a princess and they live happy ever after — information provided in as many words in the final sentence of the tale.

Here, then, we have a brisk tale where happiness is defined in terms of material wealth and is achieved through optimism, resilience, good luck and opportunism. The emphasis is on a satisfactory narrative, with no hint of moral didacticism and no need to explain Jack's actions in terms of motivation, moral or otherwise. As Propp pointed out:

In folklore, reasons, or to use the language of poetics, motivations, are not required for actions. . . . It is the action that is primary, not the reason for it. (1984, pp. 25–26)

Ideologically, there is nothing morally problematic for a peasant community in a tale which relates how a poor boy steals from a wicked, wealthy ogre so that he and his mother do not starve. First and foremost, it is an entertaining tale of fantasy, wit and wish fulfilment, where the weak triumph through intellect and cunning.

Cunning and deception are the tools of the weak against the strong, and this conforms to the moral requirements of the listener. (Propp, ibid., p. 28)

Philip is right to see Jacobs' text as a genuine oral version of the tale rather than as a revised, literary retelling based upon the Tabart text, as the Opies claim it to be.

Tabart's version is very different in many respects. It is longer, more ponderous and descriptive, with very little dialogue and much more psychological comment. The lightness of touch has given way to a more sombre, moral didacticism. Jack's mother, we are informed,

> . . . had been a widow for some years, and had only one child named Jack whom she indulged to a fault; the consequence of her blind partiality was that Jack did not pay the least attention to anything she said, but was indolent, careless and extravagant. His follies were not owing to a bad disposition but that his mother had never checked him. (Opie, 1974, p. 164)

The admonishment to the parent, 'Spare the rod and spoil the child' is barely concealed. Jack's disobedience, signalled in this opening paragraph, is later confirmed when he climbs the beanstalk despite his mother's entreaties to the contrary[3]. In order to provide Jack with moral justification for stealing from the Giant, Tabart introduces a character wholly absent from the oral version; a fairy, in the guise of an old woman, who meets Jack at the top of the beanstalk. In a story, stretching to two pages of closely-printed text, she explains how a wicked Giant had murdered Jack's father when Jack was a baby, robbing him of his castle and all his possessions and forcing his mother never to tell Jack of his true identity. The fairy informs Jack that he has been appointed to punish the Giant for all his wickedness.

> 'You will have dangers and difficulties to encounter, but you must persevere in avenging the death of your father, or you will not prosper in any of your undertakings, but always be miserable. As to the Giant's possessions, you may seize upon all with impunity; for everything he has is yours, though now you are unjustly deprived of it. . . . Remember the severe punishment that awaits you if you disobey my commands.' (ibid., p. 169)

Not only is he given justification for stealing from the Giant, he is set this as a challenge to *obey*, to atone for his past wilful disobedience that has been highlighted as one of the major flaws in his character. A series of editorial footnotes, reminding the reader of the fairy's command, permeates the rest of the tale in order to justify Jack's further ascents up the beanstalk, as they must so evidently clash with any good mother's wishes for the safety of her son. At the very end of the tale, when the beanstalk is destroyed, the fairy reappears in a final footnote.

> She first addressed Jack's mother and explained every circumstance relating to the journies up the beanstalk. Jack was now fully cleared in the opinion of his mother. (ibid., p. 174)

As for Jack,

> he heartily begged his mother's pardon for all the sorrow and affliction he had
> caused her, promising faithfully to be very dutiful and obedient to her in the
> future. He proved as good as his word and was a pattern of affectionate
> behaviour and attention to parents. (ibid., p. 174)

In this form, then, Jack's adventures up the beanstalk have not only been
presented as a test of moral courage but have also been clearly framed, however uneasily, as a lesson in obedience and filial duty.

Jack Zipes' commentary on the distinctive tradition of the nineteenth century
English Fairy Tale offers an historical explanation for the tendency of many to
be stridently moralistic in tone (Zipes, 1987).[4] The fertile legacy of medieval
English folklore, so evident in the work of Chaucer, Spenser and Shakespeare,
was suppressed under the domination of Puritan political power, which
culminated in the 'Glorious Revolution' of 1688. Puritan culture and its philosophical heir, Utilitarianism, placed an emphasis on rational judgment and
Christian principles and mistrusted the imagination, particularly in its more
fantastic forms of expression. Thus, whereas the fairy tale was able to flourish in
eighteenth century France, those few which made their way into publication
in England during the same period did so only when transformed into didactic
tales, preaching hard work and good behaviour. With the emergence of Romanticism at the end of the eighteenth century, middle-class sensibilities began to
change and the fairy tale slowly began to become more widely accepted with
Tabart, in fact, being among the first to publish them extensively.

However, the Calvinist influence remained deeply entrenched, with influential writers like Mrs Sherwood attacking fairy tales as late as 1820 as 'an
improper medium for instruction' (Zipes, 1987, p. xvii). As the fairy tale established itself as a genre, writers such as Dickens and MacDonald saw its real moral
purpose not as instruction but as a means of nurturing children's imaginations,
offering alternative, utopian visions to counter the drab utilitarianism of Victorian
industrial society. However, the tradition of didactic tales for children remained
strong and even major writers of fairy tales such as George Cruickshank continued to regard them as vehicles for moral teaching. His version of *Jack and
the Beanstalk*, for example, published in 1854, transformed the Ogre into a
drunkard and the tale into a diatribe against the evils of alcoholism (Zipes,
1987, p. 37). Such overt moral didacticism characterized another popular retelling of the tale, published by Anne Isabella Ritchie in 1868, and this tendency
persisted in the numerous retellings which appeared in chap books and cheap
anthologies throughout the nineteenth century, all of which were derivative of
Tabart's version.

Recently published versions of *Jack and the Beanstalk* are not so thoroughly or self-consciously moralistic in their tone, yet the influence of Tabart
remains strong in the cheaper, contemporary retellings to be found in the
numerous fairy tale anthologies which appear regularly.[5] The reasons for this

have been amply explained by Zipes (1993) with reference to the tale of *Little Red Riding Hood*. Anonymous chap books, often presented on single broadsheets, were a popular way of marketing fairy tales for children in the nineteenth century. Many anthologies drew upon these sources and still do so today because they are cheap and involve no copyright. These retellings were, and still are, printed purely for profit, to exploit an existing market, drawing their texts and illustrations directly from earlier publications. There is little authorial reassessment of the tales and, as such, their values persist in the retellings.

The values emphasized in the traditional, pictorial representation of Jack can be usefully gleaned from a book by Cooper Edens, which has gathered together a number of illustrations from anthologies published between 1888 and 1927. The pictures consistently depict a pre-pubescent Jack with long, curly, blonde hair, wide blue eyes, and innocent, cherubic features. Generally he shows no emotion: even while he clutches the axe and watches the giant tumble he registers only mild shock and surprise. In only one illustration is there the slight hint of a scowl, as he wields the axe and chops down the beanstalk. The images in which Jack is contextualized are pervasively nostalgic, embellishing the fairy tale world with pastoral settings, attractive old cottages, colourful cottage gardens and rich, dark interiors of the castle. They are congruent with what Zipes has noted in Victorian fairy tale writers as 'a psychological urge to recapture and retain childhood as a paradisaical realm of innocence' (op. cit., p. xx). Such images hark after a simpler, pre-industrialized past and Jack's cherubic, almost pre-Raphaelite features avoid painful or unpleasant emotion at the same time as they idealize the pre-pubescent boy whose appearance could well embody the filial virtues which resonate from the Tabart text. The nostalgic appeal to parents is, therefore, a double one, idealizing the fairy tale world they recall from their own childhood and idealizing childhood itself in the images of the little boy it offers them.

This representation of Jack as heroic cherub is at odds with the Jack of the Jacobs' text. Here we have a Jack much closer to the trickster of *Jack the Giant Killer*, wilful, cheeky, sharp and cunning. A subversive figure, he flouts authority, takes risks, causes havoc whenever he climbs the beanstalk and always wins through in the end. The comic power and ethical positioning of this Jack can best be understood with reference to Bakhtin and his theory of folk humour, which he defined as the *Carnival*, and to the characteristics of the picaresque heroes of comic drama.

Bakhtin developed his theory of the Carnival in his long study on Rabelais. Fundamentally, he believed that the spirit of the Carnival is one of liberating mockery through which official ideology and oppressive norms and taboos can be parodied and hence humanized. Carnival laughter, according to Bakhtin, can be defined as:

> 'a specific ethical attitude to reality' that allows no ideal to 'ossify in one-sided seriousness.' (Kelly, 1992, p. 47)

The spirit of the Carnival, characterized by 'inversions, parodies and discrownings' (Dentith, 1995, p. 65), suffuses the tale of *Jack and the Beanstalk*. The young, the small and the weak defeat the old, the big and the powerful. The Giant, parodying the abuse of feudal power, is 'discrowned' in more senses than one when he falls from the beanstalk. The grotesque representation of the body, a major characteristic of Carnivalesque humour, is celebrated in the figure of the Giant, who, with his tantrums and cannibalistic appetites, is as exaggerated as any offering from Rabelais. But Jack, the trickster, both in his wit and in his actions, has characteristics identifiable in the picaresque heroes of early literary works, such as the Spanish *Lazarillo de Tormes*, and in the classic comic dramas of Molière, Jonson and Congreve. Charney has defined the characteristics of the comic hero: he is cunning, resourceful and 'could never conceivably be overcome by the material forces he scorns' (1978, p. 146); he is sharp, witty, 'never at a loss for an answer' (ibid., p. 152); in true carnivalesque fashion, he is 'the enemy of all abstractions, moral principles, seriousness and joylessness' (ibid., p. 160). Furthermore, the tale itself uses the classic comic devices of deception and disguise, revelling in the ease with which Jack deceives the giantess, who, in turn, deceives the Giant. The tension as the Giant searches in vain for Jack is essentially comic, as is the irony when he unwittingly leaves all of his riches ready for Jack to run off with.

The comic spirit of the Carnival and of comic drama is identifiable not only in the form the tale takes but also in the moral meanings it conveys. In the oral folk tradition and the Carnival spirit it embodies, conventional morality is irrelevant and taboos are suspended in favour of utopian wish-fulfilment, imagined through a comic excess of feasting and material wealth. The ethic here works against oppressive, social agencies in favour of the temporary emancipation afforded by laughter. Similarly, comic drama does not celebrate conventional, social and moral norms; rather does it poke fun at the shallowness and hypocrisy that often accompanies those who preach them. The comic hero is one who can flout authority and highlight, through his wits, the bluster and stupidity of the powerful. Dario Fo's Maniac, wreaking havoc in a police station in Milan, is a distant cousin of Jack wreaking havoc in the Ogre's castle.

The literary tamperings with the oral text were bound to destroy the comic spirit of the tale as soon as it was transformed into a vehicle for conventional moral lessons. As Charney points out:

> comedy does not arise from well-adjusted, middle-class persons, decent, hardworking, sane, with . . . realistic goals and expectations. (ibid., p. 170)

The comic hero 'never truly feels sorrow, guilt, compassion, or any of the legitimate tragic emotions' (ibid., p. 176). This is certainly true of the Jack in the Jacobs' text, but very unlike Tabart's Jack, where the central theme is how he actually comes to learn to feel these emotions in the context of his relationship with his mother. The moral overlay suppresses the laughter as it converts Jack's odyssey from an anarchic adventure into one which paradoxically praises filial docility.

Most contemporary retellings of the tale lack the comic energy of the Jacobs' version whilst retaining residues of the nineteenth century moralizing which seems pious and inappropriate to modern sensibilities.[6] A notable exception can be found in Kevin Crossley-Holland's volume of *British Folk Tales*. Although the author admits to using Tabart's text as his source, he goes some way toward reintroducing the tone and energy of an oral, folk narrative, as the title of the book suggests. The prose is dense and resonant but its short sentences, tone and rhythms echo that of oral storytelling. Jack, for example, is introduced as follows:

> What a drone he was! A lie-abed and lounger, a sugar-tongued scrounger, a scattergood without a thought for yesterday or tomorrow. (1987, p. 118)

Like Jacobs, Crossley-Holland moves the plot on quickly, is sparing on psychological comment and makes extensive use of sharp and witty dialogue.

> So Jack decided to climb the beanstalk again and pay a second visit to the giant's mansion.
> 'Don't think of it,' said Martha.
> 'I am thinking of it,' said Jack.
> 'You're a fool,' said Martha. (ibid., p. 126)

Jack's mother is far from the weak, insipid figure of Tabart's text. She is assertive, sharp of tongue, is actually given a name, and has the last word in the tale.

> So that was the end of the giant; and that was the end of the beanstalk.
> 'Amen,' said Martha. (ibid., p. 131)

What makes this version particularly interesting is the tension it achieves between the differing moral meanings of the oral and literary traditions. On the one hand, it restores to Jack some of his comic energy, extending it to include his relationship with his mother, which is captured in their repartee. The spirit of the carnival is present in his antics in the Giant's castle and in the figure of the Giant himself, who is generously and comically grotesque in his appetites:

> The giant ate a monstrous supper: vegetable stew, half-a-dozen loaves, and half a pig, accompanied by a sluice of beer. 'And now,' said the giant, 'I'll have one of those children . . .' (ibid., p. 129)

On the other hand, the comedy manages to embrace rather than ignore Jack's moral flaws and the figure of the giant's wife, in particular, is problematized. More in the twentieth century spirit of tragi-comedy, she is painted as a bullied and beaten victim of her husband's violence. On Jack's last visit to the castle:

> The expression on the face of the giant's wife had changed. She looked afraid. And when at last Jack persuaded her to take him in, she was only able to limp ahead of him. 'That'll be the end,' she said. 'If he catches me.' (ibid., p. 129)

This retelling chooses to hint at moral ambiguity rather than impose a moral resolution on the contradictory values which are the legacy of Tabart's literary interventions. Wishing to use the tale as a means to explore rather than avoid these moral ambiguities, and to harness the energizing potential of its humour, I chose this version as the basis for a drama with a class of 6 and 7 year-old children who were using the tale of *Jack and the Beanstalk* at the heart of a cross-curricular project.

The Drama of *Jack and the Beanstalk*: Exploring Ethics Through Comic Playfulness

> . . . in drama, we are not teaching truths, but unteaching them, trying to reinvest the curriculum of certainty with uncertainty and ambiguity. (O'Toole, 1995, p. 80)

Tabart manipulated the story of *Jack and the Beanstalk* into a parable meant to illustrate a moral rule, the commandment: 'Honour thy father and thy mother.' Such rules have been defined by Haste as 'the grammar of social relations' (1987, p. 163). According to Aristotle, rules in ethics are important but of limited value.

> Among statements about conduct, those that are universal are more general but the particular are more true — for action is concerned with particulars. (cited in Nussbaum, 1986, p. 301)

Rules he saw as guidelines in moral development, summaries of the wise judgments of others, good for young children who lack the experience to have developed moral praxis, or practical wisdom. What is important, then, is for rules to exist alongside educational measures which attempt to develop children's powers of practical moral wisdom. Stories are ideally suited for this latter purpose; to see them as a way of enforcing rules is to misunderstand their true moral potential. The drama of *Jack and the Beanstalk* was meant to embrace and explore the ambiguities which the Crossley-Holland version had inherited from the Tabart text rather that attempt to eradicate them. In seeking to do this, I enhanced the playful, comic spirit, making it more akin to the Jacobs' version, and my analysis of the drama will concentrate on the interaction between its comic form and its moral content; and how, I believe, the two proved to be compatible.

The Drama in Summary

The school was situated in a semi-urban, village area of Warwickshire. The children were mainly white, from a mixture of private and council housing, and had some limited prior experience of educational drama. Their half-term's topic was planned around the tale of *Jack and the Beanstalk* to stimulate work in a wide range of curriculum areas and also involved the reading and telling of different versions of the tale. The teacher learned the Kevin Crossley-Holland version and told it orally in serial form over a number of days. She completed one episode with Jack climbing the beanstalk for the third time. For the subsequent episodes, drama took over as a series of three sessions, each of about fifty minutes in length. The fact that they were dominated by teacher-in-role was a conscious decision determined by the age and inexperience of the children. It also, of course, allowed me to keep a very firm grip on the direction the drama took.

At the beginning of the first session I introduced the children to the basic costume I would use to denote the various characters from the story; a black shawl and a walking stick for the old woman at the top of the beanstalk; a blue shawl for the Giant's wife, and so on. For the children to find entrance into the drama, I decided to cast them as friends of Jack from his village and began the story by narrating the discovery by Jack's mother that he had gone missing for the third time. Taking on the role of the mother, I asked them if any of them knew where he might be. When some of them suggested he might have gone up the beanstalk I replied that I didn't believe that as he had promised me faithfully he would never climb it again. But Jack was a boy who broke his promises, they told me. They all agreed that breaking promises, especially to one's mother, was wrong and they volunteered to go up the beanstalk and bring him back home. Before they did this, I made them promise not to let him steal any more money from the Ogre; it was too dangerous and, besides, we didn't need any more. This they all did and I narrated their ascent up the beanstalk. At the top, in the guise of the old woman, I informed them that the Ogre used to blame his wife every time any of his money went missing, and sometimes even hit her. The children made a second promise not to steal any money themselves if I told them the way to the Ogre's castle. I played the giant's wife as a timid, frightened woman, peering through a crack in the door, and said that I had chased Jack and mimed shutting the door in their faces. The children, however, spotted an open window, decided that Jack must have already climbed through it and quietly did the same, making their way along the castle corridors and into the Ogre's kitchen.

The second session began with the children exploring the kitchen, looking for places to hide should the Ogre come. I then took on the character of Jack for the first time and narrated my appearance out of the spout of a kettle. A long discussion ensued. The children began by trying to persuade Jack to leave straightaway, which I refused to do. Playing him very much as the trickster, I amused the children with my actions and responses and the clarity of their mission began to fade as some of them volunteered to help me escape with the money. The discussion was interrupted by the arrival of the Ogre and the children all hid and remained silent while I shouted and stamped and then counted my money. When the Ogre finally fell asleep, I stopped the drama and asked a girl to take on the role of Jack and decide whether he would take the money or not. He did.

The final session began with the children creeping out of the kitchen without waking the Ogre, only to meet his wife in the corridor. My shriek of surprise, in role as the wife, awoke the Ogre and I told them all to hide while I persuaded him to let me make him some hot chocolate so he could go back to sleep. This kept the children from being discovered and they decided to show their gratitude by helping the wife. One girl eventually suggested that we should tie up the Ogre while he slept and then make him promise to change his ways. Once 'captured' in role as the Ogre, I screamed and yelled and struggled in vain to their amusement and satisfaction. The drama ended with the Ogre, being lectured as to how, and in what manner, he ought to change his ways.

These sessions are among my fondest memories as a drama teacher. My faith in their educational worth was warmly supported by the classteacher and has since been reinforced by the responses of experienced first school teachers, with whom I have used the videoed material for In-Service work, and of a much respected colleague who has used sections of it for lecture and demonstration purposes. I believe it is, therefore, worthy of analysis but, within the following commentary, I address relevant critical questions that have been posed by those practitioners who have seen and commented on the material.

To look at improvised educational drama as moral pedagogy through the filter of comedy poses a number of problems. Literature on drama in education seldom makes more than passing references to comedy; and comedy itself is seen by many influential theorists as essentially amoral in its nature. Langer, for example, points to what she sees as Meredith's failed attempts to promote the ethical nature of comedy: 'In his very efforts to justify its amoral personages he only admitted their amoral nature and simple relish for life' (1953, p. 345). Whereas comedies go out of their way to assure us, through a happy ending, that the good will triumph, Charney (1978) suggests that virtue gets little play in the action of the drama: and concludes that: 'wit outshines, outstrips and outperforms goodness and the comic action remains essentially amoral' (op. cit., p. 59). Moreover, inasmuch as these happy endings *do* express values, they are essentially conservative and reflect the ends of society. As Ben Jonson saw it (or said he saw it), the purpose of comedy is to purge socially unacceptabe behaviour; or, in the words of Northrop Frye: 'The society emerging at the conclusion of a comedy represents . . . a kind of moral norm' (1965, p. 147), — meaning that harmony, common sense and civilized behaviour must be restored. The hero of classical comic drama may well cock a snook at conventional social morality but, at the end of the play, he is reabsorbed into the dominant social framework. The social conservatism of classical comedy is, according to O'Toole, at odds with the more anarchic comedy of the folk tradition.

Classical comedy operates at the 'rule-fixing' end of the continuum of art and play; the kind of comedy which emanates from the other, 'exploratory' end operates by calling those very rules into question, and gives a *dis*comforting experience where anarchy, immorality and misrule are temporarily validated, and may be left so. (1992, p. 153)

Here the carnival spirit is defined as essentially amoral, with no promise that any kind of social or moral order will be restored. Despite this, it is with reference to this tradition of folk comedy and its manifestation in both traditional and modern forms of participatory theatre, that most light can be cast not only on the comic representation of Jack and the Ogre in this drama but also on their potential as agents for moral education.

Jack as 'Joker'

Traditional folk drama, such as the Coventry *Hox Tuesday Drama* or the Cheshire *Souling Play* (Pegg, 1981, p. 107) is looser and more participatory in form than the classical or bourgeois theatrical traditions. The narratives are often scripted but always feature a character such as the Derby tupp (in Coventry) or the Wild Horse (in Cheshire) whose function is to cause havoc, particularly among spectators, chasing girls and generally making a nuisance of itself. Sometimes this character might be human in form, such as Tosspot in the *Pace Egg play* of West Yorkshire, and thus be free to improvise lines, draw in the spectators and generally subvert the narrative, a tradition whose influence partially persists in stage pantomime. The discomforting, subversive and comically provocative nature of such a role is analogous in spirit with Jack, the trickster of the oral folk tale, and is reminiscent of the medieval *giullare*, inspirational to the theatrical practice of Dario Fo:

The giullare was the street performer of his day, the busker of the Middle Ages, with something in common with the Shakespearean Fool, but nothing at all with the aristocratic pet who was the Court Jester. Of his very essence he was the people's entertainer, but also the people's spokesman, giving satirical voice to resentments felt by ordinary people against authority. (Farrell, in Fo and Rame, 1992, p. 6)

The role of the 'Joker' in Boal's *Forum Theatre* performs a similar function. Although the Joker is more a facilitator than a jester, his purpose is to engineer the subversion of socially and morally oppressive narratives by encouraging the audience to move from the position of passive spectators to more active spect-actors. As such, one of the roles he adopts is that of devil's advocate, disturbing the spect-actors' received values in order to challenge their thinking and empower them into enlightened forms of action. It is the spirit manifest in the dramatic function of these distinct but related roles which can best enlighten the nature of my representation of Jack, comic in form but serious in intention.

For the children, the drama was framed in the form of a moral quest. Tabart-like in their certainty, they were dispatched to carry out the mother's parental wishes, to ensure that Jack would return and keep the commandments which forbid stealing, lying and disobedience. Rules to guide moral behaviour are an important feature in the lives of young children and are particularly evident in institutionalized, social environments such as the classroom and the school; and, through the promise made to Jack's mother, they were being requested to take on a role which would involve the enforcement of these rules. When I entered in role as Jack, there was no mistaking the focus or the seriousness of their mission:

> *Girl*: You've got to come down now!
> *Jack*: I've got to come down now? Who says?
> *Many*: Your mum!
> *Jack*: My mum says?
> *Boy*: You haven't got any time to steal things yet
> *Girl 2*: Like the money . . .
> *Girl 3*: You're not allowed to steal anything
> *Jack*: What are you saying?
> *Boy*: You must go down now because your mum's *told* you to!

Children, however, have their own private, social codes, which can emphasize a different set of virtues: loyalty to one's friends, courage displayed through risk-taking and dares, quick-wittedness and a sense of humour, the ability to deceive authority and hence avoid trouble.[7] These are often, by their very nature, conflictual with conventional rules of moral behaviour. It was these qualities of the 'streetwise kid' that I was attempting to represent in the role of Jack, playing him as trickster, rebel, the subversive but likeable rogue. My costume — baseball cap worn in reverse — immediately signalled this, as did my cheerful banter and my high-status posturing.[8] I played tricks on the children and had lots of verbal fun with them. To apply MacIntyre's concept of virtues and vices embodied in social roles, if Jack as a *child* was disobedient, cheeky and dishonest, as a *friend* he was, in contrast, funny and clever; and as *son* (to his father, if not to his mother), he was courageous in seeking to avenge his father's death and reclaim his and his mother's rightful inheritance.

A justification for this interpretation of the dramatic impact of Jack can be found in comments made by the children outside the drama, in a discussion with the classteacher (see Appendix 1). The children were asked why they had risked going up the beanstalk to fetch Jack and responded that Jack was their friend, that he was brave, strong, played good games and that he was fun. When asked if there was anything not so good about him, they had many suggestions: he broke his promises, was lazy, told lies, took back things which didn't belong to him, didn't tell his mummy where he was playing and used bad language. Two conclusions can be drawn from these responses. Firstly, these children, as a group, were very clear and articulate about the basic concepts of right and wrong and could easily recognize virtues and vices in action within specific social contexts. Secondly, they show that the Jack of the drama had impacted upon them as much as the Jack of the story, interweaving with their own ideas of what made a good friend and a naughty boy. The last three examples listed above came directly from the story we created: from our discussion as to whether everything the giant owned had belonged to my father; from my complaints about Jack in role as his mother; and from my use of the word 'bum'!

Jack made a powerful impact upon the children in part because, although at the centre of the dramatic interest from the outset, his actual appearance was substantially delayed, a strategy used to great effect by Molière in *Tartuffe*. All of the contributions made by the characters the children met along the way — his mother, the woman at the top of the beanstalk, the Ogre's wife — performed the dual function of reinforcing the children's moral mission and building a consistent expectation of what Jack would be like once he did appear. When I took on the role of Jack, I worked to confirm rather than deny this expectation and used humour to subvert the moral highground from which the children began their dialogue with me. A few minutes into the scene we had the following exchange:

Jack:	So what are you going to do if I tell you I'm staying here until that Ogre comes and then, when he falls asleep, I'm going to steal something off him? (*Spoken as a dare*) What are you going to do?
Boy:	We're going to tell your mother.
Jack:	You're going to tell my mum, are you?
Boy:	Yeah!
Jack:	That I wouldn't do as she says? That I wouldn't come down? All right! (*addressing another boy*) What are you going to do?
Boy 2:	Erm, I'll help you carry whatever . . .
Jack:	Oh, you're going to help me, are you?
Girl:	Yeah, so am I!
Many:	And me! So am I!
Many:	I'm not!

By bringing alive the subversive charisma of Jack and by having it interact with the children in role, I was able to stir up dissent in order to replicate a picture of the moral conflicts within children's lives truer than is portrayed in the Tabart text. In other words, I turned a 'rule-fixing' text into an exploratory one. By adopting this stance, I was then able to encourage the children to reflect upon their moral positioning although, in the spirit of comic playfulness, this could take an unexpected turn.

Jack:	All right, those people who aren't going to break their promise to my mum, I want to know why not.
Boy 1:	Because we'll get told off.
Jack:	Because you'll get told off?

> Boy 2: And so will you when you get down there.
> Jack: (*cocky*) I can handle that.
> Boy 2: You can't.
> Jack: Maybe I can.
> Boy 1: You might not.
> Jack: Maybe I can.
> Girl: (*wagging her finger*) You'll get a smacked bum.
> Jack: Maybe I'm not scared of a smacked bum!
> (*Burst of general laughter*)

The children's laughter here points to another way through which the carnival spirit was working to energize this drama; that is, through the tension of metaxis generated by the deliberate inversion of the roles, in both a moral and a social sense. The teacher/adult was playing naughty boy whereas the children were the voice of conventional moral authority. As a result, I, the teacher, was empowered to say deliberately naughty things; whereas they, the children, were liberated to speak to me as an equal or even scold me from a morally superior position. Thus the overriding tension within the form of the drama when the children were with Jack was both comic and moral at one and the same time and the dialogical exchanges could take on the pace and mood of comic repartee.

> Jack: Well, I didn't make a promise.
> Girl: Cos you never keep promises.
> Jack: Who says I never keep promises?
> Boy 1: And you lie!
> Jack: Who says I lie?
> Boy 2: You lied to the Ogre!
> Jack: Well, he's a rotten Ogre. I've never spoken to that Ogre, anyway.
> Boy 3: You lied to your mum.
> Jack: (*flustered*) What did I say to my . . . I never lied to my mum! When did I lie to my mum?
> Many: (*in triumph*) You said you wouldn't go up the beanstalk and you did!

It is a dramatic as much as a moral necessity which energizes this short exchange, illustrative as it is of the kind of competitive status game described by O'Neill as a frequent feature of this kind of improvised event (O'Neill, 1995, p. 16). But, to paraphrase the earlier quote from Charney, here wit does not outperform goodness; in the children's eyes, *their* wit outperforms Jack's and his attempt to cover up his lies. The spirit of play is strong here but for the teacher it provides for a devil's advocate style of role-taking, long recognized by drama teachers as a valuable way of creating learning (Booth, 1994, p. 82; Neelands, 1984, p. 36). What is not generally recognized, however, is how close such an approach is to the carnival spirit. In Bakhtin's words:

The temporary suspension, both ideal and real, of hierarchical rank created during carnival time a special type of communication impossible in every day life. (Bernstein, 1981, p. 106)

According to Bernstein, this involves:

a loosening of the codes of linguistic decorum and a new readiness to mingle forms of address and speech otherwise kept strictly apart. (op. cit., p. 106)

This temporary suspension of hierarchical rank was at the heart of the moral ambivalence of teacher in role as Jack but the dramatic and educational functions remained highly ethical, intended to ensure that the children were given sufficient opportunity to explore the moral complexity of the situation. Using Beckerman's terminology, Jack rendered the action *dialectic* in nature, opening oppositional empathic alignments not, perhaps, within each individual child but certainly within the group community they were each a part of. And at the heart of this action was an issue that went beyond whether the children should simply obey rules and authority; it covered questions of responsibility for one's actions, particularly when these actions can lead to others being harmed. 'Responsibility for self and others' is defined by Gilligan as one of the six components of an ethic of care (Brabeck, 1993, p. 37) and here the 'other' gained particular form in the role of the giant's wife.

Children are used to comical images of grotesque violence from such sources as cartoons, Punch and Judy shows and fairy tale characters such as the Ogre of this tale. If the violence suffered by the wife was to be taken seriously by the children, however, it had to be played as such. Consequently, she was not represented as a comic figure. Her status as victim, hinted at in Crossley-Holland's retelling, was emphasized in this drama for, as the previous case study illustrates, such roles tend naturally to draw out a sympathetic response from children, activating the other-regarding emotions of sympathy for the victim and indignation at her oppressor. This sympathy was heightened in the third session when she also performed her narrative function of helper,[9] saving the children from being found by the Ogre. As Jack, I was able to play against this sympathy and hence encourage its articulation:

Jack: I don't like that Ogre and I don't like his wife, so I don't see why I can't take what I want from here. Have you met his wife?
Boy: His wife's nice!
Jack: Put it this way, if I take the money from this Ogre, it doesn't hurt anybody apart from the Ogre and he's horrible.
Girl: Yes it does! It hurts the wife!

She, unlike Jack, was an unambiguous or *iconic* figure, and the desire to protect her from harm was always apt to be articulated. At the climax of the children's meeting with Jack, there was a dramatic moment which illustrated this:

137

Jack: (*confused*) So should I take the money or shouldn't I?
Many: Should/shouldn't (*one girl says something which only I hear. I silence the children and ask her to repeat it to the whole group*)
Girl: I don't think you should because all the Ogre will do is hit his wife again. (*Pause. Silence*)
Jack: (*provocatively*) And I thought you said she was a nice woman.

The generally agreed reason why Jack should not steal therefore began to shift from the fear of punishment expressed in the earlier exchange to the altruistic virtues of compassion for someone who had activated the children's orectic potential, virtues consistent with Gilligan's ethic of care. Of course, this was never debated in such abstract terms, but the conflicting moral demands they engendered are what drove the dramatic narrative, gaining physical actuality through the representation of the characters and their actions.[10]

Bakhtin's theories of the carnival and of the dialogical function of the novel are related inasmuch as they are fundamental to the worldview he promotes, where human existence is a 'mixture of styles, an irreducible heterogeneity' (cited in Todorov, 1984, p. 80). In the second session, I manipulated the drama so that the caring virtues of attachment could be considered but I did not, in the manner of Tabart, impose a resolution where it triumphed, as illustrated by the fact that a child, enacting the part of Jack, still felt that he would take the money and flee. What I did do, however, was to ensure that it came into a dialogical relationship with the rule-driven ethic of the Tabart text and ensure it was added to the polyphony of voices within the dramatic narrative. 'Carnival,' writes Holquist, 'like the novel, is a means of displaying otherness: carnival makes familiar relations strange' (1990, p. 89). To have kept the violent relationship between the Ogre and his wife on the level of the grotesque, comic style of Punch and Judy may at first seem to be a more carnivalesque thing to have done; paradoxically, this is not the case as it would have detracted from the multi-voicedness of the drama and hence rendered it less ambivalent, and so less provocative and less capable of producing disturbance. Here it is worth reconsidering Bakhtin's antipathy toward drama as an inherently monological art form, briefly discussed in Chapter 6. Pechey argues, however, that we learn from his writings that Bakhtin is referring restrictively to 'pure classical drama' (1989, p. 58) and that this position, too, is a highly contentious one:

> Drama is perhaps not so much monological as *monologised* by being read as 'literature' rather than theatre. (ibid., p. 61)

In particular, Pechey presents Brechtian theatre as a 'radically novelised drama — dialogised indeed to the point of polyphony' (ibid., p. 58). Bakhtin himself, Pechey points out, noted Brecht as a representative of the 'realist grotesque' which 'reflects at times the direct influence of carnival forms' (ibid., p. 58) and adds:

> The typical roles of Brechtian theatre are . . . the rogue, the clown and the fool; images of infinite irresolution as everything they do or say is fraught with dialogical ambiguity. (ibid., p. 59)

In this sense, the drama was Brechtian in nature and, if Jack had been both rogue and clown then the Ogre was to be the fool, albeit a very frightening one.

The Ogre

Giants are among the most recognizable figures of the carnival tradition, still dominating notably famous carnival processions today, such as those which take place on Shrove Tuesday in both Belgium and in Nice. Similarly, giants and ogres are an integral part of European folklore, proliferating in folk and fairy tales, although theorists disagree as to their symbolic significance. Bettelheim argues that, for children, they may represent adults in general: 'We . . . appear to them as selfish giants who wish to keep to ourselves all the wonderful things which give us power' (op. cit., p. 27). His Freudian reading of *Jack and the Beanstalk* identifies the Ogre as 'the father who blocks the boy's oedipal desires', a figure upon which 'the oedipal boy projects his frustrations and anxieties' (ibid., p. 114). The child needs to overcome the giant at a symbolic level to grow up into a secure adult; and, of course, the particular importance of fairy tales for Bettelheim is their unique ability to fulfil that psychological need. For Zipes, on the other hand, giants are figures of socio-political rather than psychological importance. Taking his perspective from the cultural evolution of folk-tales, giants, for him, represent the tyranny and injustice of brute force and political repression which can nonetheless be overcome through communal and individual demonstrations of bravery, wit and decisive action (Zipes, 1979). Both theoretical approaches go some way towards providing an understanding of the symbolic function and moral significance of the giant/ogre within this drama inasmuch as they identify the symbolic empowerment of children with his defeat. Viewed as an archetype, the specific crimes of the Ogre are irrelevant; he is simply evil and must be overcome. In our drama, however, his defeat had more than archetypal significance. His crimes were historically specific and it was the twin other-regarding emotions they provoked — sympathy for his wife and indignation at his violent bullying — which energized the final confrontation.

In my representation of the Ogre, I was influenced by Dario Fo and dramatic creations such as Pope Boniface VIII.[11] I emphasized his grotesque qualities in speech, gesture, gait and action. He was monstrous but also comically ridiculous and, above all, he was excessive — counting a huge bag of gold, kissing the huge coins, shouting both in anger and pleasure, stomping his feet and displaying signs of enormous appetite and greed. In this sense, he was the antithesis of Aristotle's doctrine of the mean.

> The conduct which conduces to the well-being of men in human society is
> that which exhibits reasonable moderation and avoids unreasonable extremes
> of action and passion. (Carr, 1991, p. 54)

There was much comic tension, as the children stayed quietly hidden and
watched and listened to my grotesque display of appetite and evil. And, although
comic, there was a real thrill of fear in their faces as they gripped on to each
other in their various hiding places. Iona Opie has written of traditional children's games, persisting as part of our folk tradition, which, as she puts it,
'seem to satisfy a deep desire for vicarious fear expressed in dramatic form'
(1995, p. 32).

In this dramatized version of hide and seek, I was able to harness this
desire (perhaps itself another aspect of carnivalesque ambivalence) to create
a tension which allowed the children to participate safely in the experience of
his evil power. This image of a rampaging, dangerous bully was in marked
contrast to the image in the final scene where, 'tied' to a chair, I was forced
to listen and respond to their haranguing. Transcribed references from this
scene — notably and significantly from the girls — reveal that this grotesque
representation of violent, male aggression coupled with arrogant laziness was
one they could recognize and which aroused their moral indignation.

Girl: You should be a nice giant, be friendly so you don't have to hit your
wife. Look at all the jobs she does for you! And you do nothing. You
just sit around and count your money. You do nothing, just tell the
hen to lay and tell the harp to sing.

Girl 2:   Imagine if you were your wife, if you kept doing all the work. You
wouldn't like it if you had to do it all the time.

Girl 3:   You just leave your wife alone. She doesn't hurt you.

His excessiveness was what the children enjoyed but they had the satisfaction
not only of overpowering the bully but the additional challenge of trying to
transform him by telling him why his behaviour was so unacceptable. The
drama ended with them once again in possession of the moral high ground
but this time not in the role of messengers of parental authority but, within the
fiction at least, as their own agents, acting in response to the events of the
story as they had unfolded and the possibilities which I, as teacher, had been
able to interweave into the drama. In this small but significant way, the figure
of the giant was able to offer the possibility of moral empowerment; by arous-
ing the children's indignation, he could stir them into feeling and articulating
ethical values which were already deep within them.

As with the representation of Jack, however, the dramatic energy of this
scene was redoubled by the added tension of metaxis and its carnivalesque
implications. Not only was the fairy tale Ogre defeated but this defeat had
physical embodiment, being represented through the gestures, gait, in short
the *body* of an adult male. Furthermore there was the added, anarchic thrill
of the traditional classroom Ogre, the teacher himself, being symbolically

disempowered and suffering from children the haranguing and the scolding which it is normally his role to deliver. This play with power is risky within the classroom but in its riskiness lies its potency as drama and as education. Here was performed a controlled, carnivalesque ritual, the symbolic debunking of abusive power and the liberation for the children to express a different ethic as to how it should be exercised, one correlative with Aristotle's 'mean' as well as with an ethic of care and responsibility.

Conclusion

Bettelheim saw no room for moral ambiguity in fairy tale characters. For him, there was a distinct polarity between good and bad characters for this reflected the psychological need of young children if they were to learn the difference between good and evil. 'Ambiguities', he argued, 'must wait until a relatively firm personality has been established' (op. cit., p. 9).[12] A mature student who watched the videoed extract where I role-played Jack was not impressed, and for reasons very similar to those expressed by Bettelheim. These children had a clear sense of right and wrong, she said, which I began to blur for them. My duty as a teacher was to reinforce virtuous patterns of behaviour for children as young as this and not to license morally unacceptable attitudes, even in pretence. The children were too young to learn that distinctions between right and wrong were sometimes difficult. What they needed was a belief that the moral rules they were taught could be trusted and believed in. In a way, I was flattered to have my teaching arouse such passion and I can sympathize with her sentiments although disagreeing with her interpretation. Her comments are interesting, however, for to explain this disagreement is to engage with the limits of making educational drama analogous with carnival and the limits of carnival itself.

Of course I believe children need the security of moral rules that make sense to them. I was a headteacher for three years, how could I possibly *not* believe this? Even if I had wanted to unteach them the rules then I had singularly failed to do so, as was evidenced by the teacher-led discussion where the children were still able to use the language of rules to voice condemnation of Jack's behaviour soon after the offensive scene. Yet this was surely the most carnivalesque of all the sessions, it being the only one which ended without the moral order being restored, as Jack escaped with the money.

The final session, in comparison, despite its carnivalesque characteristics, ended with a purging of the giant's socially unacceptable behaviour and a reassertion of moral norms, typifying what Northrop Frye saw as a characteristic tendency of conventional comedy. So my mature student need not worry; moral anarchy was not my aim, nor was it achieved within this drama. The quote from O'Toole which I used to open this account is relevant inasmuch as the absolute truths with which the children began the drama were brought into conflict with one another, just as they are in real life. In negotiating their way through this uncertainty, moral order was restored but was not, as I have explained, based upon the same principles with which the children began the drama. Yet how can such an emphasis on moral order square with an equal emphasis on carnival?

The paradox here is inherent to the form of carnival itself. By its very nature, it might do no more than reinforce the dominant social order by temporarily allowing it to be turned upside down and distortedly emulated. There is no question that, after taking on the roles of Jack and the Ogre, I reassumed my role of teacher, called the class to order and discussed with them what had happened in the drama. Carnival is clearly temporal and temporary by nature. Like the utopian world of fairy tales, it exists as an alternative world but as one that can be actualized and lived in with the knowledge that it will not last. For educational purposes, its potential lies both within the temporary licence it provides to pursue alternative explorations of power and responsibility and within the modes it presents to enable this pursuit to happen. Certainly, within a school setting, drama as carnival is unlikely to be as revolutionary as O'Toole suggests it can be in principle; and my portrayal of Jack lacked the satirical and political bite of Fo's *giullare*. But that need not reduce it to the role of politically expedient safety valve. As Morson and Emerson point out: 'The specific forms that carnival takes vary over time and from culture to culture, and some forms exploit the generic potential of carnival more than others' (1990, p. 459).

Carnival is variable and flexible and a teacher's capacity to explore its generic potential will be limited and defined by the mix and match of values which exist within the culture of the school, embodied within the local community from which the children are drawn, the institutionalized rules of the school establishment and, crucially, within the teacher herself. The lessons described here were infused with my own value agenda, as expressed within the characters I chose to represent, the form in which I chose to represent them and the moral exploration I was deliberately trying to engender. But I could not force the children to go on this journey, only create the motivation and the structure for doing so. Hence the charm and the power of carnival, whose spirit is waiting to be tapped in the natural playfulness of young children. It is there, too, in the amorphous sense of community a classroom can generate among them, in the spirit of many of their traditional tales and in the flexible pedagogic form of process drama. Together they can generate a potent force for moral education as well as the liberating energy of laughter.

Notes

1 A casual print-our from Warwick University library in March, 1995, showed that at least forty new English language versions of the tale have been published since 1990.

2 There are earlier printed references to the tale, however. Thomas Nashe, writing in 1596, dismissed it in an attack on 'idle pedants who will find matter inough to

dilate a whole daye of the first invention of Fy, fa, fum, I smell the bloud of an Englishman'. In 1734, a skit of the tale was published by J. Roberts in London, entitled *Enchantment demonstrated in the Story of Jack Spriggins and the Enchanted Bean* (see Opie, 1974, p. 162).

3   Jack's active, adventuresome nature and his mother's passive response to his waywardness are typical of the kind of gender stereotyping common throughout literary fairy tales, thoroughly analysed by Meller et al. (1984). Although I am aware of this, gender issues are not the focus of this particular case study. They are, however, discussed in Winston (1994).

4   See Zipes (1987). The following argument is largely taken from his introductory chapter.

5   My daughter was recently given a volume entitled *Traditional Fairy Tales* as a birthday present. Published in 1990 by Tiger Books International (London), its illustrations are taken directly from an Edwardian publication and the written text, though anonymous, is obviously derivative of Tabart. For example, this is how the fairy concludes her tale to Jack: 'You are reckless but, I trust, brave and earnest. Go boldly forward, fearing neither danger nor hardship. Remember that my protection can be given to you only as long as you work boldly and faithfully' (p. 76). There is less moralizing but it is just as strident.

6   I am discounting here such postmodern works as Raymond Briggs' *Jim and the Beanstalk* (1970) and Scieszka and Smith's *Stinky Cheese Man* (1992), which are not so much versions of the tale as parodies which necessitate a prior knowledge of the tale proper.

7   See Opies (1959), Chapter 8 and Meadows (1986, p. 199). The latter examines how children are in 'the difficult position of having two reference groups within the classroom' the teacher and their peers.

8   I have been questioned as to my use of stereotype here but I am willing to argue for its justification. One critic saw my use of the baseball cap as a negative portrayal of black youth culture. In the first place, it was not at all negative as far as the children were concerned. 'You look cool!' was the immediate response of one boy, which leads to my second point. It established immediately and effectively the connotations I wanted, as evidenced in this boy's response. It also matched the archetypal role of Jack as trickster and carried with it what O'Neill describes as 'an immediate implication for action . . . easily and eagerly anticipated by the audience' (1995, p. 38). O'Neill comments further on this functional aspect of character. 'Because dramatic characters are defined precisely by their context, it is inevitable that they will partake, to some degree, of the nature of types and may remain "stereotype figures and theatrical scarecrows," as Thomas Mann called them' (ibid., p. 72).

9   The function of helper is defined by Propp (1968) as a characteristic of the folk tale.

10 It is also possible to interpret this dilemma, as a colleague has, as centring upon a conflict between Jack's *right* to his father's money (Kohlberg) versus his *responsibility* to avoid causing harm to another person (Gilligan).

11 See *Mistero Buffo* in Fo and Rame (1994).

12 Tricksters like Jack and Puss-in-Boots serve a purpose entirely distinct from moral learning, according to Bettelheim; they build character '. . . not by promoting choices between good and bad, but by giving the child the hope that even the meekest can succeed in life. . . . Morality is not the issue in these tales but rather assurance that one can succeed' (op. cit., p. 10).

Chapter 10

The Star Maiden:
Moral and Cultural Values

Moral and Cultural Values in the Story of *The Star Maiden*

In recent years, story-tellers and educationalists have perceived in the culture of Native Americans a respect and love for the land, demonstrative of the moral virtues of care and stewardship, and a spirituality which emphasizes human connectedness to the earth. Historical figures such as Chief Seattle have gained iconic status, becoming symbolic of a type of natural wisdom, expressed through communal values, which western society would do well to learn from[1]; and, as a result of this perspective, Native American stories have been retold and presented as purveyors of this wisdom (Caduto and Bruchac, 1988a, 1988b). However, the rise of post-colonial consciousness, particularly within the areas of cultural and literary studies, has raised questions regarding the ethics of appropriating stories from colonized cultures. As the native North American Lee Maracle has written:

> The truth is that creeping around libraries full of nonsensical anthropocentric drivel, imbuing these findings with falsehood in the name of imagination, then peddling the nonsense as 'Indian Mythology' is literary dishonesty. (cited in Green and LeBihan, 1996, p. 297)

The successful novelist Margaret Atwood believes that the best writing about such a group is likely to come from within that group:

> . . . not because those outside it are likely to vilify it, but because they are likely these days, and out of well-meaning liberalism, to simplify and senti-mentalize it, or to get the textures and vocabulary and symbolism wrong. (op. cit., p. 297)

Rather than being treated with respect, the stories may become subjected to misrepresentation and trivialization, their part in a complex system of thought and myth misunderstood and reduced to platitudes, their values and cultural symbols becoming polluted by those of the colonizer and by the commercial forces of post-industrial capitalism.

Barbara Juster Esbensen is an award-winning writer of children's stories who lives in Wisconsin. Many of her books are retellings of Native American stories and two of them, *Ladder to the Moon* and *The Star Maiden*, are versions of traditional Ojibway tales. These retellings are, in turn, based upon literary versions published originally in 1850, in a volume entitled *The Traditional History and Characteristic Sketches of the Ojibway Nation*, (Copway, 1978) and written by an Ojibway chief who had taken the English name George Copway. I am an admirer of Esbensen's work but a literary and historical analysis of her own and Copway's texts can serve to illustrate the argumentative force of these two, contradictory perspectives; the moral power and beauty of such tales on the one hand and the problematic issues of cultural misappropriation on the other, the latter being rendered all the more problematic when the retelling of the tale has overtly ethical intentions.

Esbensen's Tale: *The Star Maiden*

From the outset, Esbensen sets her version of the tale within the natural environment of the Ojibway nation as it was 'long, long ago, when all the tribes in the land lived in peace'. The illustrations show us a land of beauty and of plenty, of lakes, streams, woods and wildlife, a world, as the text tells us, 'rich with everything the people needed'. The Ojibway are referred to as 'the people' throughout the tale, a people who love to watch the sky at night when their work is done. One night, they notice a star, brighter than any ever seen before; and, as they watch, it falls to earth, coming to rest over a hilltop in the distance. A group of braves is sent to investigate but they return afraid because the star has refused to answer their questions. That night, however, a beautiful star maiden appears in a dream to a young brave. She tells him how tired she is of her wandering, how much she loves his people and their world, and how much she would like to live with them. In the morning, the brave tells the chief of his dream and, at a council of the wisest men and women of the tribe, the chief announces that they will welcome the Star Maiden to live with them in the form she chooses, whether as a flower, a fish or a bird. That night, the young brave leaves to find the Star Maiden and, while she drifts above him, lighting his way through the darkness, he leads her back to the village. The maiden slips into a rose, but is unhappy there as it is too far from the village and she can never see the people she loves. So she chooses a small, blue, prairie flower to be her home, but is disturbed by the trampling hooves of the buffalo. 'I cannot rest here!' she cries out in despair and, that night, the people are sad to see her return to the sky. But, hovering over the lake, she sees her reflection, and that of all her sky-sisters floating on the water. She calls to them to stop their wandering, that the quiet waters below can be their home. The people watch as the lights in the sky shake, the lake comes alive with stars and, the next morning, hundreds of water lilies can be seen floating on the lake. The Star Maiden and her sisters have found their place on earth.

The tale is written in a simple and economic poetic style, beautifully illustrated by Helen K. Davie. Through the artistry of its language, imagery, structure and illustrations, it promotes a coherent set of spiritual and moral values which can be illuminated by careful analysis.

The opening lines establish the style and the tone of the whole story.

> *Once there was a time,*
> *long, long ago,*
> *when all the tribes in the land*
> *lived in peace.*
> *There were no wars among them.*
> *Summer was always in the air.*
> *The streams were clear and pure,*
> *and filled with fish.*

Esbensen has chosen to write the tale in the form of free verse, which serves to measure the pace of the language and accentuate its rhythms. At times repetition, like the steady beating of a drum, emphasizes this effect. 'Your world calls to me', the Star Maiden announces to the brave.

> *'I love the blowing winds*
> *I love the colours I see below me.*
> *I love your rivers and lakes.'*

The words are simple throughout the narrative, the sentences short, with few or no subclauses. Similes and metaphors are striking in their simplicity and draw upon the natural world: the people love to watch the stars 'flicker their icy fire', the Star Maiden's voice is 'like a thread of silver'. When the chief speaks, his tones match perfectly those of the narrative as a whole:

> *'A star wants to live on earth,*
> *Our people will welcome her.*
> *The blue air over the prairie*
> *will fill with bird-song*
> *To honour her coming.'*

This simplicity of language may well serve the needs of a young readership but its cultural and artistic functions go beyond that; for, alongside its rhythm, pace and imagery, it matches the representations in white, Anglo-Saxon culture of the speech patterns of wise Native American chiefs such as can be seen in numerous Hollywood westerns or read in the speeches of Chief Seattle himself. In other words, Esbensen uses the language of the tale to build upon culturally received images of an idealized nature which conjure a vision of the simple but wise Indian, the 'Noble Savage'.

These values are reinforced and fleshed out by the full-page illustrations on every alternate page. Each illustration is divided in two, consisting of a large depiction of the narrative, underneath which a smaller image shows a species of wildlife — owl, deer or fox, for example — sharing the natural environment of the Ojibway people. The images are distinct but simultaneous and so emphasize the independent but peacefully co-existent relationship between the people and the other creatures of the natural world. The colourful borders which frame each page are based upon Native American patterned designs and are thus a celebration of the artistic skills of the people. In addition, the narrative illustrations throughout sustain an image of communal life, showing us men and women building a birchbark canoe together; children playing in the fields of corn; family groupings, gazing in wonder at the light in the sky; and the chief and his council dancing to celebrate their decision to welcome the Star Maiden to earth. In their work, their play, their politics and religion, the pictures show us a people who live simply but in harmony with themselves and with their environment. Women, too, are seen to share in the work and the decision-making; the pictures present images of a non-sexist society and this is reinforced in the written text by Esbensen's use of the gender-neutral pronoun *they* to describe the tribe's collective activities:

All day long, they hunted
and fished. They gathered fruits
and nuts. They made birchbark canoes . . .

Foremost of all the story's ethical messages is the value of stewardship. For a child listening to or reading the story, the personification of the water lily equates its existence with that of a recognizably human, if supernatural, life. In her three manifestations as star, woman and water lily, the Star Maiden is special, unique and beautiful. The fact that she chooses the most vulnerable of all as her final destination is an act of love and of faith in the Ojibway people. The last page of the book, for the first time, addresses the reader directly and the imperative 'Touch them gently' is repeated within the space of five lines of text. The reader is being urged to treat water lilies and, by extension, all forms of natural life which we, as humans are capable of destroying, with care, restraint and respect. The water lily may not be of material use to us, it may not feed or clothe us, but its beauty is meaningful, signifying an active and loving relationship between human kind and the natural world.

Elizabeth Tooker, in her study of the spirituality of the native peoples of North America points out that, for the Ojibway, natural phenomena, such as the Sun, are regarded not as objects but as persons of 'other-than-human-type'. She comments that:

(Ojibway) myths are not about fictitious or necessarily fabulous characters, but about past lives of 'persons', including importantly persons of the other-than-human-type. (1979, p. 24)

This gives us some perspective on the religious significance of the original tale for the Ojibway. Esbensen's rendering of the tale achieves a powerful, spiritual resonance; but, for a largely white, English-speaking readership, it is fashioned through analogy with traditional Christian mythology, in particular through the creation of images implicitly associated with the Garden of Eden and the Coming of Christ. The world presented at the beginning of the story is immediately recognizable as a form of Eden, an idealized land of plenty, of peace and harmony which the narrative implies no longer exists[2]. The coming of the Star Maiden is preluded by the appearance of a bright light in the night sky, as is the coming of Christ to the shepherds; her appearance to the brave in his dream recalls the visitation of the angels to both Joseph and Mary at the time of Mary's pregnancy; and the journey of the brave, guided by the light of the Star Maiden, has echoes of the journey of the Magi. These analogies are equally in evidence in the illustrations, where the Star Maiden, beautiful and bathed in light, hovers over the figure of the brave, or over her reflection in the lake below, with her arms outstretched like an angel, with the smile and downcast eyes of the Madonna. And when she chooses a form in which to live among her chosen people, she, like Christ, chooses to become vulnerable.

> *Water lilies! Touch them gently*
> *And remember.*

These last words of Esbensen's text are dense with meanings. She is signalling that her aim in retelling the story is the same as George Copway's, namely, to keep an important cultural artefact from disappearing. However, her intention in selecting this particular story from Copway's book has been shown to emanate from the important ethical values she believes it can convey to a contemporary young reader. So, in its most immediate sense, her use of the imperative 'remember' is an urge for her readers to bear in mind how important it is to treat the natural world with care. It is also a general reminder of how important stories are for the transmission of values. Finally, and very importantly, it confirms and emphasizes the sense of wistful nostalgia that has permeated the text since the opening sentences and which is emphasized in the pale water colours of the illustrations. It is nostalgia for a lost age of innocence, for a noble race whose simple but morally admirable way of life has vanished. To recognize this is to see Esbensen's story, in its portrayal of Native Americans and their culture, as more than a simple story for children or the manifestation of a recent educational trend; it places it in the tradition of a romantic vision of the Indian that extends at least as far back as Rousseau and James Fenimore Cooper and which has ideological as well as literary implications.

The Dangers of Noble Savagism

The phrase 'Noble Savage' was first coined by Dryden in 1670 in his play *The Conquest of Granada* but the concept it engendered was most clearly expressed by Rousseau.

> This condition, is the real Youth of the World, and . . . all ulterior improvements have been so many steps, in Appearance, towards the Perfection of Individuals, but in Fact towards the Decrepitness of the Species. (Washburn, 1964, p. 418)

Rousseau's belief in a primal age of innocence and his nostalgia for an imagined time when man was a creature of simple tastes and good instincts, uncorrupted by the tyranny of modern civilization, is notably similar to the vision at the heart of Esbensen's tale. But it is through the work of James Fenimore Cooper that this vision had the most seminal influence on European American sensibilities towards the American Indian. Rousseau's emphasis on emotion and sentimentality had a great impact on Romanticism, a movement of thought and art which confronted the philosophical belief in rationality and progress associated with the Enlightenment. The Romantics threw aside a belief in the future and embraced and glorified the past. For them, as for Rousseau, primal peoples were imagined as living in perfect harmony with nature, morally and physically ravaged only by civilization.

As creations of the Romantic movement, Cooper's (1966) 'good' Indians, such as Uncas and Chingachcook in *The Last of the Mohicans*, are literary embodiments of this depiction. However, Cooper was also writing at a time when the Native Americans were being systematically dispossessed of their territories and, despite the genuine empathy and pity he felt for the plight of the Indians, many critics see a particular ideological significance in his depiction of their heroic but doomed qualities. In the words of Seymour House:

> Since it is far easier to lament a race than to preserve it, Americans accepted Indian extinction as inevitable and indulged themselves in sentimental nostalgia for a lost cause that was assuredly lost but that had never truly been a cause. (1965, p. 61)

Slotkin has described Cooper's

> mournful treatment

of the Indians' dispossession as

> at heart, a sentimental response, covertly justifying that very dispossession.

> Through myth, we imaginatively hoard away the cake we have eaten and voice our affection for a precapitalist Eden even while we reaffirm our affiliation with the values and priorities of bourgeois society. (1992, p. 7)

Sentimental romanticism, therefore, and the presentation of the Indian as a tragic figure, noble but doomed, brings with it the dangers of a fatalistic discourse, which has no room for the expression of political alternatives. As Pearce has written: 'They (the European Americans) pitied his state but saw it as inevitable; they hoped to bring him to civilization but saw that civilization would kill him' (cited in House, 1965, p. 61).

Thus the representation of the Native American as an ideal type, the nostalgic regret for his vanished way of life, can be interpreted as part of a literary tradition which re-enforces a historical perspective confirming the dispossession and demise of the Indian as inevitable. In this sense, adulating and celebrating the Indian is a type of white man's penance for a collective sin that was really nobody's fault. Its message becomes one of inaction and regret rather than action and hope.

It is, therefore, at least arguable that significant ideological values, historically and culturally transmitted, are at the root of the nostalgia and sentiment that permeate Esbensen's text; and that, from a post-colonial perspective, she is guilty of cultural misappropriation. However, before we rush to condemn either her or her story on ideological grounds, we should not ignore the source of her tale, itself a literary artefact; nor should we neglect the life of its writer Kah-Ge-Ga-Gah-Bowh, alias George Copway, Chief of his Nation and missionary of the Methodist Church.

Copway's Tale: *The Star and the Lily*

The Ojibway, or Chippewa nation traditionally populated the land of lakes and forests which border on the prairies to the north, west and south of Lake Superior. Today, many live in Canadian Ontario or in reservations, such as Red Lake and Leech Lake, in north Minnesota. In 1850, when George Copway wrote his version of the tale, members of the Ojibway Nation living in the United States had, for fourteen years, been bound by a treaty to remove to land south of the Missouri River, a treaty which they managed to have modified by petitioning the Washington Government in 1855. The words with which they opened the petition were significant.

> We love the spot where our fathers' bones are laid and we desire that our bones may rest beside theirs also. Now Father, when our chiefs sold their land to you, your advice and counsel to us was that we should abandon our Indian habits and customs. We have renounced them and are trying to follow your advice and examples. (Washburn, 1973, p. 2510)

Their petition was successful, inasmuch as the threat of removal was lifted; in agreement, however, their tribal organizations were dissolved. They could now continue to inhabit the land of their fathers, but as individuals, not as a tribe. Such were the times Copway lived in. He himself was a native of Ontario and was thus free from the extent of the oppression endured by those members of his people who lived in the United States, coerced into consciously abandoning their cultural practices and into renouncing their capacity to organize politically. However, the life he chose appears to have been in accordance with the advice offered to the chiefs who sold their land to the Great White Father.

Copway's book was, in fact, the first volume of Native American history written by an Indian, (Indian being the term he uses himself) and from it we can pick up details of his autobiography (Copway, 1978, p. xi). His early years were spent following the traditional way of life of his people but this was broken by twenty months' schooling, conversion to Christianity and six years' residency in Boston, Massachussets (op. cit., p. viii). He appears to have divided the remainder of his life between missionary preaching among the Ojibway in the West and to pleading their cause to white Christians and philanthropists in the East.[3] In a series of letters written to the Philadelphia *Saturday Evening Post*, he is revealed as a visionary who foresaw a 'catastrophic exterminating war' on the plains of the West; and as a champion of his people's rights, albeit one who urged that their salvation lay through the civilizing processes of Christianity and an education in English language and literature (op. cit., pp. ix, 245).

In the light of this, a study of Copway's version of the story, which he entitled *The Star and the Lily*, is revealing. The accusations of nostalgia, of idealization, of sentimentality that one might level at Fenimore Cooper, or at Esbensen, are accentuated in his own narrative. The whole of his book, in fact, is suffused with nostalgia, presenting a vision of his people not too dissimilar from that of the Noble Savage. The tale is narrated in the voice of an old Indian chief and is framed by Copway's own experience of hearing it told as a child. The chief himself is presented in images evocative of peace, wisdom and simple tranquility. Before relating the tale to a group of children, he is 'sat in his wigwam, quietly smoking his favourite pipe' (p. 97). At the end, 'while tears fell fast from the eyes of all, the old man laid down and was soon silent in sleep' (ibid., p. 102). Copway then takes up the first person:

> Since that, I have often plucked the white lily, and garlanded it around my head — have dipped it in its watery bed — but never have I seen it without remembering the legend of the descending star. (ibid., p. 102)

His prose rings with cultural echoes different from Esbensen's, having more in common with Dickens than Chief Seattle. It is written with the fluency, the rhythms and the manners of the nineteenth century educated middle classes, of those white Europeans who wrote in sentimental terms about the Indians rather than in the language which Esbensen represents as that of the Indians themselves. As a man who devoted much of his adult life to the propagation of Christianity among his people, it is unsurprising that the biggest influence on the tone and imagery of his prose is recognizably that of the Bible. In his version of the tale the allusions to the Garden of Eden are explicit:

> The beasts of the field were tame, they came and went at the bidding of man. It was . . . a time when earth was a paradise and man worthily its possessor. (ibid., p. 98)

This is not the unhierarchical paradise of Esbensen's tale. Here, as in Genesis, beast is servant to man; and, as in nineteenth century capitalist America, man *owns* the land. The Indians, he tells us, loved to watch the stars:

> for they believed them to be the residences of the good who had been taken
> home by the Great Spirit. (ibid., p. 98)

Expressed in these terms, there is evidently very little difference between the Ojibway belief in an afterlife and the Christian concept of heaven. In the words chosen by the chief to close his tale, Copway makes a direct reference to heaven in a phrase which calls to mind the cadences of the *Lord's Prayer* ('Thy will be done on earth as it is in Heaven').

> 'Children! when you see the lily on the waters, take it in your hands, and hold
> it to the skies, that it may be happy on earth as its two sisters, the morning
> and evening stars, are happy in heaven'. (ibid., p. 102)

The imagery associating the Star with the coming of Christ, and the angelic appearance of the Star Maiden, are also present; like Christ, the Star Maiden will suffer little children to come unto her:

> 'Children! yes, they shall be my playmates, and I shall kiss their brows when
> they slumber by the sides of cool lakes'. (ibid., p. 101)

and she hovers 'with expanded wing' as she follows the braves to the village. Copway's stated aim may have been to preserve the stories of his people but, here, he chose to do so in the Christian vernacular. This may have been a subconscious result of his own acculturation but is more likely to have been a conscious attempt to accommodate Christian values into the traditional stories of his people. In either case, Esbensen's adaptation can be seen to have harnessed Christian religious imagery already existent in Copway's text.

The extent of Copway's Christianisation of the tale can to some extent be measured by comparing it to another version, that published in a collection by Louise Jean Walker in 1961. Walker claims in her introduction that her tales are faithful versions of those told to her in person by Chippewas themselves. Here, the Star Maiden is a spirit, one of the good fairies whom the Chippewa people respect and never disturb. She is not the vulnerable figure portrayed by Copway and Esbensen and there is a strong hint of sexuality in her decision to live in the lake.

> . . . she saw a white flower with a heart of gold shining on the waters below.
> As she looked, a canoe, steered by the young warrior who had told her
> wishes to his people, shot past and the strong, brown hand brushed the edge
> of the flower. (p. 18)

She does not seek or need the protection of the people and this mix of desire and respect is a spiritual reflection of the Chippewa's relationship with Nature, a relationship of mutual respect and sensual pleasure. Devoid of the sentiment, nostalgia, and Christian imagery, Walker's tale has a very different meaning.

Conclusion

Copway's paradox is a moving one. The nostalgic regret for the disappearance of his people's way of life is expressed in Romantic and Christian sentiments acquired from the very culture responsible for this disappearance; and, as a Methodist missionary, he was himself, in part, an agent of this culture. Yet his intentions as a writer were different from those of Romantics such as Fenimore Cooper. For right or for wrong, he saw western civilization as a force which could bring either dignity or corruption to his people, dependent upon which western values they were exposed to. Those of the Christian and the Philan- thropist (to whom he dedicated his preface) would enable the Indian 'to rise above the soil of degradation and hover about the high mounts of wisdom and truth' (1978, p. ix); whereas those of the frontiersmen would bring about the downfall of the Indian for the white man's personal profit and gain (op. cit., p. 241). Civilization as he defined it wouldn't kill his people but, at the time in which he lived, could possibly save them. As such, he did not despair for the future of his people but saw it in terms of a struggle, a cause not yet lost, and he campaigned hard for their political and educational welfare. The publica- tion of his book in 1850 had a political purpose, stated in the preface:

> ... that I may awaken in the heart a deeper feeling for the race of red-men and induce the pale-face to use greater effort to effect an improvement in their social and political relations. (ibid., p. vii)

Despite its sentiment and nostalgia, it was a work intended to provoke polit- ical action, not excuse political inaction. And the extent of his own accultura- tion into the contemporary, western, literary canon meant that he understood how to appeal in his writing to a white, urban, educated audience.[4]

James Axtell (1981) has pointed out that, when the Indian and Christian cultures met, the direction of religious change was unilinear, due to Christian- ity's aggressive and exclusive evangelism. However, he goes on to argue that to be on the defensive did not imply a total lack of initiative.

> The Indians were incredibly tenacious of their culture and life-style, but their traditionalism was neither blind nor passive ... native peoples ... were remark- ably resourceful in adjusting to new conditions, especially in using elements of European religious culture for their own purposes. (ibid., p. 86)

When preaching to the Ojibway, Copway had most probably learned to adapt the traditional tales of his tribe for missionary purposes, using them to promote Christian values. Nonetheless, his purpose in publishing was to find a white readership for the tales, to promote an appreciation for the cultural richness of his people among those Euro-Americans who could influence political action. For this reason, the integration of European cultural references within the Ojibway narrative can be interpreted not only as a conscious attempt to preserve that narrative within an aggressive, dominant culture but also as a play upon nineteenth century, bourgeois sensibilities for the intended political benefit of his people. The symbolic imagery and nostalgic aura which he contributed to *The Star and the Lily* need not, therefore, be viewed in a negative light. As Fred Inglis has written, 'Nostalgia is not a swearword. It may be as much a powerful force for good and positive action as it may be a passive or anaesthetic pervasion of the spirit' (1993, p. 46).

It is attributable to Copway's artistry and inter-cultural referencing that his book survived and that Esbensen, over one hundred years later, came to see in his version of *The Star and the Lily* a powerful vehicle for moral values, relevant to the dominant culture in a much later age. And, aware though we might be of the ideological complexity and problematic intertextuality of her tale, I would argue that the moral concerns at its heart are more a force for good than for anything else and that we should permit children the possibility to be moved by its simple poetry and the play of its images.

Moral and Cultural Values in the Drama of *The Star Maiden*

The work described and analysed below was taught over five sessions, of approximately one hour each in length. The children were a Year 5 class in a Roman Catholic Primary School situated on the outskirts of a city centre. My analysis of the story has indicated that, unlike the previous case studies, I had identified its ethical values as a source I wished to tap into rather than to problematize but that there were nonetheless problems concerning the cultural representation of Native American people and the appropriation of their mythology. My broad intentions in the drama were, therefore, twofold. Firstly, to explore the moral agenda of the tale — issues of stewardship, of care for the environment — through enhancing the poetic symbolism, not disturbing it, and by harnessing the powerful emotional pull of the tale. Secondly, to de-mythologize the representation of the Noble Savage by presenting historicized models of dispossessed Native Americans, framed within a contemporary context. The drama was intended to explore an ethical tension between economic pressures and cultural identity and hence introduce further moral dimensions. I was aware that this was an ambitious project and, in the event, the drama which ensued worked most effectively through the moral resonances of its symbolism while throwing up further ambivalences concerning cultural, moral and spiritual values and their manifestation in drama. Yet this uncertain outcome is what makes it worthy of analysis.

In the first session, I read the children the story, first of all giving a brief introduction to its source, its age and to the importance of stories for the Native American peoples. We then studied the illustrations and I followed this with an origami exercise, making a water lily out of two squares of coloured paper and promising to come into the school to work in small groups with all those children who would like to make their own. We then began to work together on a dance which told the story of *The Star Maiden* through movement. I taught the opening sequence and choreographed the rest, which was devised from the children's own movements. The dance was completed and performed to music in the second session. Following this, we created a composite calligram, in the shape of a star, using phrases from the final two pages of the book, and experimented with different ways of reading it (see Appendix 2).

The drama proper took place during the third and fourth sessions, spread over two days, in the following week. First of all, the children took it in turns to lay the lilies they had made over some blue paper which I had placed in a corner of the hall. They then sat in a semi-circle before it and recognized that they had created a representation of the lake where the Star Maiden lived with her sisters. We recapped the significance of the story and I then showed an illustration of a modern day, teenage Native American, which depicted clearly the poverty of life on a reservation.[5] I briefly related how the white settlers had dispossessed the Indians of their land. I then told the children that we would begin to make our own story, set in the modern world, about the people to whom the story of *The Star Maiden* belonged. We would make this in the form of a drama which began with a dream. I simultaneously narrated and enacted the dream, explaining that it was the recurring dream of the young Chief of his tribe. In it, he would see himself signing a contract in exchange for money, and then, dressed in a smart, new suit, floating in a canoe on the lake beside which he had lived as a child. He would stoop to pick a water lily, which he would then crush in his hands and drop into the lake, awakening suddenly and in a sweat. After discussing and analysing the dream image in great detail, the children worked in groups to create a dramatic image which might explain this dream in terms of recent events in the Chief's life. All images depicted the Chief selling the land and the lake without the consent of his people.

At the start of the next session, we sat around the lake and re-opened the discussion of possible reasons as to why the Chief might have decided to sell the land and why he now felt so guilty about it. I then took on the role of the Chief's grandfather and told the children how I had travelled to the city to speak with my grandson, who worked there as a successful businessman; and I explained how the people in the offices there had ignored and been rude to me; and how I pitied them, for they were not at peace.

After creating the atmosphere of those offices as it must have felt for the old man, the children then played out, in collective roles, the meeting of the son and his grandfather, at the end of which the son agreed to meet with his people and explain his decision. For this meeting, I took on the role of the Chief and insisted that the money from the sale would be used to build houses and provide jobs and amenities that my people could enjoy and benefit from. At the end of the meeting I came out of role, stood at some distance from the lake and asked the children to position themselves either around the lake, close to me, or in-between, depending upon where their sympathies as members of the tribe now lay. All grouped closely around the lake. We discussed how the Chief must have felt to experience such rejection; then, as the drama had begun with a dream, I asked them to end it with a dream. In small groups, they were asked to think how the story might end and to create a dramatic image, this time from the dream of a member of the tribe, which would hint at what this ending was. After viewing and discussing these, I asked the children what they thought we could learn from the story we had created.

The following week, in a final, classroom session, the children created their own star poems. Given the phrase *Touch Them Gently*, they were asked to compose the poem by naming and describing things in the world of today, or in the traditional world of the Native Americans, which they thought needed to be treated with care (see Appendix 3).

These lessons were not ideal models of sustained good practice. There were two boys in the class with behavioural problems who were never disruptive, but only intermittently involved in the drama or its accompanying classwork; overall, the children's lack of experience with the medium affected their ability to create effective dramatic images. I made a very basic error of judgment by thinking the children would be able to manage the scene where, in role as the Chief, I visited the office environments they had created. However, I felt at its conclusion that, on the whole, the children had worked with commitment and serious moral engagement, creating a strong sense of group identity, a view supported by the spoken and written comments of the teacher. In addressing where, why and how it worked as moral education, I will not be neglecting the ambivalences which make it, in the end, a difficult drama to evaluate. The framework established in Case Study 2 is still pertinent to its analysis and I will make direct use of it but will begin by proposing and analysing a further category: that of ritual.

Ritual Enrolment and Moral Involvement

Even to say it in one word, ritual, is asking for trouble. (Schechner, 1993, p. 228)

The dynamic of the drama was dependent upon the children being able to feel, understand and articulate the moral issues contained within the symbolisms of the tale and why it might be of significance to a particular culture. Consequently, the main intention of the first two sessions was to help them internalize and care for the story and for this I deployed strategies which were ritualistic in form. As the above quote from Schechner suggests, however, the concept of ritual is a slippery one and recently theorists within the field of process drama have attempted to define its characteristics in greater depth. O'Neill usefully draws our attention to the nature and function of rituals in social life and to how many plays, particularly by Shakespeare, contain examples of them, ranging from processions, feasts and coronations to weddings, trials and funerals. Such rituals she defines as: 'a way of understanding and celebrating our own lives in the context of our communities' and emphasizes their purpose in the theatre as bearers of 'harmony and fulfilment' (1995, p. 147).

In process drama, however, the term *ritual* is used not only with reference to the imitation of such real life rituals but to define specific conventions intended to serve similar communal purposes within the contextualized, structural needs of a particular dramatic event. These commonly include the use of a conch to ritualize turn-taking and the deployment of theatre forms such as trials and public meetings. O'Neill sees a significant function of both kinds of ritual as the 'distancing and containing (of) emotion' (ibid., p. 149). For O'Toole, ritual in process drama is characterized by 'the formalised and ceremonial sharing of a moment perceived to be significant by all those concerned' (1992, p. 29). He sees its use at the beginning of a drama as: '. . . part of the enrolment, as a way of committing the participants to each other and to the drama' (ibid., p. 160). One of the ways it manages this is to involve the participants in a task in which there is a tension implicit to its very undertaking. Neelands and Goode stress the differences in drama between ritual and mere entertainment. For them rituals 'establish a community of ideas, beliefs and values' (1995, p. 17) and ritual experience 'actualizes . . . through symbols the spiritual and material aspirations of a community' (ibid., p. 18).

In the drama of *The Star Maiden* there were three enrolling events which I would classify as ritual theatre: the creation and performance of the Dance; the creation and reading of the communal Star Poem; and the creation of the water lilies and the lake, the visual 'set' for the drama. All were communal, formalized experiences meant to enrol the children into the spirit of the drama by generating commitment and by creating a shared feeling of significance, harmony and fulfilment. The success of these rituals was most powerfully evidenced by the children's involvement in and responses to the dance.

The movements of the dance depicted the story and used the book's illustrations as stimuli. The opening phrases, which I taught, consisted of stylized movements suggesting how the Ojibway people used to live: hunting, fishing from the lake, gathering fruit. The children's own motifs were structured around the journey of the young brave to meet the Star Maiden, the descent of the stars from heaven and their transformation into water lilies. The music — *Red Wind*, by Gabrielle Roth and the Mirrors — was characterized by soft but heavy rhythms, resonant of Native American drumming.[6] The tensions implicit to the creation and performance of this dance involved the children in measured movement through space; in working in unison, as individuals yet as one; in groups which changed formation and where touch, support and teamwork were necessary; and in shared, repetitive spatial and temporal patterning. It was learning achieved and demonstrated through the body.

> The body . . . is the place where humanity achieves the ritualization of motion in an artform called 'dance' . . . the most important and pervasive means by which primal peoples celebrate living. (Highwater, 1982, p. 133)

Jamake Highwater is a contemporary Native American writer who has explained the spiritual, ritualistic force of dance in the experience of primal people and argues that only recently has western culture begun to rediscover an understanding of the significance of dance to the communal emotional and spiritual life. Recent writing by western theorists and educationalists on dance would support his argument. (For example, Hanna, 1979, Spencer, 1985). Boas is one theorist who stresses the transformative nature of dance, defining it in terms of an aesthetic available to all:

> ordinary gestures and actions can become dance if a transformation takes place within the person; a transformation which takes him (sic) out of the ordinary world and places him in a world of heightened sensitivity. (cited in Spencer, 1985, p. 2)

Understood in these terms, dance has the potential to become a powerful, sensitizing, communal experience and, after creating, rehearsing and performing the *Star Maiden* dance, the children were questioned as to its emotional impact upon them. Their responses were immediate:

Girl: It makes me feel peaceful inside, nice and calm.
Girl: Happy.
Girl: Special.
Boy: It looked like the stars in the night, in a nice night, like seeing it with a nice sunset.
Boy: I feel like I'm in the tribe, like I'm in the story, cos the music fits in with my idea of the people.
Girl: I feel comfy.
Girl: It reminds me of lilies, floating about on the water.

Performing the dance, therefore, enhanced the emotional impact of the story by distancing and containing this impact within a strong, artistic form.[7] It conjured up positive feelings of well-being associated with a web of imagined images which had the story at their centre, helping the children to care, not necessarily, in any deeper sense, for each other but for the story, the focus of the dance itself. An emotional bond, encouraged by ritual, now linked them more firmly to the fiction and to the symbolic figure of the Star Maiden. Consequently, within the drama that followed, children were more readily able to participate in serious, symbolic play, where care for the story as a cultural belief came to be at the heart of the moral confrontation between the Chief and his people.

However, it is interesting to reflect once again on Williams' contention that 'drama . . . is neither ritual which discloses the God nor myth which requires and sustains repetition' (Chapter 3, p. 30). The *Star Maiden* dance exhibited both these features of ritual and emphasizes that the drama was to have a different function, one intended to dialogize the experience of the dance. In the event, as subsequent analysis will suggest, the success of the dance as ritual provided an emotional imbalance which worked to the detriment of the intended dialogism of the drama. To appreciate why this should have happened, it is helpful to remember that I was not working in a value-free, cultural vacuum. This was a Catholic school and a class in which all bar one of the children were Catholic and where, according to the teacher, 70 per cent of them were regular church-goers. In other words, these were children whose lives were attuned to ritual; whose school community was defined largely by the importance it attached to the ritual of the Catholic mass; and who consequently understood ritual as a serious and significant event. The children's firm grounding in Christian mythology needs to be borne in mind as an important contributory factor to this particular drama with these particular children. Rather than the ritual creating their ability to work with the story, it is more precise to see it as working in congruence with an already existent sensitivity to the story's symbolism and its potential significance to a people. Although Christian terminology was never used or referred to throughout the drama, I will argue that its resonance, skilfully interwoven by Copway into the text of *The Star and the Lily* and inherited by Esbensen, greatly facilitated the children's capacity to work fictionally and with integrity in a cultural context different from their own. At the heart of this was their ability to work with the symbolism of the story and the drama.

Responding to the Dramatic Image as a Source of Moral Reflection

> It is the play's central image that remains, its silhouette, and if the elements are highly blended this silhouette will be its meaning, this shape will be the essence of what it has to say. (Brook, 1968, p. 152)

Ezra Pound has defined the poetic image as 'that which presents an intellectual and emotional complex in an instant of time'. He writes: 'The image is more than an idea. It is a vortex or cluster of fused ideas and is endowed with energy' (cited in Rogers, 1978, p. 7). These characteristics — complexity, fusion of intellect and emotion, energy — give us some clue as to the power of imagery to generate moral reflection and to capture moral conflict as it is most truly experienced; as a complex nexus of contradictory reasons passionately argued and emotions passionately felt. The sensorial qualities of symbolic imagery carry with them the necessary charge to convey this; and, in the words of Iris Murdoch: 'Metaphors often carry a moral charge which analysis in simpler and plainer terms is designed to remove' (1970, p. 77).

The meaning of this drama hinged upon the dramatic image which gave form to the Chief's recurring dream, used at the beginning of the third session. The image portrays the Chief, dressed in a smart suit, signing a contract for the sale of land and water and being handed money in dollar bills; then, as dreams do, the location shifts to the lake where he grew up, the contract now being used as an oar to steer him across the lake in a birchbark canoe. As he stoops to pick the lily, the words of a proverb taught him by his grandfather resound through his head:

> *Our people will live until the waters turn sour*
> *Until the land is scorched by the Sun*
> *And the Star Maiden loses sight of her sisters above.*

As the words fade, he crushes the lily and drops it into the lake, awakening in a sweat and covering his face with his hands.

Dreams are a common convention in non-naturalistic drama and O'Neill has shown how they can be used by practitioners of process drama.

> Words, actions and sounds in a dream can be patterned and distorted in a grotesque but highly significant manner. The dream also provides a strong temporal orientation — a reliving of a happy or painful past incident or a premonition of future happenings. (1995, p. 146)

The dream suggests a tension between the tribe's past and the Chief's desire to make a different future.[8] It also served the aesthetic function of placing symbol, and the interpretation of symbol, at the heart of the drama, thus creating a congruence with the poetic form of the original story and allowing for a dialogical interplay between their symbolisms. The ambivalence integral to these symbols provided a holding form with sufficient space to accommodate a polyphony of related meanings which the children could supply; and the fact that these meanings had moral connotations allowed the symbol to carry a moral charge, as defined by Iris Murdoch. Semiotically the image signalled just such a moral conflict through somatic responses indicative of feelings associated with the discomfort of anguish, guilt and remorse. Finally, its unfinished, unexplained ambivalence had the appeal of a mystery, providing the impetus to engage the children's imaginative energies in the task of interpreting its meaning. Ambivalence, described by Ushenko as 'a coprescence of contextually controllable and integral alternatives' is seen by the same theorist as the motor of the imagination, which he defines as 'the power to envisage, or visualize, ambivalence and ambiguity' (cited in Nowottny, 1962, p. 147). Given such a stimulus, the children's analysis of the dream image proved to be striking, not only as a demonstration of their ability to make moral sense of it but also for the complexity of moral meanings they could justifiably interpret from it. For this reason, I present their responses in detail below, slightly editing my contributions as teacher, followed by an interpretive commentary.

G 1:   Well, it's the contract, like, asking them for water lilies.

B 1:   Someone's asking for his land and he gives it to them.

T: Does he give it to them?

G 2:   No, he gives in and sells it.

G 3:   He thinks he's been a traitor to his people for selling the land.

B 2:   I think he's really selfish. The clothes are just for himself. And he sells the land without telling anybody else. He just sells it.

T: He sold the land where his people lived? Without telling them?

B 2:   They won't have anywhere to live because he sold the land.

T: Right, OK.

G 4:   He's fed up being poor and not having good places to live. He thinks, 'I'm fed up with all this, I need to do something better!' But, really, the better thing was wrong.

T: . . . What do you think he did, then?

G 4:   Well . . . he realized it was wrong.

G 1:   Well, the thing was, he crushed the water lily so afterwards, like, he realized what he had done and he was really mad with himself.

T: It's a dream, it's not necessarily anything he's done. What do you think this means? (*picks up the lily and crushes it. Hands shoot up*)

G 5:   It's the Star Maiden.

T: So what's he done to her?

Many: He's killed her.

T: Why do you think that's the last thing in his dream, when he wakes up he goes . . . ? (*covers his face with his hands*) What does it mean? What's it making him feel?

G 5:   Angry.

G 6:   Mad.

B 3:   Like someone's telling him off.

B 2:   I think that the water lily is like his land and he's crushed it when he's sold it, like he's got rid of it, just for himself.

. . .

B 4:   It's freedom, getting away from things . . . hard things . . . things like, living like tramps all around the place and not having good food.

T: . . . Does anyone think he might have sold the land not just for himself but he's still feeling bad about what he's done? . . . (*several hands go up*)

B 5:   He might feel, to help people cos he's got the money to make, like, the power to improve their lives, giving them water and things and stuff like that.

T: . . . So why might he still feel so bad about it?

B 1:   He may have fallen out with his people, with his tribe, then he took the land away from them. Now he knows what he's done and he can't give the land back to them.

> *G 1:*   I think he's done something bad to his people and without asking
> them what they wanted. But, like, he's just gone and made this
> decision and didn't ask them and he might have done the opposite
> to what they want.
>
> *B 4:*   He's betraying the Star Maidens cos he's leaving them.
>   . . .
> *B 6:*   I think that his grandparents said that their people would stay until
> the water's gone sour, like they'll keep on going until, like, it's all
> gone but he's changed that, by taking the land and water from them
> and giving it to someone else for money.
>
> *B 3:*   He's scared cos his grandma and grandad made a rule and he feels
> that he's breaking it.
>
> *G 6:*   I think he wants to sell the land because he knew his tribe were poor
> and probably he thought, like, because we're poor I should sell the
> land. But just because his people are poor, it doesn't mean that they
> don't want to live on this land.

It is to be emphasized that all of the children's comments were, and were understood to be, speculative, in the mode of 'perhaps', even though they often chose to express these speculations as substantive statements.

Immediately, the contract, a formal symbol of a social, moral code, is seen to be at the heart of the tension and the vice of moral cowardice, of giving in, is offered to account for the Chief's discomfort. Girl 3 sees it as deeper than this; the Chief has betrayed his people and failed in his obligations as their leader. Boy 2 detects selfishness in the contrast between the Chief's own display of wealth and his people's poverty; and also in his despotic action and aggressive individualism. His crime, in this boy's eyes, is to be incriminated in the dispossession and resulting homelessness of his community. Girl 4 is the first to describe a motive for the Chief's action but sees his own desire for personal betterment as unjustifiable, sensing that a subsequent realization of this has caused his sense of remorse.

The Chief's crushing of the water lily is first interpreted as a projected act of aggressive destruction, directed really at himself but is then seen very lucidly by Boy 2 as entirely symbolic. It is interesting that the children's responses throughout show that they understand the feelings associated with guilt but never articulate it as a concept. It is sensed in the Chief's body language, as the anger which expresses the shame and frustration that a child can experience when scolded by an adult; hence the Freudian depiction of guilt here, which envisions a parental figure censuring the Chief. Boy 4 expresses with some sensitivity an understanding of the harshness of life on the reservation and sees that the money could be used to buy freedom, which he defines in economic terms. There is a swift response when the Teacher suggests that there might be a possible altruistic explanation for the Chief's act. This is voiced by Boy 5 and recognizes that the Chief could have been acting in the economic interest of his tribe. Boy 1 speculates that it might, in fact, have been a vindictive action, regretted after the event, while Girl 1 passes judgment on the Chief's qualities of leadership. Boy 4 returns to the concept of treachery, this time evoked through the symbol of the Star Maiden while Boy 3 sees the fact that the Chief's grandparents uttered the proverb as particularly significant. This, to him, gives it the status of a rule and suggests that the ties of kinship are significant but have been disrupted. Finally, Girl 6 gives a very concise and balanced appreciation of the fact that this could be a story of a conflict between economic interests, as defined by a leader, and the historical and cultural attachments of the people he is trying to serve.

The image itself was 'imposed' by the teacher but its meaning was not; and the children's interpretations were so many possible stories, speculative and communal, clustering around a variety of *thick concepts* and evoking a number of interweaving moral themes. The children could see stories of cowardice, of treachery, vindictiveness, tyranny, and unjust dispossession. They could also see the story of a clash between economic and cultural forces, of stability and change, of well-intentioned but flawed leadership. This latter point illustrates MacIntyre's argument: that it was within the Chief's social role as leader that children identified his moral function — to do right by his people and uphold the traditions of the tribe. They articulated this by suggesting different narratives to explain the dream which, to use Louis Arnaud Reid's term, were *apprehended* rather than comprehended from the resonance of the symbolism (Reed, 1980). J.H. van der Hoop has described symbols as:

> the chief means by which the human mind expresses not so much those ideas which it has outgrown, or wishes to conceal, but those which it has not yet mastered. (cited in Nowottny, 1962, p. 174)

To rephrase this insight speculatively, perhaps it is through symbolism that children can appreciate and learn to express ideas they have not yet mastered. With this in mind, it is worth examining how the children made dramatic use of the starflower — the symbol linking our improvised story dialogically with the original — as an aid to making moral sense of the drama.

The starflowers the children made were of tissue paper. Like a real water lily, they were pretty but fragile. The ritual of bringing them into the hall and laying them on the paper at the start of each of the final two sessions was a physical reminder of this and of the story's closing words. 'Touch them gently.' I had, in fact, made my own starflower and had placed it on the 'lake' but not all of the children realized this. So when I picked it up and crushed it, the effect was marked as the metaxis was so acute. Here was I, a teacher, destroying something, perhaps the work of a child in the class. The fictional act of destruction was represented by a real act of destruction and the children's faces initially registered shock; for not only had the moral of the initial story been contravened but so, they felt — for an instant — had the moral code of the classroom.[9] Comments in the transcript above reveal the extent to which, on the fictional level, the children were able to identify this act of destruction as a symbolic act of violence against the Star Maiden, against the land where the Chief's people lived and, by analogy, against their values and beliefs. This, I believe, persisted in their minds as the moral touchstone throughout the rest of the drama. In the fourth session, when the Chief spoke in collective role with his grandfather, the following exchange took place:

Chief: You'll be breaking the Star Maiden's heart.
Gran: You're the one who'll break the Star Maiden's heart by selling the land.
Chief: Why?
Gran: Because she came here to settle and we let her in and now you're taking all that away from her. That is no longer her land and she is one of us.

This was echoed soon after in the scene where, in role as their Chief, I addressed the children as my people:

Boy: You sold the land. Get it back, or you are not an Indian, you're a city person.
Tchr: Are you saying I will not be one of you?
Boy: Yes.
Tchr: I'll always be one of you.
Girl: If you destroy our lake and the lilies in it, you are actually killing a person. Someone that we loved and she loved us.
Tchr: A person (*pointing to the lake*). But they aren't people, they're flowers.
Girl: Have you forgotten what they mean?
Tchr: What do they mean?
Girl: They're a star from the sky.
Tchr: But that's a story, it's just a story.
Girl: It isn't. Us Indians believe in it. If you are an Indian, you should, too.
Tchr: In the city, if you told them that story, they would say, 'It's a nice story.' If you said you believed it's true, they'd laugh at you.
Girl: Let them laugh. It's our beliefs.

The words of the girl in this exchange resonate with spiritual significance. At this moment in the drama, the Star Maiden and her story are defined as something sacred, as a symbol of the values and beliefs of a people and their betrayal by the Chief is seen as a betrayal of his own cultural identity. Once again we need to remember that such an understanding was perhaps not difficult for this Catholic child; for, if she could believe in reality that a wafer of bread could be transformed into the flesh of the Son of God then she could manage a fiction where to kill a lily was, indeed, to kill a person. This does not diminish the effectiveness of the dramatic symbolism but emphasizes that its power lay in its ability to activate and transform, through art, values which were already present within the participants.

Cultural Representation and Moral Interpretation

In a previous case study I argued that Heathcote's brotherhood code could be deployed by teacher-in-role to make simplistic moral meanings represented in archetypal characters more expansive. In this drama, matters were more complex as both characters were new creations and their meanings were built not from their representations within the text of the original story but by their dialogical relationship with the values it embodied and the symbols it contained. If the Grandfather was in the brotherhood of all those who are victims of prejudice and of economic 'progress' and of those who resist change, he was also in the brotherhood of those attached to historical values and traditions; who have faith in religious stories; who place spiritual values above material values. The Chief, on the other hand, was in the brotherhood of all those who embrace material values; who believe they have the understanding to act in the best interest of others. He was also in the brotherhood of those who reject the beliefs upon which they were raised; who compromise their cultural identities; who embrace material values at the expense of spiritual values.

My intention was to create these characters as historicized, non-mythic figures, with the Grandfather and the Chief finding each other on opposing sides when encountering the historical forces of cultural and economic change. This would, I hoped, work against the flawed image of the noble savage and engage children, in role as members of the tribe, with a genuinely historicized moral conflict. The final confrontation between Chief and tribe would become the scene in which this conflict would be articulated. It was, and it was powerful, but not in the manner I had intended and it is debatable as to how far the drama became historicized in any real sense.

When introducing the Grandfather into the drama I used the convention of the spoken stage direction, focusing carefully on each item of costume before I put it on.

> This hat is an old hat, white with age. The grandfather can't afford another. He needs this hat to protect his head against the rain. It is not an Indian hat but he uses it. . . . A blanket, woven by his wife, many years ago. A traditional Indian blanket which keeps him warm in winter. . . . A stick. He's old, not as strong as he once was.

These descriptions emphasized the status of the old man as victim and the items of costume acted as deictic signifiers of this fact throughout his appearance. The fact that he represented a world under threat was reinforced by his speech. I spoke in short, simple sentences, similar to those of the Esbensen text, echoing its nostalgic tones and the cultural references evoked through its rhythms.

> People in the city, they are not at peace. They shout, they move too fast, they
> appear to me to be angry. My people used to like to sit in the sun, to listen
> to the sounds of the natural world, to live by running waters.

On reflection, these examples reveal the danger of replacing one sentimental-
ized, cultural stereotype — the noble savage — with another — the equally
noble and wise, old Indian. If the hat and the blanket were meant to historicize
the old man then they did so in a very imprecise way. They were not chosen
from any knowledge I had of the modern Ojibway tribe but were drawn from
cultural representations of Native American people I could recall from documentary and film and were used primarily for functional reasons. The bowler
hat, in particular, could be artfully contrasted with a newer, smarter version
worn later by the Chief, bearing the different connotations of a city businessman. There was a tension, therefore, between artistic efficiency and cultural
accuracy and I was cavalier in my approach to the latter for the sake of the
former. If the two men were represented with a lack of historical and geo-
graphical precision then so, too, was the conflict they evoked. This was an
entirely fictional representation, drawn from a knowledge that there exist in
Canada and the USA Native Americans who have become millionaires from
running gambling casinos on their reservations, as well as those who continue
to suffer poverty from their historical dispossession.

In my defence, I can argue that my aim was not precise, historical accuracy but the representation through dramatic fiction of an historically plausible
moral conflict, using those resources I could best muster. If the drama lacked
a certain kind of truthfulness based upon cultural specificity, it was, perhaps,
specific enough for these children, thousands of miles away and in another
culture. Nevertheless, the extent to which the children were able to appreciate
this conflict remains debatable; and if, as I have argued, the moral power of the
story's symbolism can be largely explained by its Christian analogies, we need
to view the nature of any moral learning which took place within this final
session not only from within the form of the drama but from within the boundaries of the children's own cultural identities.

The old man may have become a cultural stereotype, verging on the
mythic, but despite this — or possibly because of it — he proved to be a very
efficient dramatic creation.[10] When given the chance to hot-seat him, the children were quick to convey their sympathy in questions which denoted a moral
standpoint as well as a sense of emotional connectedness.

> *'Do you think people ignore you because of your colour?'*
> *'Apart from your grandson, is there any other family you could turn to?'*
> *'Since he's been in the city, do you feel alone?'*
> *'How do you feel about the way you live, like in shacks?'*
> *'How do you feel now that the land's been taken away from you?'*

These questions reveal sympathy for the Grandfather as a victim of racism,
loneliness, poverty and dispossession, sympathies aroused by the visual and

sensorial qualities of his embodiment as much as by the sense of the words he spoke. Stereotype he may have been, but he was nonetheless a clear poetic symbol, containing a powerful, moral charge. For what intrigued the children most of all when questioning the old man, was the conflict between grandfather and grandson. In particular, their kinship took on symbolic importance as it deepened their sense of treachery.

> '*Do you feel angry because your grandson has betrayed you?*'
> '*Do you still count him as a Native American?*'

The grandfather was seen as a victim in the same sense as was the Star Maiden and the children evidently *did* understand that he embodied a whole set of values at odds with those being represented by the Chief. As his grandfather, I offered some sympathy for the Chief's actions when they questioned me about them:

> 'You think he has betrayed us by selling the land? He is my grandson. I am sure what he does he does because he thinks it is good for us.'
> 'In his dreams he will always be one of us, though in his life he may try to pretend not.'

However, when they met him, the Chief failed to win their sympathies in the way the grandfather had done.

When addressing the tribe as Chief, I spoke briskly, confidently, authoritatively but passionately and with conviction. I was respectful, listened and found numerous ways to project my argument. I admitted to being saddened by their accusations of betrayal and conveyed, through gesture, feelings which echoed the remorse and inner conflict the children had witnessed in the dream. None of this was enough to move the children from a position of hostility and an unshifting expression of support for the values represented in the figure of the old man and in the symbol of the Star Maiden. As the Chief's arguments in favour of a hospital, new housing, jobs and better prospects for the young fall on deaf ears time and time again, the words of the children in role carry echoes of those used earlier by the Grandfather; references to ancestors and to a love of the land resonate throughout as the children in role pass judgment on the Chief, condemning him as a destroyer of tradition and as an outcast of his tribe.

> '*We've lived here for centuries. Now everything is going to be demolished*'
> '*At the end of the story it says remember and you're not remembering any of it. You're just destroying the Star Maiden*'
> *You say you want to be one of us all the time. But you're not, because you're doing things all wrong*'
> '*You sold the land. Get it back or you're not an Indian.*'

It is obvious, on reflection, that there was a dramatic imbalance in favour of the Grandfather's position. Not only was he cast in the powerfully sympathetic role as victim but, as guardian of the Star Maiden, he was an embodiment of the values which I had spent so much pedagogical energy in cultivating, through drama and through ritual. The Chief, on the other hand, had been seen to destroy a starflower, the moral touchstone of the drama. As a dramatic creation, he may have been more than a cultural stereotype but I singularly failed to arouse any sympathy for his dilemma. Consequently, the climax which was meant to engage the children in history rather than myth, however contentious this version of history might have been, failed to do so.

Perhaps the children were too young to sympathize with the moral conflict of the Chief, although in an earlier part of the drama one boy at least had shown some appreciation of his motives and could feel for his dilemma. When analysing an image created by a group of girls showing the Chief being coerced by businessmen to sign the contract, he had suggested that the Chief was thinking 'Whatever I do, it's wrong.' When pressed, he explained that the tribe would be happy if the Chief did not sell the land but without the money he couldn't help his people. This was a sensitive dramatic insight, casting the Chief in the role of tragic agent. 'The tragic agent', writes Martha Nussbaum, 'senses that no matter how he chooses he will be left with some regret that he did not do the other thing' (1986, p. 27).

However, this understanding was not at all general. I had assumed that the children would have no problem in understanding his altruistic concerns for the material needs of his tribe but one boy's comments at the end of the session were revealing. '*Well,*' he said, '*the ideas about the hospitals and the houses were good but we still like the land the way it used to be.*' For him, myth in this drama had clearly triumphed over history and, in his imagination, he was living more in this mythical past than on the present day reservation. On reflection, this is hardly surprising; the idyllic life portrayed in the images of the book and celebrated in the dance was a far more appealing, utopian vision for a 10 year-old to linger in than the Chief's promised world of hospitals, houses and schools. The dialogue in the final scene, however, indicates that there was a further, perhaps more significant undercurrent running in favour of the myth and this was further emphasized in the discussion after the drama. '*What's more important than money?*' I asked and a girl replied '*Their stories, because the Star Maiden story is like a symbol of their life, cos that's what you believe in. You've got to stick up for what you believe in.*' Such an insight, I would hazard, did not emanate from the drama alone but primarily from this child's understanding of her own religious faith. The achievement of the drama was to help her articulate an appreciation that people of cultures other than her own might feel the same way about their beliefs as she did about hers.

If previous examples have shown that the children's own moral and spiritual values had helped them engage deeply with the drama, here they can be seen to have informed the moral meanings it constructed. And the collective moral statement which resulted was a powerful one, consisting of a strong affirmation of the moral and spiritual values central to Esbensen's tale. In being presented with a version of a myth more analogous to their own than to Ojibway mythology, the children could nonetheless learn and articulate respect for cultural difference; and this illustrates the self-other continuum, referred to in Chapter 5, at the heart of drama's potential for moral learning.[11] It was the world of otherness which activated and stretched the children's own moral resources into a dramatic statement which became an example of iconic rather than dialectic action. The minds of the children were not changed and their responses reveal an affirmation of belief rather than a change in belief; but in this affirmation there lay the possibility of cathartic illumination, for developing what Nussbaum has defined as: 'a richer self-understanding concerning the attachments and values that support the responses' (1986, p. 388).

Conclusion

Rustom Bharucha has been largely responsible for bringing arguments concerning the politics of cultural representation into the arena of modern performance studies and, in doing so, has mounted a strong attack on Peter Brook's production of the *Mahabharata*. What western critics acclaimed as a triumph of inter-cultural performance, celebrating a masterpiece hitherto neglected by Eurocentric, global culture, Bharucha denounces as a continuation of British economic misappropriation of India's cultural resources. From his own cultural perspective, he mounts a sharp and astute analysis of what he sees as the conceptual and performative shortcomings of Brook's adaptation, which he sees as exemplifying:

> . . . a particular kind of western representation which negates the non-western context of its borrowing. Brook has not grown up with the epic in his childhood, unlike most Indians, who have internalized the *Mahabharata* through a torrent of emotions, thoughts, taboos, concepts and fantasies. (1993, p. 70)

If the internalization of the *Mahabharata*'s spiritual concepts and values is what renders it comprehensible to those who have grown up with it in the Hindu faith, any western director must, Bharucha argues, confront the meanings of such an elusive text within its own cultural context. He hints that Brook found this impossible and suggests that, instead of misrepresenting 'other' cultures, he should: '. . . focus attention on his own cultural artefacts, the epics of western civilization like the *Iliad* or the *Odyssey*, which he is more likely to understand' (op. cit., p. 70).

Bharucha's criticisms of Brook should act as a tart warning to anyone wishing to use stories from other cultures for dramatic purposes and are very much in line with the criticisms of Miraclee and Atwood, voiced earlier. My attempts to dialogize the story of *The Star Maiden* in order to address some of the problems of cultural representation were, in accordance with Bharucha's arguments, bound to fail. The drama did not attempt to strip the tale of Christian analogies in order to gain an understanding of the story's real significance for its original tellers, the Ojibway people. Here there remained a deep and obscure heart of darkness. Without meaning to, I did quite the opposite; I harnessed and enhanced the Christian symbolism and the moral meanings imposed by Copway and Esbensen respectively.

Moreover, in the teeth of a perspective which must regard this as cultural misappropriation, I have argued that these cultural accretions were what provided the story and the drama with moral and symbolic power for these particular children. My aims to historicize the story through drama were possibly misconceived and certainly did not work; and a member of the Ojibway people may well have found them deeply insulting. On the other hand, like the values within the Esbensen text, they were of ethical importance to our contemporary world and it encouraged the children to articulate attitudes of non-racism, stewardship and respect for the beliefs of others.

In the final analysis, I am happy to argue that this, at least, should not be offensive to right-minded people; and if this constitutes the judgment and aspiration of one of Atwood's 'well-meaning liberals', so be it. To paraphrase Inglis, liberalism need not be a swear-word. It may be as much a powerful source for good and positive action as it may be a deceptively complacent pervasion of the spirit. And so too, I suggest, were the story and the drama of *The Star Maiden.*

Notes

1 Although there is currently some doubt as to whether Chief Seattle ever delivered the speech for which he has become famous, its influence persists. See, for example, the resource pack published by the United Society for the Propagation of the Gospel (1984).

2 Sally Hunter, a professor of Children's Literature who lives in St. Paul, USA, insists that there is no Eden-like story in Ojibway mythology. I am grateful for Barbara Juster Esbensen for this information.

3 Op. cit., p. viii, where he specifically addresses the preface of his book 'To the Christian and the Philanthropist'.

4 Copway openly declares his love for English literature and, on p. viii of his preface, indicates his admiration for the literary styles of Irving and Macauley.

5 This was taken from the teaching pack *Indians and Pioneers*, 2D Publications.

6 I have since developed this dance in workshops with students and teachers. A teacher whom I greatly respect voiced his doubts about it, suggesting that the movements and music amounted to a form of insulting, cultural tokenism. The problem of cultural representation will become a major theme of this case study but, in this case, I remain unconvinced that there is an argument to answer. The dance was illustrative of the story and did not purport in any way to emulate how the Ojibway might themselves have danced or represented the story. If the objection

is essentially to *any* form of working with the story, it is an issue I address in the conclusion.

7   This paradoxical capacity for art to make us feel emotion through achieving distance from its object was briefly discussed and referred to in Chapter 5. O'Toole (1992, p. 110) defines those tasks where participants work as artists as those which achieve maximum role distance.

8   This is a reference, of course, to Suzanne Langer's phrase where people in drama are defined as 'makers of the future'. See Langer, 1953, p. 307.

9   For another example of how a simple, destructive act in drama can attain strong, moral significance, see the earlier case study on the tale of *The Brahmin and the Thief.*

10 Stafford and Branston (1996, p. 90) make the point that, although the word stereotype tends to always carry pejorative associations, a stereotypical representation need not, per se, have negative effects. They define stereotyping as a 'process of categorization necessary to make sense of the world'.

11 See Appendix 3, where children illustrate their work with iconic references from their own religion.

Conclusion

The issues which have driven this study are being increasingly recognized as significant. I have already referred to work by Baird Saenger (1993) and Zipes (1996) in the United States and, in Britain, recent publications by Murris (1992) and the Citizenship Foundation (Rowe and Newton, 1994) show concerns and approaches which are illuminating in the ways they reflect and diverge from the arguments developed over the previous chapters (see also Fox, 1996). Both British projects are aimed at primary schools and are presented as teachers' packs, with stories as their central resource. Murris, in particular, is openly indebted to the work of Lipman (1980, 1988) and the *Philosophy in Schools Project* he inspired. As such, moral philosophy is one of its major concerns and its pedagogy is almost entirely centred on classroom discussion aimed at encouraging children to move from the particularity of the stories into a consideration of 'the universal laws that govern our thinking' (Murris, 1992, p. 10). She comments:

> A philosophical discussion can start off with personal, emotional experiences, but should move on quickly to get to the more general rules about how people should behave — rules resulting from an enquiry based on reason. (ibid., p. 10)

So, for example, in work related to Sendak's *Where the Wild Things Are*, children are questioned about issues relating to *Mischief, Manners* and *Punishment* and asked to consider, for instance, whether wolves are bad, whether they know the difference between good and bad and to postulate on different meanings of the word 'bad'. The emphasis it puts on rules, universal laws and objective rationality are clearly distinctive from my own work.

The Citizenship Foundation's publication entitled *You, Me, Us* is a major government initiative, sponsored by the Home Office and specifically aimed at developing social and moral responsibility in primary schools. For this reason it merits rather more detailed attention. It, too, adopts moral reasoning as its chief pedagogical approach to understanding the issues raised by the stories it offers. Whereas Murris makes use of published picture books, including many in the fairy tale tradition, *You, Me, Us* uses tales in a variety of genres, all of which have been especially written for the pack. Once again, Lipman's influence is openly acknowledged and so, too, is the work of Kohlberg. In fact, the rationale provided in the teachers' notes identifies five progressive stages entirely dependent upon Kohlberg's developmental categories and great stress is laid upon the kind of reasons children offer in support of their beliefs, with teachers being urged to:

> pick up on the higher or more aware thinking and subtly reinforce it by offering it back to the group for further consideration. (Rowe and Newton, 1994, p. 9)

This strategy is the one proposed by Kohlberg for encouraging children to move on to a higher stage of moral reasoning. A clear distinction is made between the cognitive and affective sides of moral awareness, with the ability to care for others and empathize with them being identified as 'another important factor' which has an influence on people's moral actions (ibid., p. 10).[1] Universal moral principles (or *Golden Rules*, as they are referred to) underlie teaching modules such as those on *Rules* and *Property and Power* and the stories provided in each section have clear, didactic purposes, similar to those provided in Assembly books. So, for example, the module on *Property and Power* includes a school story entitled *A Lucky Break* intended to provoke a discussion into the reasons why stealing is wrong.

The *You, Me, Us* material is engaging and very well-targeted, with interesting and varied pedagogical approaches to supplement the classroom discussion. Its intentions are unlike my own, however, inasmuch as its stories have clearly focused, predetermined moral agendas aimed at encouraging a particular pattern of social and moral behaviour. This didacticism is also apparent in its suggestions for drama work. Whereas Murris' ideas for drama are in the manner of diversions, with little relevance to the philosophical or moral agenda being pursued in the discussion work, the *You, Me, Us* pack makes use of drama to reinforce its didactic intentions. Having worked on the story *A Lucky Break*, for example, children are asked to make up a play to show the possible effects, both mental and physical, of stealing on a victim (op. cit., p. 136). More sustained role plays are suggested, such as an entire module where children are to pretend they have been shipwrecked and are required to invent the rules for their new society and deal with a series of moral and social dilemmas which subsequently arise (op. cit., pp. 90–96). Here, the intention is clearly to teach children about the need for social rules and the workings of democracy.

There are, therefore, some fundamental differences in approach between the *You, Me, Us* material and the the work described in this study. I have been sceptical of stories being used for simple didactic purposes and have deliberately worked with a genre of story where moral values are often obfuscated or contradictory. I see drama, its potency and its effectiveness, as ambiguous, at times risky, and regard the whole area of understanding and working with values as at once inescapable but deeply problematic. In addition, the philosophical base from which I argue a view of moral education is in the broader area of neo-Aristotelian ethics rather than the post-Kantian morality system.

It is important, therefore, to consider how such an approach might inform a primary school's moral education policy and the key, I believe, lies in relating two principles paradoxically at the heart of the *You, Me, Us* project — that of encouraging moral enquiry while building community — with the philosophical premises promoted by Williams (1985) and MacIntyre (1981). Essentially this would involve schools consciously regarding themselves as communities which attempt to define, promote and enquire into the virtues.

I am aware as I propose the idea of schools as 'communities of virtue' that, as Williams points out, such language today has an air of reactionary 'priggishness' about it and that it is liable to be misapprehended. At first glance, it might appear to aspire to the views of William Bennett, whose recent publication *The Book of Virtues* (1993) seeks to teach children what he defines as 'moral literacy' through a selection of stories from the western historical and literary canon intended to inculcate a fixed list of virtues. Stories such as Horatio's defence of the bridge are offered alongside passages such as Baden Powell's *The Duties of a Scout* as definitions of a prescribed set of virtues, in this case those of Courage and Duty (op. cit., p. 217, p. 470). 'The purpose of this book', Bennett writes: 'is to show parents, teachers, students and children what the virtues look like, what they are in practice, how to recognize them and how they work' (1993, p. 11). They are, therefore, a fixed moral code, embodied in the cultural heritage of the western tradition and schools are strongly criticized for failing to teach them.[2] This is very much the same tone and perspective I problematized in my introductory chapter. MacIntyre's perspective, which informs my own views, is different. Virtues exist and are defined by the communities which practise them. They are, indeed, understood as part of a tradition which these communities inherit but they are only vigorous when their nature and their relationship to one another are the source of argument and debate. Defining the virtues — and hence the good life — is a struggle and different communities in history have recognized and cultivated different virtues in different ways. The virtues exist factually, as Williams points out, inasmuch as we share a common vocabulary through which we can negotiate our understanding of them. These thick concepts are the vocabulary of ethics but if they are encapsulated within traditions and the stories which are part of these traditions, then we must understand the concept of tradition as an argument, an evolving conversation to help create the future, not as a set of rigid principles to which we must conform. Being located within history is not the same as being its slave.

The concept of community is, however, like most of the concepts debated in this study, complex and problematic. In a simple sense, my community is one of place, and equates with my neighbourhood or my local area. But it might also be determined by my work. As a drama teacher, I might regard the teachers with whom I work as my immediate professional community and those other drama teachers who share common interests and beliefs as my extended professional community. There are also family communities, ethnic communities, religious communities and other communities of shared interests, whether political or cultural in nature. Overarching all of these, is the western community of liberal capitalism. I belong to several of these communities at once. Some I choose, some I inherit, each with its own perspectives on particular virtues which can come into opposition with one another.

Many teachers understand, for example, the conflicts that can exist between the family and the professional community and the difficulties involved in attempting to be a good parent and a good professional at one and the same time. The school is the forum where different communities of interest meet and one of its fundamental challenges is to forge itself into an institution conscious of its role as a community where certain agreed virtues are cultivated and learned. In fact, in an era when communities of family, work and place are increasingly unstable, the school remains one of the fixed, communal spaces where this cultivation can be trusted to take place.

There is nothing new or revolutionary in this idea. Williams identifies that the cultivation of the virtues, whether this terminology be used or not, has long been an aim of moral education, socialization and education in general (1985, p. 10). In fact, schools must of necessity define and promote particular virtues such as industry, responsibility, honesty and respect for others and draw up either implicit or explicit rule systems to encourage conformity to them. As Sullivan has explained:

> The school is now, and has always been, an institution immersed in values.
> In fact, it legitimates current societal values and consolidates them for a new generation. If we are facing a value crisis . . . it is a crisis of legitimacy of the values that our culture holds. (Modgil, 1985, p. 239)

This latter point underlines the difficulties that schools face but values nonetheless remain an area they cannot avoid. The language of the virtues is a common language, however, and can be used to negotiate meaning. The virtues present us with a perspective which sees moral values as *neither* absolute and prescribed *nor* relative and negotiated. Such a perspective recognizes that communities share common values; that truthfulness, honesty and justice, for example, are common virtues but that understanding their nature in practice may well vary from communal context to communal context. Issues of how and which virtues are to be recognized and encouraged within a particular school emerge from argument and discussion, to be agreed and defined in policy and aims statements which evolve and are subject to review, taking account of the needs and interests of the different communities the school serves.

Mechanisms for such procedures already exist in UK schools. This process aspires to create the moral ethos of a school which serves, as we have seen, to *initiate* children into moral knowledge. Such knowledge, however, as Stenhouse informs us, is only one aspect of learning and for a full moral education children need, in addition, training, instruction and *induction* into moral knowledge. All four aspects are important, all have different emphases and a school should map out in its policy documentation in which areas of the curriculum the different emphases will occur.

I have indicated that, in its emphasis on group cooperation, on listening, sharing and respecting the work of others, as well as through the opportunities drama provides for children to fictionally practise the virtues, that drama can make an important contribution to the social and moral training of young children. But the main preoccupations of this study have been in the more problematic area of *induction* to moral knowledge and the opportunities drama can offer for enabling children to explore the nature of the virtues and vices as thick concepts, manifested in particular social actions, played out within particular social roles. If stories are the means by which we learn hermeneutically about the virtues, vices and the nature of the moral life, we have seen, too, that, as teachers, we need to remain alert to exactly *what* they are telling us. Drama can be the means through which these values are opened up to question and are actively conversed with through enactive, narrative story-making. Hornbrook is right when he argues that drama's collective, moral discourse does not stem from 'the private preferences of emotivism' but is located upon the 'stage of critical judgment' (Hornbrook, 1989, p. 139). Through drama, the classroom can become this communal, public stage where the virtues can be problematized, played with, subverted, reframed, or brought into conflict with one another. Through generating moral engagement and active inquiry, drama can deepen a child's sensitivity to and understanding of the complexities of the moral life.

To advocate that teachers mine the rich seam of traditional stories from within a variety of cultural sources is, of course, partly an ethical response to the reality of postmodern, global culture and the ethnic and cultural diversity within contemporary Britain. But it is more than this. The project began with a pragmatic observation — that dramas using such stories as pre-text could contain a powerful, moral charge. In the process of the inquiry, I have suggested some theoretical explanation as to why this should be the case but, at its conclusion, I remain aware that these suggestions remain partial and incomplete. I have only touched upon what O'Neill describes as the close relationship between characters and plots within mythic stories and those within drama, and this remains an area, I believe, worthy of further research. It is in the nature of a reflective inquiry such as this that further questions should be raised, further lines of inquiry suggested. In turning my attention to what I consider these might be, I will attempt to address the different parties whom I hoped would benefit from this research at its outset; practitioners and academics, interested in drama, traditional stories, moral education and reflective inquiry.

It could be of use to primary teachers in general to research into ways in which the material compiled by the Citizenship Foundation could be supplemented to engage children in the kind of drama and moral learning experiences I have promoted here. For example, the key ideas in the unit on *Property and Power* are listed as *stealing, trust, punishment* and *fairness*, all of which pertain to the drama work pursued around the stories of the *Brahmin, the Thief and the Ogre* and *Jack and the Beanstalk*. The appeal of such a project is that it would be informed by material which practising primary teachers have found useful, covering concepts which have proved to be relevant to children's moral lives. Such an inquiry could include a broader investigation into the kinds of thick ethical concepts children find it rewarding to explore at different ages and in different social circumstances. These should spread beyond those concerned with the development of good citizenship and could include courage, loyalty and compassion as well as stewardship, tolerance and fairness. The intention would not, of course, be to create an alternative stage system to Kohlberg's but a loose framework informed by professional experience, evaluation and reflection. It would be valuable, as well as exploring new resources of stories which teachers might find useful, to look at those that are already in widespread use and build them into such a project.

This work, aimed at primary teachers in general, could be complemented by related inquiries of interest to specialist practitioners of drama. Throughout the study, I have ventured a number of hypotheses which could be taken further. For example, in the first case study I used a framework of six categories where drama could be seen to provide a pedagogy for ethical inquiry; in Chapter 5 I proposed that Beckerman's distinctions between iconic and dialectic action could provide a non-ideological approach to understanding moral engagement in drama; and, although venturing into the area of comedy, I emphasized that this remains a greatly underresearched area in the field of process drama. All three areas could become foci for more extensive research, particularly with primary school children more experienced in the practices of the art form, or with older children or students, whose concerns have not impinged at all on this particular inquiry.

In suggesting that MacIntyre's theories present a valuable and fresh perspective from which drama teachers can plan for moral education, I have implied a certain theoretical position. The principle underlying this position recognizes the virtues as inherently social and communal and that it is open to argument as to how they are best manifested in particular contexts. Children should, by implication, be encouraged to explore the virtues and the vices in action from within specific social roles — those of a mother, a leader, or a journalist, for example — in order to understand them as thick concepts, not as abstract principles. Such explorations should embrace ambivalence and avoid didacticism, not only because drama derives its power from such ambivalence but because this matches the ethical life as it is experienced at its most acute. As stories are the form through which this understanding is most effectively conveyed, drama should approach moral issues obliquely, through stories, rather than directly, through overtly issue-based lessons. Dramas of this sort should allow children to linger in the complexities of particular situations and not seek to draw out prescribed maxims or rules as lessons which the drama has taught; rather should such stories illustrate that, in situations where right and wrong answers are elusive, there can still be better or worse ways of living one's life. However, this theory is not offered in any instructional sense but as a testing ground which has emerged from my own theory in practice, a skeleton in need of flesh which can only be nourished by further research *into* practice.

Throughout this inquiry, in issues of theory and practice, form and content, values have been problematically but unavoidably at the heart of things. The model of reflective practitioner research I have provided was adapted to my own particular circumstances within the demands of a specific focus of inquiry. It may prove useful in informing the thinking of fellow practitioner-researchers through the methodology it offers but, more significantly, through its underlying principles and ethical concerns. Fundamentally, these accept the inescapability of values but refuse to be paralysed by their ubiquity or blind to their plurality. Rather both research and practice are portrayed as activities where we must embrace what Scheffler has called a 'double consciousness . . . resoluteness under uncertainty', an attitude prepared for 'the redirection of such resoluteness with changing evidence' (1985, pp. 114, 115). Such an attitude recognizes that, although grand theory may no longer be the objective of our inquiries, *phronesis*, or practical wisdom, remains our goal; and that, although we can only ever partially obtain it, the knowledge we gain while searching can sustain us on our quest.

Notes

1   Interestingly, Lipman's writings reject both moral developmental stage theory, which he sees as 'incompatible with philosophy and legitimate moral discussion' and the separation of the affective and cognitive in moral education, which, he comments, is 'to misunderstand the nature of learning'. See Lipman et al. (1980), p. 154 and p. 162.
2   Bennett has written two books to this effect: *Our Children and Our Country: Improving America's Schools and Affirming the Common Culture*; and *The De-Valuing of America: The Fight for Our Culture and Our Children*.

Bibliography

Sources

COPWAY, G. (1978) 'The Star and the Lily', in *Indian Life and Indian History*, New York: AMS.

CROSSLEY-HOLLAND, K. (1987) 'Jack and the Beanstalk', in *British Folk Tales*, London: Orchard.

EDENS, C. (1990) *Jack and the Beanstalk*, California: Green Tiger Press Inc.

EDGERTON, F. (1965) 'Brahmin, Thief and Ogre', in *Panchatantra*, New Delhi: Orient Paperbacks.

ESBENSEN, B.J. (1988) *The Star Maiden*, London: Little Brown.

EURIPIDES (1974) *Hippolytos*, BAGG, R. (transl), London: Oxford University Press.

JACOBS, J. (1993) 'Jack and the Beanstalk', in *English Fairy Tales*, London: Everyman.

SAKI (1986) 'The Storyteller' in *The Complete Saki*, London: Penguin.

TABART, B. (1974) 'Jack and the Beanstalk', in *The Classic Fairy Tales*, OPIE I. and P. (ed), Oxford: Oxford University Press.

THOMAS, V. (1992) 'The Brahmin, the Thief and the Ogre' from *More Stories from the Panchatantra*, New Delhi: Hemkunt Press.

WALKER, L.J. (1961) 'The Star Maiden' in *Red Indian Legends: Tribal Tales of the Great Lakes*, Long Acre, London: Odhams Press Ltd.

WERTENBAKER, T. (1989) *The Love of the Nightingale*, London: Faber and Faber.

Playtexts

AESCHYLUS (1988) *The Oresteian Trilogy*, VELLACOTT, P. (transl), London: Penguin.

ANOUILH, J. (1951) *Antigone*, GALANTIERE, L. (transl), London: Methuen.

BOND, E. (1979) *The Woman*, London: Methuen.

BRECHT, B. (1963) *The Caucasian Chalk Circle*, STERN, J. and T. (transl), London: Methuen.

BRECHT, B. (1967) *Mother Courage and her Children*, BENTLEY, E. (transl), London: Methuen.

BRECHT, B. (1974) *The Good Person of Setzuan*, WILLETT, J. (transl), London: Eyre Methuen.

BRECHT, B. (1980) *Life of Galileo*, WILLETT, J. (transl), London: Eyre Methuen.

CHURCHILL, C. (1990) 'Top Girls', in *Plays: Two*, London: Methuen.

CHURCHILL, C. (1990) *A Mouthful of Birds*, London: Methuen.

EURIPIDES (1972) *Electra*, VELLACOTT, P. (transl), Harmondsworth: Penguin.

EURIPIDES (1973) 'The Trojan Women', in *The Bacchae and Other Plays*, VELLACOTT, P. (transl), London: Penguin.

Fo, D. and RAME, F. (1992) *Plays: One*, London: Methuen.

GIRAUDOUX, J. (1935) *La Guerre de Troie n'aura pas Lieu*, Paris: Bernard Grasset.

MOLIÈRE (1969) *Tartuffe*, Paris: Bordas.

SARTRE, J.-P. (1947) *Les Mouches*, Paris: Gallimard.

SHAKESPEARE, W. (1951) *Julius Caesar*, London: Harper Collins.

SHAKESPEARE, W. (1951) *Macbeth*, London: Harper Collins.

ZOLA, E. (1989) *Thérèse Raquin*, Bath: Absolute Classics.

Critical Texts

ADELMAN, C. and JENKINS, D. (1976) 'Re-thinking Case Study: Notes from the Cambridge Conference', *Cambridge Journal of Education*, vol. 6, no. 3.

AHLBERG, A. (1984) *Please Mrs Butler*, London: Penguin.

ARIES, P. (1979) *Centuries of Childhood*, Bungay, Suffolk, UK: Peregrine.

ARNAUD REID, L. (1980) 'Meaning in the Arts', in *The Arts and Personal Growth*, Oxford: Pergamon.

ARTAUD, A. (1964) *Le Théâtre et son Double*, Saint-Amand (cher): Gallimard.

ARTS COUNCIL OF GREAT BRITAIN (1992) *Drama in Schools — Arts Council Guidance on Drama Education*, London: ACGB.

AVERILL, J.R. (1985) 'The Social Construction of Emotion: With Special Reference to Love', in *The Social Construction of the Person*, GERGEN, K. and DAVIS, K. (ed), New York: Springer.

AXTELL, J. (1981) *The European and the Indian: Essays in the Ethnohistory of Colonial North America*, New York: Oxford University Press.

BAILEY, J. (1981) *Themework*, London: Stainer and Bell.

BAIRD SAENGER, E. (1993) *Exploring Ethics Through Children's Literature*, Pacific Grove, California: Critical Thinking Press.

BARTHES, R. (1973) *Mythologies*, London: Granada.

BARTHES, R. (1977) *Image, Music, Text*, London: Fontana.

BBC (1996) *Today*, 6 July.

BECKERMAN, B. (1990) *Theatrical Presentation*, London: Routledge.

BENJAMIN, W. (1992) 'The Storyteller', in *Illuminations*, London: Fontana.

BENNETT, W.J. (1993) *The Book of Virtues: A Treasury of Great Moral Stories*, New York: Simon and Schuster.

BERNSTEIN, M.A. (1981) 'When the carnival turns bitter', in *Bakhtin: Essays and Dialogues on his Work*, MORSON, G.S. (ed), University of Chicago Press.

BERNSTEIN, R. (1976) *The Restructuring of Social and Political Theory*, Philadelphia: University of Philadelphia.

BEST, D. (1992) *The Rationality of Feeling*, London: Falmer.

BETTELHEIM, B. (1976) *The Uses of Enchantment: The Meaning and Importance of Fairy Tales*, London: Penguin.

BHARUCHA, R. (1993) *Theatre and the World*, London: Routledge.

BLOOM, A. (1987) *The Closing of the American Mind*, London: Penguin.

BLUM, L. (1993) 'Gilligan and Kohlberg: Implications for Moral Theory', in *An Ethic of Care*, LARRABEE, M.J. (ed), New York: Routledge.

BOAL, A. (1979) *Theatre of the Oppressed*, London: Pluto Press.

BOLTON, G. (1979) *Towards a Theory of Drama in Education*, Harlow, UK: Longman (Harlow, UK: Longman.)

BOLTON, G. (1984) *Drama as Education*, Harlow, UK: Longman.

BOLTON, G. (1992) *New Perspectives on Classroom Drama*, Hemel Hempstead, UK: Simon and Schuster.

BOND, E. (1995) 'A Blast at our Smug Theatre', *The Guardian*, 28 January 1995.

BOOTH, D. (1994) *Story Drama*, Ontario: Pembroke.

BRABECK, M. (1993) 'Moral Judgment: Theory and Research on Differences Between Males and Females', in *An Ethic of Care*, LARRABEE, M.J. (ed), New York: Routledge.

BRANSTON, G. and STAFFORD, R. (1996) *The Media Student's Handbook*, London: Routledge.

BRIGGS, R. (1973) *Jim and the Beanstalk*, London: Puffin Books.

BRODKIN, M. (1934) *Archetypal Patterns in Poetry: Psychological Studies of Imagination*, London: Oxford University Press.

BROOK, P. (1968) *The Empty Space*, London: Penguin.

BROOKER, P. (1988) *Bertolt Brecht: Dialectics, Poetry, Politics*, London: Croom Helm.

BROWNING, R. (1993) *The Pied Piper*, illustrations Andre Amstatz, London: Orchard.

BRUNER, J. (1960) 'Myth and Identity' in *Myth and Mythmaking*, MURRAY, H.A. (ed), Boston: Beacon Press.

BRUNER, J. (1986) *Actual Minds, Possible Worlds*, Cambridge, Massachusetts: Harvard University Press.

BRUNER, J. (1990) *Acts of Meaning*, Cambridge, Mass: Harvard University Press.

CADUTO, M. and BRUCHAC, B. (1988a) *Keepers of the Earth*, Colorado: Fulcrum Press.

CADUTO, M. and BRUCHAC, B. (1988b) *Keepers of the Earth: Teacher's Guide*, Colorado: Fulcrum Press.

CAMPBELL, J. (1949) *The Hero with a Thousand Faces*, Princeton, NJ: Princeton University Press.

CAREY, G. (1996) 'Morality is more than a matter of opinion', *The Daily Telegraph*, 5 July.

CARR, D. (1991) *Educating the Virtues*, London: Routledge.

CARR, W. (1986) 'Theories of Theory and Practice', in *Journal of Philosophy of Education*, vol. 20, no. 2.

CARR, W. (1987) 'What is an Educational Practice?', *Journal of Philosophy of Education*, vol. 21, no. 2.

CARR, W. and KEMMIS, S. (1986) *Becoming Critical*, London: Falmer Press.

CARROLL, J. (1996) 'Escaping the Information Abattoir: Critical and Transformative Research in Drama Classrooms', *Researching Drama and Arts Education*, TAYLOR, P. (ed), London: Falmer Press.

CHARNEY, M. (1978) *Comedy High and Low*, New York: Oxford University Press.

CODE, L. (1991) *What Can She Know? Feminist Theory and the Construction of Knowledge*, Ithaca: Cornell University Press.

COLBY, R. (1982) 'Drama as a Moral Imperative', *2D*, vol. 2, no. 1.

COLBY, R. (1987) 'Moral Education through Drama', *2D*, vol. 7, no. 1.

COLES, R. (1986) *The Moral Life of Children*, Boston: Atlantic Monthly Press.

CONNOR, S. (1989) *Postmodernist Culture*, Oxford, UK: Basil Blackwell.

CONNOR, S. (1992) *Theory and Cultural Value*, Oxford UK: Basil Blackwell.

COOPER, J.F. (1966) *The Last of the Mohicans*, London: Dent.

COURTNEY, R. (1980) *The Dramatic Curriculum*, London: Heinemann.

COX, T. (1970) 'The Development of Drama Education 1902–1944', M.Ed. Thesis, University of Durham.

CULLINGFORD, C. (1992) *Children and Society: Children's Attitudes to Politics and Power*, London: Cassell.

DAVIES, G. (1983) *Practical Primary Drama*, London: Heinemann.

DAY, J. (1991a) 'The Moral Audience: On the Narrative Mediation of Moral 'Judgment' and Moral 'Action', *Narrative and Storytelling: Implications for Moral Understanding and Moral Development*, San Francisco: Jossey-Bass.

DAY, J. (1991b) 'Role-taking revisited: Narrative and cognitive developmental interpretations of moral growth', *The Journal of Moral Education*, vol. 20, no. 3.

DENTITH, S. (1995) *Bakhtinian Thought*, London: Routledge.

DICKINSON, H. (1969) *Myth on the Modern Stage*, Urbana: University of Illinois Press.

DONALDSON, M. (1978) *Children's Minds*, London: Fontana, pp. 19–24.

DRAIN, R. (ed) (1995) *Twentieth Century Theatre: A Sourcebook*, London: Routledge.

EDMISTON, B. (1993) 'What have you travelled?', *Drama*, vol. 1, no. 3.

EDMISTON, B. (1994) 'More than Talk: A Bakhtinian Perspective on Drama Education and Change in Understanding', *The NADIE Journal*, vol. 18, no. 2.

EDMISTON, B. (1995) 'Discovering Right Actions: Forging Ethical Understandings through Dialogic Interactions', *Selected Readings in Drama and Theatre Education*, Brisbane, Australia: NADIE Publications.

EDMISTON, B. and WILHELM, J. (1996) 'Playing in Different Keys: Research notes for Action Researchers and Reflective Drama Practitioners', *Researching Drama and Arts Education*, TAYLOR, P. (ed), London: Routledge.

EISNER, E. (1985) *The Art of Educational Evaluation*, London: Falmer Press.

EISNER, E. (1991) *The Enlightened Eye: Qualitative Inquiry and the Enhancement of Educational Practice*, New York: Macmillan.

ELIADE, M. (1963) *Myth and Reality*, New York: Harper and Row.

ELLIOTT, J. (1991) *Action Research For Educational Change*, London: Open University Press.

ERIKSON, E. (1977) *Childhood and Society*, London: Paladin, pp. 222–43.

ESSLIN, M. (1984) *Brecht: A Choice of Evils*, London: Methuen.

ESSLIN, M. (1987) *The Field of Drama*, London: Methuen.

EWEN, F. (1970) *Bertolt Brecht, His Life and His Times*, London: Calder and Boyars.

FLANAGAN, O. and JACKSON, K. (1993) 'Justice, Care and Gender: The Kohlberg-Gilligan Debate Revisited', *An Ethic of Care*, LARRABEE, M.J. (ed), New York: Routledge.

FLEMING, M. (1994) *Starting Drama Teaching*, London: David Fulton.

FLETCHER, H. (1995) 'Retrieving the Mother/Other from the Myths and Margins of O'Neill's "Seal Wife" Drama', *NADIE Journal*, vol. 19, no. 2.

Fox, R. (1996) *Thinking Matters: Stories to Encourage Thinking Skills*, Exeter, UK: Southgate.

FREEMAN, M. (1991) 'Rewriting the Self: Development as Moral Practice', *Narrative and Storytelling: Implications for Moral Development*, TAPPAN, M. and PACKER, M. (ed), San Francisco: Jossey-Bass.

FREEMAN, M. (1993) *Rewriting the Self: History, Self, Narrative*, New York: Routledge.

FRYE, N. (1957) *Anatomy of Criticism*, Princeton, New Jersey: Princeton University Press.

FRYE, N. (1965) 'The Mythos of Spring: Comedy', *Comedy*, CORRIGAN, R.W. (ed), New York: Chandler.

GEERTZ, C. (1988) *Works and Lives: The Anthropologist as Author*, California: Stanford University Press.

GÉRARD, A. (1993) *The Phaedra Syndrome: Of Shame and Guilt in Drama*, Amsterdam: Rodopi.

GERGEN, K.J. (1991) *The Saturated Self: Dilemmas of Identity in Contemporary Life*, New York: Basic Books.

GILLIGAN, C. (1982) *In a Different Voice*, Cambridge, Massachusetts: Harvard University Press.

GLASER, B.G. and STRAUSS, A.L. (1967) *The Discovery of Grounded Theory: Strategies for Qualitative Research*, Chicago: Aldine.

GOLDBERG, S. (1993) *Agents and Lives*, Cambridge, UK: Cambridge University Press.

GRAVES, R. (1960) *The Greek Myths, vol. I*, London: Penguin, p. 165.

GRAY, R. (1976) *Brecht, the Dramatist*, Cambridge: Cambridge University Press.

GREEN, J.R. (1994) *Theatre in Ancient Greek Society*, London: Routledge.

GREEN, K. and LEBIHAN, J. (1996) *Critical Theory and Practice*, London: Routledge.

HALL, C. (1988) 'Addressing Racism through Drama', *2D*, vol. 7, no. 2.

HANNA, J.L. (1979) *To Dance is Human: A Theory of Non-verbal Communication*, University of Texas Press.

HARDY, B. (1977) 'Towards a Poetics of Fiction', in *The Cool Web*, MEEK, M. et al. (ed), London: Bodley Head.

HASTE, H. (1987) 'Growing into Rules', in *Making Sense*, BRUNER, J. and HASTE, H. (ed), London: Methuen.

HEATHCOTE, D. (1984) *Collected Writings on Education and Drama*, JOHNSON, L. and O'NEILL, C. (ed), Cheltenham, UK: Hutchinson.

HEATHCOTE, D. and BOLTON, G. (1995) *Drama for Learning: Dorothy Heathcote's Mantle of the Expert Approach to Education*, Portsmouth, NH: Heinemann.

HEKMAN, S.J. (1995) *Moral Voices, Moral Selves: Carol Gilligan and Feminist Moral Theory*, Cambridge: Polity.

HERSH, A. (1992) 'How Sweet the Kill: Orgiastic Female Violence in Contemporary Revisions of Euripides' "The Bacchae"', *Modern Drama*, vol. 35.

HIGHET, G. (1957) *The Classical Tradition; Greek and Roman Influences on the Western World*, Oxford: Clarendon Press.

HIGHWATER, J. (1982) *The Primal Mind*, New York: Harper and Row.

HOFFMAN, M.L. (1976) 'Empathy, Role Taking, Guilt and Development of Altruistic Motives', *Moral Development and Behaviour*, LINKNONA, T. (ed), New York: Holt, Rhinehart and Winston.

HOLQUIST, M. (1990) *Dialogism: Bakhtin and his World*, London: Routledge.

HORNBROOK, D. (1989) *Education and Dramatic Art*, London: Blackwell.

HORNBROOK, D. (1995) 'Mr Gargery's Challenge: Reflections on NADIE Journal International Research Issue', *NADIE Journal*, vol. 19, no. 1.

HOYLES, M. (1989) *The Politics of Childhood*, London: Journeyman Press.

INGLIS, F. (1986) 'Popular Culture and the Meaning of Feeling', *Dutch Quarterly Review of Anglo-American Letters*, vol. 16.

INGLIS, F. (1993) *Cultural Studies*, Oxford, UK: Basil Blackwell.

JOYCE, K. (1987) 'Confronting Sexism through Drama', *2D*, vol. 6, no. 2.

KELLY, A. (1992) 'Revealing Bakhtin', *New York Review of Books*, 24 September.

KENNY, R., GROTELUESCHEN, A. (1984) 'Making the Case for Case Study', *Journal of Curriculum Studies*, vol. 16, no. 1.

KEYSSAR, H. (1991) 'Drama and the Dialogic Imagination', *Modern Drama*, vol. 34, p. 95.

KIRK, G.S. (1970) *Myth: Its Meaning and Function*, Cambridge, UK: Cambridge University Press.

KIRK, G.S. (1974) *The Nature of the Greek Myths*, London: Penguin.

KITTO, H. (1973) *Greek Tragedy*, London: Routledge.

KOHLBERG, L. (1971) 'Stages of Moral Development as a Basis for Moral Education', *Moral Education: Interdisciplinary Approaches*, BECK, et al. (ed), Univ. of Toronto Press.

KOHLBERG, L. (1981) 'Moral Development and the Theory of Tragedy', *Essays in Moral Development, Vol. I: The Philosophy of Moral Development*, San Francisco: Harper and Row.

LANGER, S. (1953) *Feeling and Form*, New York: Charles Scribner's Sons.

LANGFORD, G. (1985) *Education Persons and Society: A Philosophical Enquiry*, Basingstoke: MacMillan.

LAWRENCE, C. (1981) 'Teacher and Role: A Drama Teaching Partnership', *2D*, vol. 1, no. 2.

LAWRENCE, C. (ed) (1993) *Voices for Change*, Newcastle-upon-Tyne: National Drama Publications.

LIPMAN, M. et al. (1980) *Philosophy in the Classroom*, Philadelphia: Temple University Press.

LIPMAN, M. (1988) *Philosophy Goes to School*, Philadelphia: Temple University Press.

LITTLE, A. (1967) *Myth and Society in Attic Drama*, New York: Octagon.

LOEVINGER, J. (1976) *Ego Development*, San Francisco: Jossey-Bass.

LUCAKS, G. (1968) *The Historical Novel*, London: Merlin Press.

LURIE, A. (1990) *Don't Tell the Grown-ups*, London: Bloomsbury.

MACINTYRE, A. (1967) *A Short History of Ethics*, London: Routledge, Kegan and Paul.

MACINTYRE, A. (1981) *After Virtue*, London: Duckworth.

MEADOWS, S. (1986) *Understanding Child Development*, London: Routledge.

MELLER, H. et al. (1984) *Changing Stories*, London: NATE Publications.

MORGAN, N. and SAXTON, J. (1987) *Teaching Drama*, London: Hutchinson.

MORSON, G. and EMERSON, C. (1990) *Mikhail Bakhtin: Creation of a Prosaics*, California: Stanford University Press.

MURDOCH, I. (1970) *The Sovereignty of Good over Other Concepts*, London: Routledge and Kegan Paul.

MURRIS, K. (1992) *Teaching Philosophy with Picture Books,* London: Infonet.

MUSSER, L. and FREEMAN, E. (1989) 'Teach Young Students about Native Americans: Use Myths, Legends and Folktales', *The Social Studies*, Jan/Feb.

NARAYAN, K. (1991) 'According to Their Feelings', *Stories Lives Tell*, NODDINGS, N. and WITHERALL, C. (eds), Columbia University, New York: Teacher's College Press.

NEELANDS, J. (1984) *Making Sense of Drama*, Oxford: Heinemann.

NEELANDS, J. (1992) *Learning Through Imagined Experience*, London: Hodder and Stoughton.

NEELANDS, J. (1994) 'Theatre without Walls', *Drama*, vol. 2, no. 2.

NEELANDS, J. and GOODE, T. (1995) 'Playing on the Margins of Meaning: the Ritual Aesthetic in Community Performance', *Drama*, vol. 3, no. 2.

NICHOLSON, H. (1993) 'Postmodernism and Educational Drama', *Drama*, vol. 2, no. 1.

NICHOLSON, H. (1995) 'Performative Acts: Drama, Education and Gender', *NADIE Journal*, vol. 19, no. 1.

NODDINGS, N. (1984) *Caring: A Feminine Approach to Ethics and Moral Education*, Berkeley and Los Angeles: University of California Press.

NODDINGS, N. and WITHERELL, C. (1991) *Stories Lives Tell*, Columbia University, New York: Teachers' College Press.

NORMAN, R. (1983) *Moral Philosophies: An Introduction to Ethics*, Oxford: Clarendon Press.

NOWOTTNY, W. (1962) *The Language Poets Use*, London: Athlone.

NUSSBAUM, M. (1986) *The Fragility of Goodness*, New York: Cambridge University Press.

OAKESHOTT, M. (1962) 'Poetry and the Conversation of Mankind', *Rationalism in Politics and Other Essays*, London: Methuen.

ODDIE, D. (1994) 'The Actor and the Teacher', *Drama*, vol. 2, no. 3.

O'HARA, M. (1996) 'The Drama of Drama in Education: Questions and Issues', *Drama and Theatre in Education: Contemporary Research*, SOMERS, J. (ed), North York, Ontario: Captus Press.

O'LEARY, J. (1996) 'Man Who Wants Schools to Focus on Right and Wrong', *The Times*, 6 July.

OLIVER, D.W. and BANE, M.J. (1971) 'Moral Education: Is Reasoning Enough?', *Moral Education: Interdisciplinary Approaches*, BECK, C.M., CRITTENDEN, B.S. and SULLIVAN, E.V. (eds), New York: Newman Press.

O'NEILL, C. et al. (1976) *Drama Guidelines*, London: Heinemann in association with London Drama.

O'NEILL, C. and LAMBERT, A. (1982) *Drama Structures*, London: Hutchinson.

O'NEILL, C. (1994) 'Here Comes Everybody: Aspects of Role in Process Drama', *NADIE Journal*, vol. 18, no. 2.

O'NEILL, C. (1995) *Drama Worlds: A Framework for Process Drama*, Portsmouth NH: Heinemann.

OPIE, I. (1995) 'Fear and Tension in Children's Games', *Dramatherapy with Children and Adolescents*, JENNINGS, S. (ed), London: Routledge.

OPIE, I. and OPIE, P. (1959) *The Language and Lore of Schoolchildren*, London: Oxford University Press.

O'TOOLE, J. (1992) *The Process of Drama*, London: Routledge.

O'TOOLE, J. (1995) 'The Rude Charms of Drama', *Selected Readings in Drama and Theatre Education*, NADIE Research Monograph, no. 3, Brisbane, Australia: NADIE Publications.

PECHEY, G. (1989) 'On the borders of Bakhtin: Dialogisation, decolonisation', *Bakhtin and Cultural Theory*, HIRSCHKOP, K. and SHEPHERD, D. (eds), Manchester University Press.

PEGG, B. (1981) *Rites and Riots: Folk Cultures of Britain and Europe*, Dorset, UK: Blandford Press.

PHILIP, N. (1992) *The Penguin Book of English Folktales*, London.

PIAGET, J. (1932) *The Moral Judgment of the Child*, London: Routledge, Kegan and Paul.

PRATT, A. (1982) *Archetypal Patterns in Women's Fiction*, Brighton, UK: Harvester Press.

PRING, R. (1984) *Personal, Social and Moral Education*, London: Hodder and Stoughton.

PROPP, V. (1968) *Morphology of the Folktale*, Texas Press.

PROPP, V. (1984) *Theory and History of Folklore*, Manchester University Press.

RABEY, D.I. (1990) 'Defining Difference: Timberlake Wertenbaker's Drama of Language, Dispossession and Discovery', *Modern Drama*, vol. 33.

RAWLS, J. (1977) *A Theory of Justice*, New York: Oxford University Press.

READMAN, G. and LAMONT, G. (1994) *Drama in the Primary Classroom*, London: BBC Publications.

REIM, R. (1994) *Greek Tragic Theatre*, London: Routledge.

ROBINSON, K. (1980) 'Drama, Theatre and Social Reality', *Exploring Theatre and Education*, ROBINSON, K. (ed), Heinemann, London.

ROBINSON, K. (1981) 'A Re-evaluation of the roles and functions of drama in secondary education with reference to a survey of curricular drama in 259 secondary schools', Ph.D thesis, University of London.

ROGERS, R. (1978) *Metaphor: A Psychoanalytic View*, Berkeley and Los Angeles: University of California Press.

ROWE, D. and NEWTON, J. (eds) (1994) *You, Me, Us: Social and Moral Responsibility for Primary Schools*, London: Citizenship Foundation.

SCHECHNER, R. (1993) *The Future of Ritual*, London: Routledge.

SCHEFFLER, I. (1985) *Of Human Potential*, London: Routledge and Kegan Paul.

SCHEFFLER, I. (1991) *In Praise of the Cognitive Emotions*, London: Routledge.

SCHEFFLER, S. (1996) 'Against the System', *The Times Literary Supplement*, no. 4846, Feb. 16th.

SCHÖN, D. (1987) *Educating the Reflective Practitioner*, New York: Jossey-Bass.

SCIEZSKA, J. and JOHNSON, S. (1991) *The Frog Prince (continued)*, New York: Viking.

SCIEZSKA, J. and SMITH, L. (1992) *The Stinky Cheese Man and other Fairly Stupid Tales*, New York: Viking.

SELMAN, R.L. (1976) 'Social cognitive understanding: A guide to education and clinical practice', *Moral Development and Behaviour*, LIKONA, T. (ed), New York: Holt, Rinehart and Winston.

SEYMOUR HOUSE, K. (1965) *Cooper's Americans*, Ohio State University Press.

SLADE, P. (1954) *Child Drama*, University of London Press.

SLADE, P. (1993) 'Avoiding delinquency: The arts and moral education', *Arts Education*, June.

SLOTKIN, R. (1992) 'Myth and the Production of History', *New Essays on 'The Last of the Mohicans'*, PECK, B. (ed), New York: Cambridge University Press.

SOMERS, J. (1996) 'The Nature of Learning in Drama in Education', *Drama and Theatre in Education: Contemporary Research*, North York, Ontario: Captus Press.

SPENCER, P. (1985) *Society and the Dance*, Cambridge: Cambridge University Press.

STENHOUSE, L. (1975) *An Introduction to Curriculum Research and Development*, London: Heinemann.

SULLIVAN, E. (1985) 'Kohlberg's Stage Theory as a Progressive Educational Form for Value Development', *Lawrence Kohlberg: Consensus and Controversy*, Philadelphia: Falmer Press.

TAPPAN, M. (1991a) 'Narrative, Authorship and the Development of Moral Authority', *Narrative and Storytelling: Implications for Understanding Moral Development*, San Francisco: Jossey-Bass.

TAPPAN, M. (1991b) 'Narrative, Language and Moral Experience', *The Journal of Moral Education*, vol. 20, no. 3.

TAPLIN, O. (1985) *Greek Tragedy in Performance*, London: Routledge.

TARLINGTON, C. and VERRIOUR, P. (1991) *Role Drama*, Ontario: Pembroke.

TATAR, M. (1992) *Off with Their Heads! Fairy Tales and the Culture of Childhood*, New Jersey: Princeton University Press.

TAYLOR, C. (1989) *Sources of the Self: The Making of the Modern Identity*, Cambridge: Cambridge University Press.

TAYLOR, P. (1995) *Pre-Text and Storydrama: The Artistry of Cecily O'Neill and David Booth*, Brisbane, Australia: NADIE Research Monograph Series no. 1.

TAYLOR, P. (1996) 'Rebellion, Reflective Turning and Arts Education Research', and 'Doing Reflective Practitioner Research in Arts Education', *Researching Drama and Arts Education*, TAYLOR, P. (ed), London: Falmer Press.

THOMPSON, S. (1977) *The Folktale*, Berkeley and Los Angeles: University of California Press.

THOMSON, A. (1996) 'Carey urges parents and teachers to set an ethical example for all', *The Times*, 6 July.

TODOROV, T. (1984) *Mikhail Bakhtin: The Dialogical Principle*, Manchester University Press.

TOOKER, E. (ed) (1979) *Native North American Spirituality of the Eastern Woodlands*, New York: Paulist Press.

TROYNA, B. (1994) 'Reforms, Research and Being Reflexive about Being Reflective', unpublished paper.

TURNER, G. (1988) *Film as Social Practice*, London: Routledge.

UNITED SOCIETY FOR THE PROPAGATION OF THE GOSPEL (1984) *Testimony, Chief Seattle*.

WAGNER, B.J. (1979) *Dorothy Heathcote: Drama as a Learning Medium*, London: Hutchinson.

WALVIN, J. (1982) *A Child's World: A Social History of English Childhood, 1800–1914*, London: Penguin.

WASHBURN, W.E. (1964) *The Indian and the White Man*, New York: Random House.

WASHBURN, W.E. (1973) *The American Indian and the United States: A Documentary History (Volume IV)*, New York: Random House.

WHITE, H. (1981) 'The Value of Narrativity in the Representation of Reality', *On Narrative*, MITCHELL, W.J.T. (ed), University of Chicago Press.

WILLETT, J. (1974) *Brecht on Theatre*, London: Methuen.

WILLIAMS, B. (1985) *Ethics and the Limits of Philosophy*, London: Fontana/Collins.

WILLIAMS, R. (1968) *Drama from Ibsen to Brecht*, Harmondsworth: Penguin.

WILLIAMS, R. (1975) *Drama in a Dramatized Society*, Cambridge: Cambridge University Press.

WINSTON, J. (1994) 'Revising the Fairy Tale through Magic: Antonia Barber's 'The Enchanter's Daughter', *Children's Literature in Education*, vol. 25, no. 2.

WINSTON, J. (1995) 'Careful the Tale You Tell: Fairy Tales, Drama and Moral Education', *Children and Society*, vol. 9, no. 4.

WITHERELL, C., POPE-EDWARDS (1991) 'Moral versus social-conventional reasoning: a narrative and cultural critique', *The Journal of Moral Education*, vol. 20, no. 3.

WOLFE, D.T. (1978) 'Educational drama and moral development', in BAIRD SHUMAN (ed.) *Educational Drama for Today's Schools*, Metuchen, NJ: Scarecrow Press.

WOOLLAND, B. (1993) *The Teaching of Drama in the Primary School*, London: Longman.

WRIGHT, N. (1980) 'From the Universal to the Particular', *Exploring Theatre in Education*, ROBINSON, K. (ed), London: Heinemann.

ZIPES, J. (1979) *Breaking the Magic Spell*, London: Heinemann.

ZIPES, J. (1983) *Fairy Tales and the Art of Subversion*, London: Heinemann.

ZIPES, J. (ed.) (1986) *Don't Bet on the Prince* Aldershot: Gower.

ZIPES, J. (ed.) (1987) *Victorian Fairy Tales*, London: Methuen.

ZIPES, J. (1993) *The Trials and Tribulations of Little Red Riding Hood*, London: Routledge.

ZIPES, J. (1994) *Fairy Tale as Myth, Myth as Fairy Tale*, Lexington: University Press of Kentucky.

ZIPES, J. (1996) *Creative Storytelling: Building Community, Changing Lives*, London: Routledge.

Appendix 1

The following is extracted from transcripts of the discussion the teacher had with the class in between the second and third session of the Jack and the Beanstalk drama. Editorial cuts are shown by dotted lines.

T: You were all pretending to be children of the village who were friends with Jack. You all went up the beanstalk to get Jack down, which was a bit of a risky business, wasn't it?

Chn: Yeah!!

T: A big, high beanstalk which had a Giant at the top. Now, why did you agree? Jack's mother asked you to go and bring him back. Why did you agree to do that for her? Karen.

Ch: Because he's our friend.

T: Because Jack's your friend. OK. Why are you friends with Jack, then? . . . . . What sort of things do we know about him that makes him one of our friends?

Ch: He's nice to me and he lets me play in his garden and in his house.

T: Right, I think it might be helpful if we make a list of things that we know about Jack. Let's think first of all about all the good things about Jack. Keely?

Ch: He plays.

T: He plays with you.

Ch: He's kind.

T: He's kind.

Ch: He's nice.

T: He's nice.

Ch: He plays with me in my house.

Ch: He looks after you when you've fallen over.

Ch: He's rich.

T: Yes, he's got a lot of money now, hasn't he?

Ch: He's brave.

T: Brave, because he keeps going back up that beanstalk, doesn't he? . . . Somebody says that he's . . .

Chn: STRONG

T: That's right, he must be very fit, mustn't he? Some more good things about him. Richard?

Ch: He's friendly.

T: Friendly, right.

Ch: He plays good games.

T: He plays good games, does he, he's lots of fun to be with?
Ch: Yeah.

. . .

T: OK, Let's think about some of the things about Jack that aren't so good. Christopher?
Ch: He breaks his promises.
T: He breaks promises, to his mother particularly. Ian?
Ch: He's lazy.
T: He is a very lazy boy, isn't he? Cara?
Ch: He tells lies.
T: Right. Hannah, what did you say?
Ch: I said he steals.
T: He does, he steals from the Giant, doesn't he?
Ch: Cos he takes back things that don't belong to him.
T: Yes?
Ch: He doesn't . . . sometimes . . . (*too soft to hear*)
T: He doesn't tell his mummy where he is playing, right?
Ch: He isn't helpful.
T: He isn't helpful at all, is he? When his mummy needs him to do jobs.
Ch: He's always daydreaming.
T: He'd rather daydream, wouldn't he?
Ch: He's tired and lazy.
Ch: He lets his mum do all the work.
Ch: He's naughty.
  . . . (*Teacher stops the tape. She told me later that one child now suggested that Jack swore and that there was some dispute over this and that the child finally said that 'bum' was a swear word.*)
T: When we stopped a minute ago, some of you said that Jack was naughty. I wonder if you can give me any examples of why Jack's naughty? What's he done that's naughty?
Ch: He told a lie.
T: What lie has Jack told? Think back to the story. Think about things that Jack's done. When has he told a lie to someone?
Ch: To the Giant's wife.
T: He lied to the Giant's wife, didn't he. What did he say?
Ch: He wouldn't cause her any trouble.
T: Right. He told her he was only coming in to have a look round, that he wasn't going to steal anything.
Ch: But he did!
T: But he did, right.

. . .
. . .

Appendix 2

The Star Poem
Star sparkle
Blue sky
Star sisters
Star light
Water lilies
Touch gently
Creamy petals
Star Maiden
Blue lake
Night long

This poem was created in the form of a calligram, a five-pointed star. The phrases were all taken from the last two pages of the book *The Star Maiden*. It is possible to begin the poem at any point of the star, so the version above is just one of ten possible readings.

Appendix 3

Calligram 1 of *The Star Poem*

Calligram 2 of *The Star Poem*

because it is gentle.

Beliefs which we believe is because we feel they are true

Some very young babies

because they are fragile

A great gift of love

because that won't come again.

A wonderful dog

A wonderful tree

because they give oxygen

TOUCH
THEM
GENTLY

Index